L. Riggleman

Problems of College and University Administration

Problems of College and University Administration

BY

FRANK L. McVEY

*Former President of
The University of North Dakota and
The University of Kentucky*

AND

RAYMOND M. HUGHES

*Former President of Miami University
and Iowa State College*

THE IOWA STATE COLLEGE PRESS
AMES, IOWA

378.1
M253p

*Copyright, 1952, by The Iowa State College Press.
All rights reserved. Composed and printed by
The Iowa State College Press, Ames, Iowa, U.S.A.*

Preface

The two authors of this book have enjoyed a friendship of thirty-five years, enriched by occasional visits and conversations at meetings of educational associations. They were college teachers with more than twenty-five years of experience and they have served a period of fifty-six years as presidents of four institutions of higher education.

After retirement from active service, they agreed at the close of one pleasant visit to join in writing a book based on their experience and observations of the various problems which arise in college administration. It is their hope that such a book might be of use to deans, heads, and other administrative officers, as well as presidents, in meeting some of *their* problems. The two colleagues present in this book more than a hundred aspects of college administration as they have met them while in office or as they have reached conclusions about those problems in recent years.

In planning the book it was agreed that each author would write on any topic suggested which interested him, whether he agreed or disagreed with his colleague. Each topic has been initialed to identify the writer.

The comments are not always closely related. The theme

of the book, based on experience and observation, is not a continuous narrative. It is really a reference book and different aspects may be covered in several sections. It attempts to deal with many of the problems met by college presidents and other administrators.

We are indebted to Mrs. John G. Park, of Lexington, Kentucky, for reading the manuscript and for making helpful suggestions.

FRANK L. MCVEY
RAYMOND M. HUGHES

December, 1951

Introduction

This land of ours, covering three million square miles, includes a population of 150 million people. Located among them are 1,850 colleges and universities attended by 2,600,000 students and staffed by more than 240,000 teachers. The amount spent on higher education exceeds one billion dollars annually, which brings college education into the brackets of a great and important national enterprise.

The first college in the United States was Harvard, founded in Cambridge, Massachusetts Bay Colony, in 1638. Other colleges followed slowly, and by the opening of the American Revolution there were a half-dozen institutions of college level. The growth of colleges in numbers, in endowment and income, plants, faculties, and students since then, particularly in recent years, has been amazing.

Each year three or four hundred new presidents and many more deans and directors are appointed in the 1,850 institutions. This turnover may be laid to retirement, resignations, and death, and in some cases to removal through trustee action. New presidents are coming into the educational field, most of them well trained in education or highly experienced in a profession or business. Most of them, however, are wholly new to the job of president of a college and inexperienced in conducting a considerable educational organization.

The presidency of a college or university is a many-sided job. No man is equally capable of handling all of its many duties. Some features of the task are entirely new to any man. That is one place where this book may help. Of course it does not cover every question a president or dean will meet. But where it does it will either suggest a solution or give a turn to the inquirer's thinking that may prove valuable.

With many men appointed as presidents, deans, and directors each year, the average term of presidents is too short, about six years. It should be longer, perhaps eight or ten years, for the best interest of our institutions. Perhaps such a book as this may make it possible for more administrators to avoid difficulties which could develop into serious problems. It might, in fact, make some administrations run more smoothly and give them a longer life.

Certainly the colleges need no dictators as president and fewer men who build their ego on authority. There is a need for more leaders who, through democratic procedures, withdraw from controversial positions. Some of the policies developed in this book might well lead to improvements in the administration of higher education.

The opinions arrived at may be contrary to those of the reader, but even so he will find something with which he may test his own opinions.

Table of Contents

1. **The New President**   3
   Inaugurals 4
   What Is Expected of the President?—McVey 6
   What Is Expected of the President?—Hughes 7
   Possible Advances a New President May Be Able To Make . . 8
   The Students 8
   Student Activities 9
   Other Student Relations 9
   The Faculty 9
   Finance 10
   Alumni and Public Relations 10
   The President's Time—McVey 11
   The President's Time—Hughes 15
   Further Comment on the President's Time—McVey . . . 17
   The President's Secretary 18
   Intangibles and Imponderables 19
   The President's Personal Influence 20
   Prayer, a Great Source of Strength 21
   The President's Wife—McVey 22
   The President's Wife—Hughes 24
   To the President's Wife 25
   The President's House—McVey 26
   The President's House—Hughes 27
   Is There a Dog in the House? 29
   Entertainment Problems 30
   Some Exceptional Expenses 32
   Some Puzzling Problems 34

Table of Contents

    Help From Outside Consultants 37
    Public Addresses—McVey 38
    Public Addresses—Hughes 39
    Responsibility for Leadership 40
    How Long Should a President Serve?—Hughes 41
    How Long Should a President Serve?—McVey 42
    The Effects of an Old President on an Institution 43
    How To Utilize a President Emeritus 43
    The Attitude of the President Emeritus 44

2. The President and the Trustees   47

    McVey and the Trustees 47
    Hughes and the Trustees 49
    The President and the Trustees 52
    A New President's Opportunity 54
    The Size of the Board 56
    Relations With the Legislature—Hughes 57
    Relations With the Legislature—McVey 59
    Formulation of College and University Policy 62
    The President as Chairman of the Board 64
    Assistants Whom the Trustees Should Provide for the President   65
    The President's Need for a Wise Counselor—Hughes 70
    The President's Need for a Wise Counselor—McVey 71
    The Age and Origin of Three Hundred Presidents on Election   72
    The Previous Employment of Presidents 73
    The Selection of a President 73
    Evidence of a Good President 75
    Undesirable Presidents 77
    How Can an Undesirable President Be Removed? 79

3. Problems of Administration   83

    The College and University Parliament—McVey 83
    The College and University Parliament—Hughes 86
    The Chief Financial Officer—McVey 88
    The Chief Financial Officer—Hughes 92
    A Provost, or a Vice-President of Faculty and Curriculum . . . 93
    College Deans — Appointment and Contributions 94
    College Deans 98
    Dean of Women—McVey 100
    Dean of Women—Hughes 102
    Dean of Men 104
    Department Heads 107
    The Registrar and His Functions 108
    Importance of an Able Admissions Officer 113
    The Maintenance of the Plant 116
    Clerical Services — A Stenographic Bureau 125
    Making Use of the Inventory Clerk's Records 127
    The Budget 127

Surveys of Colleges and Universities—Hughes 129
Surveys of Colleges and Universities—McVey 131
College Catalogs 134
College and University Advertising 135
A Twenty Year Plan 136
Attendance at Professional Meetings 137
Public Relations 138

4. The Campus, Buildings and Plans   **141**
Campus Sites 141
A Landscape Architect Should Plan the Campus 143
Preparing Building Plans in Advance of Need 145
Architecture Is Important 146
Faculty Housing as a University Project 148

5. The President and the Faculty   **151**
The President Should Know His Staff 151
Recruiting New Faculty Members 152
Interviewing Prospective Staff Members 155
Judging the Value of Faculty Members 156
Pensions—McVey 158
Pensions—Hughes 161
Sabbatical Leave 161
Teaching and Research 163
Guilds Control Higher Education 166
Democracy in College Administration 167
Two Faculty Committees 170
The Salary of the Football Coach 173
The College Teacher Has a Good Life 174

6. The Status of Students and Their Relation to the College   **179**
Occupations of the Fathers of Students 179
Education of Fathers and Mothers 180
One Reason for the Increase in College Enrollment . . . 181
High School Grades and Success in College 181
Progress of Students 183
Failure of Able Students 186
Upper Class Students Who Make Low Grades 187
What Proportion of Students Work up to Their Ability? . . 188
Fraternities—McVey 190
Fraternities—Hughes 192
Organization of Non-Fraternity Men and Women 194
Auditing Student Activity Accounts 196
YMCA and YWCA 197
The Ship Is Greater Than the Crew 198
Student Publications and Faculty Control 200
Transfer Students 201
Securing Positions for Graduates 201

Table of Contents

    Student Activity Tickets 203
    Scholarships and Grants-in-Aid 203
    Student Loan Funds 204
    Student Loan Funds and Scholarships 206
    How a Student Can Get off Probation 208
    Intramural Athletics 210
    Intercollegiate Athletics 211
    Student Health Service 212
    Board and Rooms for Students 213
    Student Boarding 214
    Dormitories 215
    Our Leaders 218

7. The President and the Alumni   **223**
    The Alumni 223
    The Individual Alumnus 224
    Working Relationship 225
    Established Aids in Alumni Work 226
    The Alumni Secretary—McVey 226
    The Alumni Secretary—Hughes 227
    Elements of an Effective Alumni Program 229
    The Alumni Association—McVey 229
    The Alumni Association—Hughes 231
    Alumni Clubs—McVey 231
    Alumni Clubs—Hughes 232
    Alumni Reunions—McVey 233
    Alumni Reunions—Hughes 234
    Alumni Publications—McVey 234
    Alumni Publications—Hughes 235
    The Alumni Register 235
    The Class Secretary 236
    Class Contributions—McVey 236
    Class Contributions—Hughes 236
    Alumni Can Provide a Living Endowment 237
    Alumni Are a Source of Large Gifts 238
    Financial Campaigns 238
    Placement of Graduates 238
    Recent Graduates as Critics of Teaching 239
    An Alumni Advisory Council 240
    Alumni Can Send Able Students 240
    Alumni Can Aid With the Legislature 241
    Alumni May Nominate Trustees 241
    Alumni of Especial Importance 242
    Distinguished Alumni 242
    Publication of an Alumni "Who's Who" 245

8. The Importance of Teaching   **247**
    Teaching Is a Faculty Matter—Hughes 247

Teaching Is a Faculty Matter—McVey 248
The Articulation of Students 249
Teaching 252
How the Work of a College May Be Judged 255
Lecturing—Hughes 257
Lecturing—McVey 259
Visiting College Classes 260
Fellowships for Promising Young Teachers 260
The Doctorate as a Requirement for a Professorship . . . 261
What Does It Cost To Graduate a Student?—McVey . . . 263
What Does It Cost To Graduate a Student?—Hughes . . . 265

9. Graduate Work and Research   269
Research and Its Importance 269
Cost of Research in Time 272
Cost of Research in Money 273
Further Observations on Research 274
Allotment of Research Funds 275
When Should an Institution Enter on Graduate Work? . . . 276
Admission to the Graduate School 278
Financial Assistance to Graduate Students 280
Authorship in Publishing Results of Doctoral Theses—Hughes . 281
Authorship in Publishing Results of Doctoral Theses—McVey . 283
Joint Research—Interdepartmental Committees 284
Writing Books 285
University Research Foundations 286
Wider Use of University Foundations 288

10. College Chapel, the Library, and Other Matters   291
College Chapel—Hughes 291
College Chapel—McVey 292
The Library—Hughes 293
The Library—McVey 293
The Library Stack Room 299
A University Press 303
Art in College Halls 304
Art on the Campus 305
A Cultural Course for Students 307
A Creative Artist on the Campus 308

Appendix   311
Detailed Study of Occupations of Fathers of Members
    of Class Entering in Fall of 1937 313
Basis for Determining What Rank in Scholarship Any
    Given Student Should Attain 315
Personnel Leaflet 320

Index   323

The office of college president is an interesting and stimulating post in which the incumbent has some power and considerable influence in shaping the development of an institution. Among the essential qualities for the job are vision and imagination tempered by judgment. It can be said, by and large, that holders of such an office do not vision the future in large enough terms; their horizon is too narrow. To visualize the future with anything like accuracy necessitates a thorough knowledge of drifts and trends. Intuition is of some value, but a true perception of future possibilities depends upon vision and wisdom.

1.
The New President

When a man is asked if he is interested in the presidential post of a college and he has an inclination to accept the position, he is faced with questions of great importance.

He may assume that because the institution is a college it must be a desirable place in which to live and work. However, there are, in fact, a series of questions that should be answered for his satisfaction: What are the reputation and standing of the college? — which includes its past history and the reasons for its founding. Does its charter limit freedom of teaching and does that instrument restrict faculty appointments by sectarian creeds or beliefs? Is the board of trustees a self-perpetuated body with no great responsibility to any organization outside of itself? Among the members is there a majority of liberal-minded men who possess some wisdom? Are the members really interested in the college as an educational institution? Has the board by its past actions shown an understanding of the place of the institution in the area in which it is located?

The candidate should make other queries relating to the support and maintenance of the institution. He will want to know what endowments the college has, how they are invested, and whether or not they are tied to particular types of enterprise that might be questioned by supporters of the college. How much of the income is derived from endowments and how much from student fees; if largely from the fees, how is the income affected by depressions and to what extent? What is the proportion of income devoted to salaries of the teaching staff as against the maintenance of property?

Is the plant well kept or does it need expensive repairs? Is the obsolescence account a mere fiction or is there a real attempt to face the future when buildings are to be replaced? Does the board have plans for the development of campus and buildings, and are these plans thoroughly worked out and well understood by the board?

What is the clientele of the institution? If publicly maintained, the problems of the relation to students, alumni and state are quite different from those involved in the ties that bind a private institution to its supporters. But the question of the value and strength of the relationship is the same. Is it cordial and hearty, or is the tie a loose, ineffectual one? If morale is low in faculty and students, it is sure to be reflected in the attitude of the public beyond the campus boundaries. This is vital, and knowledge of the situation may save much heart searching and worry, since morale is something that can be built up if one knows where the weakness lies.

Often staff morale is dependent upon teaching loads, salaries, tenure, leaves of absence and retirement plans. If the stipend for teaching is low and the teaching load heavy, members of the staff become discouraged and tend to supplement their salaries by doing odd jobs that take their minds away from the main purpose of their position on the college faculty.

M.

Inaugurals

In the twenties, the inauguration of a college president was often quite a regal affair, lasting as long as three days. An elaborate program of speeches and exhibits was carefully prepared, and beautifully engraved invitations were issued to prominent citizens, alumni, and heads of colleges. Sister institutions responded generously by sending their delegates to the inauguration. With the decade of depression and the war following it, inauguration proceedings were materially reduced and limited to a two-hour program, or at most one day. The delegates now, for the most part, are members of the staff and lay alumni living in the vicinity. Often they have been students in the college and as such accept the invitation.

As a matter of good sense, the reduction of an inauguration to one day is to be commended. However, the celebration of the founding of the college at its quarter century anniversary might very well be the inspiration for a larger program. In that case, the inauguration could well play its part with the emphasis placed on some phases of education for the purpose of bringing to the attention of the public the objectives of the institution.

I have pondered many times over the proper content of a speech to be given by the man inducted into office on inauguration day. What should he say on such an occasion? My colleague thinks the new president should say what he has in mind for the institution to which he has been called as its administrative officer. My reply would be in the form of a question. How can he make such pronouncements when his acquaintance with the college is limited, unless he has been a dean or professor there and is being promoted to a high office? The new president might well stress what he thinks a college can do, but to be specific in stating his views under such circumstances might produce misunderstandings which would create obstacles at the very beginning of his term of service. After all, a college is a democracy which requires consultations and agreements, if its function is to be successful.

As a matter of procedure, it might be as well if some national figure would make the address on the inaugural occasion. Thus the new president could accept the office with a few words of appreciation, leaving his program to a later period when he had familiarized himself with the processes of the institution. At the dinner or luncheon which inevitably is a part of inauguration doings, he might make a gracious speech of not over fifteen minutes, which if seasoned with a few witty comments would win him plaudits. The one objection is the limited audience at any dinner or luncheon. Even this can be overcome by good publicity and newspaper coverage. The committee in charge of the inauguration program will insist upon a set speech. Who remembers much of anything he has ever heard on such an occasion? The usual remark is that the new president conducted himself with great dignity. Let him accomplish this briefly.

M.

What Is Expected of the President?

Many years ago, an English professor lectured at Cornell University on European and American Universities. "The president of an American educational institution," he said, "has his suitcase packed ready to go anywhere, at any time, for anything." This incident recalls the comment on the general who, when the battle began, mounted his horse and rode off in several directions at one and the same time. The American college president is supposed to be a scholar, a good speaker, a financial wizard, all things to all men, and a good fellow.

The presidential intendant would do well to ascertain what is expected of him. Is he, for example, to be a teacher, a campus president, or a traveling salesman for the college? It is certain that as the burdens of administration increase, he won't do much of anything in the teaching field. It is also certain that he can't spend too much of his time in attending dinners, conventions, meetings and the like and still serve the college as an administrative officer. Finding out where his main responsibility lies usually proves to be a hunt for an *ignus fatuus*. Some selections must be made, and the wise man will find the way and emphasize the important things if his educational philosophy is a sound one.

In early days, a minister of the gospel was usually chosen for the post of president on the basis that he had high ideals and a religious zeal for the welfare of youth. Much of this emphasis has passed. For a time the selection of economists was the vogue; then men trained specifically in education held the stage; and today there is a drift toward lawyers, businessmen, and scientists for the position of college president. Boards of trustees may feel, too, that a man high in public office brings prestige to an institution. After all, the position can be well filled when character, training and experience fitted to the needs of the place are kept in mind.

The unsolicited applicant for a presidential vacancy gets small consideration from boards of trustees, although business executives are accustomed to receive and give consideration to applications. A man who applies for such a position is regarded as one who needs a job. The English system of finding heads of colleges and professors is to ask all who are interested to send their credentials to a person designated in an advertisement appearing in leading periodicals. There is much to be said for the English system. It will be seen that any board of trustees must follow a hard road in seeking a president for their institution.

M.

What Is Expected of the President?

As Dr. McVey has indicated, what is expected of a president has changed greatly over the years. In early days college problems were relatively small, confined largely to raising enough money to pay the meager salaries. At Miami University, from 1824 to 1872, the total budget never rose to $20,000 in any year; yet in 1873 the trustees closed the institution for twelve years for lack of funds.

With the growth in the size and resources of colleges, the problems increased and competent officers were appointed to carry most of the financial burdens. Increasing numbers of institutions employ executive deans or vice-presidents to deal with all faculty and curriculum problems, still further releasing the president's time.

The trustees increasingly recognize that the president must

be relatively free from routine to deal effectively with unexpected issues, with institutional policies and with the public. The evolution of the college president has followed at a distance the evolution of the president of the United States. George Washington dealt with all problems that presented themselves, in reasonable leisure. Today, the burden is divided among a large group of able men, each relieving the president in certain areas; yet he is desperately pressed for time.

I should say the trustees desire as president a man of such character, judgment and wisdom as can adequately represent them and the institution before the public. They expect him to so control the college or university that a minimum of trouble or criticism will reach them. They also expect him to guide the various interests of the school so that it will hold its own creditably among sister institutions, and, if possible, show advances in some activities.

H.

Possible Advances a New President May Be Able To Make

It is impossible to find a new president with the same abilities as his predecessor. It is most desirable that each man, in his eight to twelve years of service, leave the institution stronger in some particulars than he found it.

Most men who have reached an age when they may be considered for a presidency estimate their own strength and weakness rather well. A new president should be able to judge his own ability to serve usefully in the new post.

There are four main areas in which a president can hope to strengthen his institution: the students, the faculty, finance, and alumni and public relations.

The Students

A. Raise the quality of undergraduates by denying the unfit admission.

B. Improve the quality of graduates by (1) dropping loafers quickly, (2) improving requirements for graduation, (3) instituting final general examinations for honors.

(If Graduate Work Is Offered) :

C. Raise the quality of students admitted to study for the master's degree.
D. Improve services to the public schools by (1) adapting the work for the master's degree to public school needs, (2) maintaining high standards for the course.
E. Provide more suitable training for teachers who are candidates for the doctor of philosophy degree.

Student Activities

A. Reduce the number of students overburdened with student activities.
B. Make adequate scholarship requirements for participation in student activities.
C. Reduce the number who take no part in student activities.
D. See that finances of student activities are well handled.

Other Student Relations

A. Improve service in rooming and boarding for students as provided by the institution.
B. Introduce or improve placement of graduates.
C. Improve and make closer the personal relations of faculty and students.
D. Improve health and physical development facilities for students.

The Faculty

A. Improve the faculty:
   1. As regards teaching skill and inspiration.
   2. As regards research.

B. Improve the human relations of the faculty. Increase good feeling. Reduce gossip. Reduce campus politics.
C. Make the library as strong and as useful to the faculty as possible — both in management and in books.
D. See that equipment and supplies are adequate and in good condition.
E. See that offices and classrooms are all used to the highest efficiency and that all are in good repair and kept clean.
F. See that blackboards are washed daily.

Finance

A. Increase annual income:
   1. Secure larger public support.
   2. Secure large additions to endowment.
   3. Secure larger contributions to current operations, living endowment.
   4. Secure gifts for buildings.
   5. Raise student fees and increase the number of scholarships, if feasible.
B. Improve use of current income:
   1. Eliminate every unnecessary expense.
   2. Raise salaries of valuable professors.
   3. See that the business office provides the president with complete and understandable information.

Alumni and Public Relations

A. Bind the alumni more closely to the college:
   1. Improve alumni magazine.
   2. Increase services of alumni office to alumni.
   3. Organize visiting committees of alumni for each department, making the chairman of each departmental committee a member of an alumni committee for the college as a whole. After organization, these committees can be maintained on an efficient basis by the efforts of the department heads.

4. Bring alumni into closer relation to the administration.
B. Become acquainted with the leading members of the legislature, or, in a private institution, with leading prospective donors to the college.

H.

The President's Time

There is more of everything in these days of the machine and the atomic bomb except time. There are still but twenty-four hours in which to meet increasing duties and multiplying activities that compel a careful budgeting of the hours and minutes, not only of businessmen and followers of professions, but particularly of the president of a college. Building operations are keyed to a schedule; salesmen are required to maintain a quota; hours are measured and standardized for mechanical procedure. In all of these instances there is a marked trend toward order, saving of time, and the maintenance of effort. The president of a college knows this, but his time has a way of slipping by. He is caught in a program of meetings that last longer than he expected and callers who stay over their allotment of minutes, and the day ends with much left undone.

I have thought, in going over schedules for a day and agenda set up for meetings, that the president's secretary should keep a log book of what happens throughout an office day — what, in fact, was accomplished. Such a log, concise and accurate, carefully studied, might be of great value in budgeting time. The effort in keeping such a log would be small compared with the information gained about the president's habits, his use of time, and the results attained. He would learn who comes frequently, the urgency of such visits and the amount of time taken to dispose of minor matters.

It goes without any undue emphasis that a well-organized office with a helpful, sympathetic and able staff is worth much in formulating the best use of a president's time. A first-class filing system is of great help in making letters, reports, and memoranda available when they are needed. Ammunition dumps in the rear of the army are not of much aid to the men on the front if munitions cannot be brought up promptly to the battle line when needed. In a word, a poor filing system is a cause of much irritation and delay.

In this article on the president's time it was not my purpose to write about the heavy obligations that his office imposes, but rather to comment on the time he should use for recreation, family life, meditation, reading, and diversion. Undue devotion to his office and the college in the matter of running errands, talking, planning, and the like, may detract from his efficiency. He must have some time for his family; for after all, a serene home is a great sustainer of morale, and it is easy to push this part of his life to one side. The hospitality of his house requires several hours a week, but when carried too far, may lay an undue burden upon him. The question as to where the line runs between too much and too little entertainment is a good one.

A president must keep up on his reading. As an educator, he will find a great mass of material that has professional value coming from many organizations, associations, and individuals. The president cannot ignore this and must keep in touch with the important developments in the educational field. He, of course, can rely upon the experts on the college staff to analyze and evaluate the details and minutiae, but he must know something about the subject. An instance of this point is found in the changing attitude toward the use of the I.Q. as a means of judging student ability. Many questions come up for reconsideration in the educational field. Besides professional reading, a president should follow what is happening in the national and international spheres, because what he says and what he believes influence the opinions of others.

It is a good thing for a president to have a hobby; that is, the right kind of hobby. Collecting stamps and playing chess would not qualify, in my opinion, as hobbies of a diverting type. Chess is a bit solitary and a great time consumer. The playing of a musical instrument offers many possibilities for enjoyment and relaxation. An interest in music has given some presidents a resultant pleasure and much beneficial relaxation. In my own case, I took up painting two decades ago. The practice of the painter's craft carries me out of doors on many a Saturday afternoon. Through the years I have found that painting requires the full attention of those who follow it. Everything is pushed aside in the concentration required in the making of a picture.

A presidential follower of the arts may not become a good artist and may never attain even mediocrity, but he will have a lot of fun. His family will enjoy talking about the picture he has brought home from his field trip. Thus he becomes a kind of sportsman who has snared something from nature more durable than a catch from the waters or the birds killed in a hunt. Golf is justly celebrated as an exercise and means of relaxation and enjoyment; however, I have found the game too time-consuming. To be a good golfer, even a fair one, requires two or three afternoons a week. The game has its points, which include outdoor exercise and fellowship with pleasant companions. The talk on the course during a golf game is largely limited to scores, the last hole and the bad plays. In some respects it is a discouraging game, requiring a lot of time.

Again, a president must have opportunity for meditation so that he can measure values and consider the real purpose of the institution he serves. He can do this on walks, if alone, or in his study, if he is not interrupted. It is then he can measure results, the value of staffs, drifts in student opinion, their work and earnestness. Now and then an idea may flash into his mind which he tries to evaluate as an important factor in his own growth and in the development of the college. Often he will find that he can see the whole pattern more clearly — the framework of the college and its growth — when he is away from the campus. Sometimes on a train, alone with his own mind and soul, he can sense the height and depth of his work. If he is honest in his mind and not given to rationalization, such sessions with himself will give him greater courage and a larger purpose in carrying on. Henshaw Ward invented a word, "thobbing," which is made up of the first letters in thought, opinion, and belief. Thought based upon opinion and belief is a process largely followed, but highly dangerous for a college president to indulge in at any time. So, it is wise to beware of meditation that drifts into "thobbing."

A vacation is a need, not a luxury, for a college president. Some like to spend time in a big city going to plays, attending major league ball games, perhaps visiting museums and libraries. This sort of vacationing has its pleasures, but it can hardly be called restful. Living in city hotels for a period in the summer months certainly is not my idea of a vacation. Others like to pursue a strenuous outdoor life, even to the extent of climbing mountains. President Winthrop Ellsworth Stone of Purdue was an ardent climber, but he lost his life on his last expedition. It can be said, however, that more people die in bed than any other place, and many die on golf courses.

Fishing has much to commend it as a restful, healthy, and satisfying way to spend a vacation, though when continued too long may prove a bit boring. A really exciting and stimulating sport is sailing. The president who owns a good craft on a fair-sized body of water is in for a lot of fun. This sport requires skill and a good knowledge of boats, water, and wind. A long catalog could be made. The important thing is not to overdo, to take things as they come, where each day develops new adventures that are mild, but stimulating. A vacation should not be a pleasure exertion experience, but a rest of mind and body.

Some time ago in talking of vacations, Robert Hutchins said, "I went to a place in Maine where many trustees of colleges lived during the summer. The talk among those men, when I was present, was mainly about education and, for me, nothing but shop talk. It wasn't much rest." When he had finished his comment, he asked where I went. I told him I vacationed on a fair-sized lake in Northern Michigan, where we lived in a small cabin. The village, three miles away, was inhabited by two hundred persons. Many of them were convinced I was a horse doctor, and I never told them otherwise. Thus discussions on education were confined to my wife and myself.

As I have thought about vacations, I would say they are

usually not long enough. A month should be the minimum and six weeks is better. About two weeks are used up in reaching a relaxed state, two more in vegetating; and two weeks later, there comes an increasing response to ideas. At the end of such a period away from a campus, the head of the institution should be in first-class condition to meet all comers, and to carry his duties easily and well. Yes, a good vacation is worth the time and money to the man who takes it, and particularly is it worth while for the college he serves.

And, a final word: Work from the campus should not follow a president by mail, telephone, or telegram, unless urgent.

M.

The President's Time

Any estimate of the way the president's time is spent can have interest only as it gives a survey of the different things he is called on to do. No two men would spend their time in the same way.

Assuming, as we should, that he takes a full month's vacation and does no work on Sundays, we subtract 79 days from 365 and have 286 days. To translate these figures into percentage, it is clear that 1 per cent of his total time is 2.86 days of 8 hours, or about 23 hours.

	Percentage of time
With the governor, legislature and legislative committee	4
With trustees, trustee committees and preparing for same	8
With deans, directors and vice-presidents, if any	6
With faculty and faculty committees	4
Individual conferences with faculty members	7
" " " non-faculty members	3
" " " alumni	3
" " " students	3
" " " parents of students	2
Conferences on state problems of different kinds	4
Preparation of the annual budget	7
Attendance at educational meetings out of town	4

16   The New President

Attendance at alumni meetings out of town	4
Correspondence	15
Social occasions	5
Welcoming addresses	2
Preparing public addresses and speaking	6
Conferences with prospective staff members	3
Leadership in state education, study, and activity	5
Leadership in national education, study, and activity	5
	100

This schedule allows no time for reading or for much thinking outside of regular work, but the man's evenings are free, according to the schedule. Unfortunately, many evenings are not free.

A consideration of this tentative schedule will show that any reduction of the number of items that can be made is all to the good, as is any reduction of the time allotted to each. Yet all these things demand attention, or did in my day. I cut out all leadership in state and national education while at Iowa State. This was a mistake. Before that I had been quite active in both. Certainly a college president should give time to leadership in these areas.

In Dr. McVey's discussion of the imperative need for a vacation for every college and university president, I most heartily concur. In my own case I have had hay fever since I was twenty-one — an added excuse. For the last twenty years of my active life, I have taken five or six weeks off each year in August and early September. During most of this period my wife and I went to Ojibway Island in the Georgian Bay, some 200 miles north of Toronto. It is a beautiful place for rowing in the many channels between the islands. Mrs. Hughes and I loved rowing, and each morning and afternoon we were away on one of the beautiful channels. So, as I do not care for fishing, I would add rowing to Dr. McVey's list of pleasant vacation opportunities, but it must be in a place where rowing is possible, safe and pleasant. On earlier summers we went to Old Mission on Madeline Island, in Lake Superior. This is a lovely place, but not for rowing.

I would like to add a few things to Dr. McVey's discussion: Apparently I was never missed by anyone either at Miami or Iowa State while I was away. When I returned, everything was always in excellent shape. One summer at Iowa State, a large cattle barn was struck by lightning and entirely destroyed. All the cattle were rescued safely, however. I wired the acting president to proceed with the matter as seemed wise, and he did so. The trustees expressed no criticism of my somewhat long vacations. I believe they fully approved them.

Another thing, and to me it was important: I am not one who can be content for five or six weeks without work. So I always took quite a few odds and ends and generally worked on them three or four hours a day. A regular summer task which usually required ten days was the preparation of an address to the faculty for the opening of the college in the fall.

My predecessor, Dr. Guy Potter Benton, had instituted this opening address at Miami. I carried on the custom but made it somewhat more important by including three things: (1) discussing the several problems and abuses to which I thought the faculty should give attention during the year; (2) listing the advances made at Miami during the preceding year; (3) giving the objectives on which I was intent for the coming year. I always felt that outlining the advances I contemplated was an inspiration to the faculty to co-operate and gave me their support in realizing them.

To me, over the years, this preparation of an opening address to the faculty was an important and worth-while summer task. I felt that the opportunity to contemplate the institution from a remote spot, far away from business or pressure, was valuable to me and to the institution. In some ways I did more to earn my salary while on vacation than at any other time.

H.

Further Comment on the President's Time

In his schedule of a president's time, Dr. Hughes has attempted a difficult and, as he wrote in an accompanying letter, "a futile answer," but the list is, nevertheless, suggestive. The basis of it is an eight hour day over a period of 283 days. This result is reached by subtracting Sundays and a thirty day vacation; having done this, the schedule is made of percentages of time directed to various duties.

In the list I find no time allowance given for the study of diverse and sundry reports that must be read and pondered by a president. The assignment of one-seventh of his time to correspondence is not far from the actual time consumed, but it is too much. Nearly one-half of his time is assigned to various types of conferences. So with conferences and correspondence, the head of a college has used sixty per cent of his time under the Hughes schedule. When such cold facts are faced, the president must do something about it. A good secretary can reduce the correspondence by almost one-half, and an assistant or vice-president can do as well as the president on many of the conferences that are numerous and pressing. This age should be called The Paper-Conference Era.

Some accounting might well be made of the eighty-two days that are left in a year out of the Hughes schedule. It is in this period that the president has some time to think about the problems of the college with less interruption than on weekdays spent on the campus. It may be presumed that the eight hour day is not the limit of time a president devotes to college matters aside from his normal requirements of recreation, family life, and sleep. Considering this subject as a whole, I am reminded of Dr. George Vincent's comment made a good while ago when he said, "The post of a university president is becoming an impossible one."

M.

The President's Secretary

After having an able secretary for sixteen years and five far-from-able secretaries, one after the other, for eight years, I have strong opinions about the president's secretary. A truly able secretary almost doubles a man's value. A secretary who is little more than a stenographer can increase his value only ten per cent. Any college president should be allowed to spend $2,500 in this way; and if his own salary is fairly large, he should feel free to spend one-fourth to one-third as much for a secretary. In any case, he can probably secure some efficient person who is worth more than the salary since the job of being secretary to a college or university president is an attractive one.

A first-class secretary, with slight direction, can do all the thinking about what persons one should see. All the president has to do is to meet those whom the secretary calls in.

An able secretary quickly wins the confidence of the faculty, and she can answer many questions quite as satisfactorily as the president himself.

While I have known two secretaries who served ably under three presidents, and exceptional women can do this, it is usually more satisfactory for a new president to install a new secretary, unless he brings his own secretary with him from his previous post.

H.

Intangibles and Imponderables

The tax authorities use the word intangibles to cover such personal property as stock certificates, bonds, mortgages, notes, trust holdings, and the like. In the education field, the word appears now and then to designate those indescribable things such as spirit, curiosity, imagination, and personality in a human being. The intangibles of the business world are identified with material things; those of education appear in the individual as he grows in grace and spiritual qualities. So a university is defined as a place, a spirit.

An old hand in the educational field may get an inkling of the spirit prevailing on a campus. He may find there an attitude of competition, of pride in athletic progress. College spirit is an intangible value, but is the most important intangible in a university. On the other hand, one may observe a serious purpose among the students and an earnest zeal in faculty members. In the latter instance, there is a sense of reaching out, of seeking, of earnest inquiry.

An imponderable is immeasurable, since the force of the idea to which the word is applied cannot be weighed. It may be said that imponderables are contained in the educational process. As such forces and trends come to be known, they cease to be imponderables, but remain intangibles, hard to grasp and to understand. The college head must therefore be capable of sensing these unseen trends, forces, ideals, and spiritual drifts. Unless he has some appreciation of what these mean to a college, he will fail to give that institution over which he presides the quality that will make it great. He is assisted by faculty attitudes, student response, and the contributions of gifted men and women to the campus life and thought.

In these days of larger student attendance and increasing public functions, a president is confronted by duties that are quite unrelated to the real purpose of the institution. In addition, he finds on his desk many problems pertaining to construction, endorsements, appointments, and questions of administration. In consequence, the intangibles and the imponderables are left for other days and times. The institution may grow in plant, student body, and size of staff; but if the spirit shrinks, mediocrity will be written into its history. There should be no such thing as a mediocre college, yet there are many where the leaders have forgotten or neglected the intangibles and imponderables.

M.

The President's Personal Influence

A college or university president is like a clergyman in one particular. His personal relations and his private life are always on review. The standards he maintains are to a considerable extent regarded as the standards of the college.

Occasionally, a president is heard to remark that he cannot constantly live up to the office and must have some respite from it.

He certainly should have generous vacations, but the standards of his office go where he goes, and he will be judged at home by his actions abroad. There are always observers quick to report back to the college town any slight letdown in a president's conduct.

On the other hand, a man of high principles and noble conduct reflects these attitudes all over a campus. He tends to hold the deans and department heads — those who know the president — up to his standards. In turn, they reflect them farther on down the line.

In the small college of five hundred or less, this influence is all pervasive. The larger the institution, the further everyone is away from the president's influence, and the less it counts.

The faculty demands absolute integrity of its president, and any deviation is widely reported. It is astonishingly easy to injure one's reputation by just trying to be polite and not saying bluntly what is meant. Any professor coming to the president with a plan or request requiring his support is likely to accept a courteous hearing, without direct disapproval, as approval. If his project is later turned down, he charges the president with being a liar. It is always better to be direct and positive.

Easy accessibility and a patient, courteous hearing give faculty members confidence in a president's desire to serve both their interests and those of the institution. When his duties make it difficult for him to extend a full hearing to all faculty members who desire to see him, it is greatly to the advantage of the institution that a vice-president be appointed and given full authority to deal with all faculty and departmental matters. A fine man in this post can contribute greatly to the contentment of the faculty and also to the relief of the president.

H.

Prayer, a Great Source of Strength

For me, prayer was a valuable resource through the twenty-five years I served as a college president. I was dealing all the time with people. It was very important for me to understand their situations and do everything that could be done to meet their respective needs.

I prayed constantly for an open mind and for understanding of the matters that came before me. Prayer is a most mysterious thing, but I know in my case it gave me peace of mind and confidence.

For many years I read a chapter in the Bible and prayed when reaching the office. Often throughout the day I would ask for help. It certainly brings affairs into true perspective to present one's problems to God. In this way really fair decisions can be reached.

Professors, instructors, students, parents and others have problems which they desire to present to a president. Many are simple problems, but some are very puzzling. To maintain one's balance and patience throughout the day and make each person who has called leave the office with a feeling of having been helped, even where it was impossible to grant the request, is a real responsibility.

One must try to realize that each person's problem is of utmost importance in his own eyes. To protect the standards of the institution and yet give all possible consideration to each applicant was much easier for me when considered in the presence of God.

H.

The President's Wife

Seldom is a man called to a presidential post who has not reached middle age. Since this is the case, he has already achieved the marital state or through misfortune is either a widower or a bachelor. Whatever may be his status in that regard, he established his household and chose his mate with little idea that he would become a college president and therefore would be in need of a capable wife to support and to aid him in his difficult task. This is not to say that men seldom marry capable women, but that this particular post makes a great demand upon a president's wife. I shall endeavor to set forth in this commentary what I believe to be the qualities needed in the woman who is called upon to play that role.

First of all, good health is highly desirable, as it helps her materially to endure the stress and strain of a heavy social program, long evenings, extended dinners, luncheons, calls, and house guests. Good health is behind the impression she gives of interest and joy in whatever she is doing. Beyond good health, this woman should be well educated, preferably a college graduate. From my observation I would say that a teaching experience gives her an understanding of the purposes of a college, making her more sympathetic with the problems of teachers and the shortcomings of students. It is well that she keep up her reading and have some knowledge of current events, because she will have again and again important guests whose good will can be greatly increased by an intelligent hostess. What every woman would like to have is charm, and that quality smooths many a difficult path. Perhaps I might add that appearance is the standard by which strangers judge a person they are seeing for the first time. This means good grooming, a quiet but modest taste in dress, and a pleasant voice and manner. Dowdiness should be avoided even at the cost of considerable expenditure at the costumers. These requirements for a successful and helpful presidential mate are outwardly important but by no means enough.

After all, this woman whom I am writing about must possess character and, if possible, have reached an inward serenity. Fundamentally this means a kind person who really loves people and who can suffer fools gladly. Naturally she is a tactful person who knows what is the right thing to do and does it with wisdom. The ability to keep counsel and to hold her peace when controversy raises its sometimes ugly head adds much to her value as a good soldier in the academic citadel. She withholds criticism of people, especially of faculty members. Soon she learns to avoid consorting with cliques, of which there are many on a campus where large faculties are engaged in teaching and research. This is always difficult, since each group would like to claim her for its own. Friends are desirable and necessary, but anything approaching favoritism leads to comment and criticism, since such persons are regarded as being near to the throne and are supposed to have the ear of the president.

There is a material side to the work and duties of a president's wife involved in the management of a considerable establishment. It may be assumed that she will have the aid of at least one servant, and in a large house, several. Even so, it calls for more than average administrative ability, including a knowledge of good housekeeping. The care of a family is a big job in itself, and the additional one of hostess in a president's house means a heavy load of responsibility for one pair of shoulders. So health, education, personality, charm, tact, and wisdom are all to the good in filling the position of the wife of a college president today.

If the college faculty and trustees recognize the size of the burden, they can assist by not pressing too hard on the president's house as the place where college entertainment is centered. The trustees will provide funds for the maintenance of the house, and the faculty will not ask to hold receptions there. The development of student unions and guest quarters on most campuses will bring welcome relief to many a president's wife.

M.

The President's Wife

The strain of office on the wife of a president is greater than it is on the president himself. While he has a secretary who can protect him from telephone calls and visitors at undesirable hours, his wife usually has no such protection.

Along with the heavy burden of managing a household, often with inadequate help or no help at all, she is looked up to by the faculty wives as their adviser, their leader and often as their intermediary with the president. Their calls come at all hours over the telephone and in person and are often extended. To wedge these in with household duties, marketing and care of children requires great stamina and unusual ability as an organizer. Many women just don't have what it takes.

It means a great deal to be able to bring guests home to lunch or dinner. Often these guests are unexpected and cannot be announced long in advance. A meal in the president's home with a chat afterwards can afford much to a worried professor or visitor. An efficient housekeeper will make this possible. Today, the extreme difficulty in securing competent service adds greatly to the problems of a president's wife.

While politics is sometimes played among faculty members, it is safe to say there is nearly always politics among the faculty wives. To keep clear of this and to do what can be done to reduce it to a minimum is no easy problem. Admission to the many campus clubs, securing the offices, gaining promotion and higher salaries for their husbands, and many other matters, all are involved in the politics of faculty wives. Much of this would be reduced if their lot were made easier. Living at the level of a college professor on a limited salary taxes their ingenuity. Reasonable desires for domestic help, suitable clothes, school and college expenses for children, vacations, books, social life — all require money. It is always hard to compress demands within income. And yet what is more necessary for the effective work of a college professor than a happy home? Anything that a president's wife can do to allay discontent is of enormous value to an institution.

An able, acceptable college president is invaluable, but the worth of a president's wife who is equal to her responsibilities is above rubies.

H.

To the President's Wife

In case McVey and I have been a bit discouraging to any president's wife, let me add this. The trustees hope your husband has all the gifts and virtues we have suggested would be valuable for *you* to have and, in addition, that he knows how to manage a college or university successfully and make it operate smoothly, and keep the students, faculty, and alumni happy. We feel sure he falls short of these standards quite as much as you may find yourself lacking in some of our suggested gifts of personality.

H.

The President's House

On hundreds of campuses throughout this country there are residences of many types and various ages designated as the president's house.

When I went to the University of North Dakota in 1909, the president's house had been built a few years before under the direction of a local architect. The building had many good points, but a three-story house with great pillars in front did not fit into the terrain of a prairie country. The public rooms were too small, though the dining room and kitchen were commodious and well placed.

In my second presidency, at the University of Kentucky, the trustees had bought an old house with considerable land for lawn and yard space. As a newcomer, I was allowed to advise the architect on the family needs and the requirements for entertaining. The result of this combination of architect and resident was the reconstruction of an old house into a pleasant, livable residence, with ample facilities for entertainment. In contrast to this pleasant old house, many presidential residences have an institutional atmosphere. They are not really homes and in consequence lack that air of friendly welcome so essential to true hospitality.

I am sure that a house equipped with furniture, rugs, and pictures purchased by a committee can never possess a home atmosphere unless there are intelligent and experienced women in that group. Too often the furnishing of such a building is left to a decorator or to a local dealer. On the other hand, if the matter of cost is to be borne by the occupant, he will find it very burdensome to buy the furniture needed for such a place. As a consequence, an air of emptiness or even shabbiness may result.

The question arises then, What is the real function of a president's house? Is it a home, a hotel, or a combination of both?

On some campuses elaborate houses have been erected that are very expensive to operate and burdensome to the hostess who may preside over them. Servants are required in kitchen, garden, dining room, and chambers — a costly enterprise. A more modest establishment is better adapted to the use of such a home and place of occasional entertainment. It is desirable to have facilities for a few overnight guests; beyond that, the college should provide a guest house, or guest rooms in a dormitory. Often a lecturer or distinguished guest would much prefer the privacy of special outside rooms rather than make the effort to fit into the regime of a family household.

Other types of entertainment, such as large receptions and banquets, should be held in one of the assembly rooms provided now by most colleges in their student union building. Such an arrangement removes from the shoulders of the president's wife the recurring burden of preparing for large parties and dinners. Although faculty members and students prefer to go to the president's house, in these days of staggering student enrollment and extensive faculties it is no longer a possibility.

M.

The President's House

The idea in providing a house for the president has changed somewhat throughout the years.

In earlier days, when many college towns lacked good hotels, the president was obliged to take care of all distinguished visitors. Before the days of unions, faculty clubs and other suitable places, the president was expected to entertain extensively in his home with dinners and receptions. Domestic help was plentiful then and reasonable in cost. Also, the other demands on a president were not so great as those of today.

To provide a handsome ten or twenty room house for the college president is to load him with a home impossible to maintain without servants, and to secure such domestic help is sometimes difficult. This condition has been recognized in a few cases where the president has declined to live in the residence provided by the institution.

The whole matter is far different than it was at the turn of the century, or even in the 1930's.

Certainly, where the old conditions still prevail, with a college in a small town without proper hotel facilities, it is desirable to provide the president with an adequate house and to secure for him competent domestic service. Personally, I never believed it wise for the college to provide service for the president. On the other hand, many institutions do so provide and pay for such service.

In any case, where adequate entertainment is available in hotel or union, it is questionable whether a president's home should be provided at all. When service is scarce, a large house makes a drudge of the president's wife. This should not be. If a moderate house, adequate for a president and his wife, can be provided, it would be welcome and fitting. It is rare for a man under forty-five years of age to be appointed to a presidency, and usually his children are away from home.

Certain entertainment is definitely desirable for the morale of the faculty and students. A reception for the entire faculty, early in the fall, at which new members may be presented to their associates, is necessary. This should be paid for by the college and if the faculty is large, held in some adequate place outside the president's home.

If the college is small and the senior class is manageable, a reception to the class is certainly appropriate in the spring. Inevitably the president will do a good deal of simple entertaining at lunch and dinner for various individuals and small groups throughout the year. Personally, I feel that these are best paid for by the president, and that his salary should be adequate for this purpose.

If there is a president's house, it should be suitably furnished. As has been observed many times, the average official life of a president is only five or six years, and he should not be forced to furnish a house provided by the institution. On the other hand, any man chosen for such a position will almost always own some household goods which he prefers to use.

If the president's house is on campus, it is fitting that the grounds be cared for, and that heat, light, and water be provided by the institution.

Quite certainly the day has passed when an expensive and elegant house is desirable or even an asset to any college president. Such a home carries with it the obligation for generous entertaining, very difficult to maintain today. A newly appointed president should look carefully into the matter before agreeing to live in the president's house. If it means undue physical labor for his wife, he certainly should decline the honor.

H.

Is There a Dog in the House?

The house in question is the president's residence on a college campus and the canine is the household pet. Should he, the dog, have a place and a part in the president's menage?

I am really serious about this as a factor of importance in the administrative family, because I have seen what a dog can do on many occasions to ease the stilted beginnings of social contacts. Students come to the president's house diffident and shy; it is hard for them to adjust themselves to the situation. Often they do not know more than two or three among those present and feel they are involved in a serious and difficult social affair, though the intent has been to make the occasion informal. It is at this point that the dog comes in. At once he is the center of attention, and in a dog's friendly way he responds to the advances made to him. The host tells a story or two about the dog's exploits; the ice is broken, and the party gets off to a good start.

It is not every canine that can meet the demands thus made upon him. In many ways the Scotch terrier fills the bill better than most breeds. He has dignity, some reserve, but responds like a gentleman to the greetings of a guest. He seldom runs, barks, or makes a nuisance of himself. There are other breeds, such as the cocker spaniel, but he is more sensitive than the Scotty. As a subject of conversation, a dog is much better than the weather.

My wife told a story about a dog Miss Wylie had in her house on the Vassar campus. When students came in for a group visit, the dog was there stretched out before the cheerful fire. After the talk was well started, Professor Wylie would say to her pet, "That is all, Toots, you may go now." Whereupon, according to the account given me, the dog would leisurely and quietly retire.

The name of the dog should be chosen with some care. The one who knows the Scotty would never call him Fido or Carlo, for there are more descriptive names. Angus, Sandy, Danny, Tammy, or Tim fit him better and give him more personality. There is a real place for the right dog in the president's house.

M.

Entertainment Problems

When I was made acting president of Miami in 1911 at $4,000 a year, I continued to live in our eight room house and had no thought of moving out. I was definitely acting president, and entertainment was no responsibility. During that year I helped the board all I could in the consideration of a number of men for president.

At the end of that year no decision had been reached. I was re-appointed at the same salary. I moved over to the president's home, but we did very little entertaining. The third year, I was elected president of the university at a salary of $5,000 a year. Mrs. Hughes and I tried to do our part socially. We served tea to the faculty on the lawn when college opened in September. Throughout the year, as there was no desirable hotel, we entertained a good many guests of the university. We also invited various faculty members to dinner from time to time. In the late spring we held a reception for the seniors. This routine was maintained during the remaining thirteen years of my service.

When we went to Iowa State College at Ames, Mrs. Hughes

was not very strong and I impressed upon her that the board had elected me as president and that no responsibility rested upon her beyond her strength. However, she wanted to do her full duty socially, so far as possible.

Early in the fall a reception was given at the Memorial Union to all members of the faculty and staff. We entertained rather frequently at dinner throughout the year. I always felt free to take anyone home to lunch: students, faculty or guests of the college. In the spring, at the close of the year, we gave a dinner for the older alumni.

At Iowa State, the numbers were too great for wholesale entertainment. However, during the first half of the summer term, we had a conveniently sized group; about one hundred were graduated at the close of the first summer term. We would entertain this group at breakfast on the lawn, and it was always a pleasant party.

Nothing elaborate was attempted, and the cost of all entertainment came out of my own pocket until my last two years. The expense of our large reception to the entire staff, which amounted to some hundreds of dollars, was paid thereafter by the college.

In all this entertaining experience, I learned two interesting facts: I had read once that if a meeting was called at which every person present was desired to participate, not over seven should be asked. I found that seven at a table proved to be most satisfactory. At our breakfast for seniors, we arranged to have a faculty man or wife at each table with six students; here all six students took part in the conversation.

When a distinguished visitor was invited to dinner, the number of guests was unimportant. The guest with a little encouragement, would do the talking and entertain the party, which was just what we wanted.

Any man who works eight hours a day in the president's office does not have the energy to entertain a great deal. Presidential homes, large and equipped for elaborate entertainment, seem to me enough to discourage any man from accepting the social responsibility such a house demands.

I knew one president, Dr. Hollis Godfrey of Drexel Institute, who solved the social problem very wisely. He and Mrs. Godfrey lived in a comfortable apartment. They entertained various groups for dinner at the Art Club in Philadelphia. Their large receptions were held in the Institute.

A college president and his wife must maintain a home that is open to friends of the institution. They must entertain some of their own friends and some members of the staff. But to expect one as heavily burdened with problems as the president of a college to carry on an extensive social program is unreasonable.

H.

Some Exceptional Expenses

The president's salary often seems exorbitant to the members of the faculty. It is my best judgment that it should be twice the highest professorial salary. Usually, and I believe properly, a president's home with heat, light, and water is provided. I have opposed any additional support for entertainment, automobile, house service, and such extras. It seems sounder and more satisfactory for the board to provide for exceptional entertainment or other expensive activities by an increase in salary above twice the professorial level.

There are, of course, several sound reasons why a president should receive a comparatively large salary. The most evident is that no one with extensive executive experience can be secured for less. There are, however, other reasons. Of necessity, the president does considerable entertaining. This requires an adequate domestic staff and a good table. He also has many expenses that a professor is not called upon to meet.

At Miami, in the small town of Oxford, I found that I was expected to head most subscriptions. This proved to be so formidable an undertaking that I was shortly driven in self-protection to limit my benevolence to ten per cent of my salary. After that was exhausted, I would explain my position to any solicitors who importuned me. I told them if they would return after

July first, the end of my year, I would be glad to make a contribution. This reasoning appeared to be unanswerable. The custom of giving away ten per cent and keeping accounts to make this amount certain has proved a most satisfactory method throughout my succeeding forty years.

Traveling expenses always exceeded the sum I felt free to submit to the state auditor. Vic Donahay, auditor of Ohio in my day, made his political success, later leading to the United States Senate, by a blast in the newspapers about a state employee who spent forty cents for a baked potato. I always limited my expense account to items which I believed could not be criticised, and paid the balance myself. I felt it to be undesirable that the traveling expenses of the president of a state institution should come up for criticism at the state house.

There were also for me each year a number of exceptional expenses of various kinds, unusual charges against the college which I did not wish to submit to the board, which sometimes amounted to several hundred dollars a year. One minor expense resulted from the students having placed the cow of a poor Negro woman on the belfry tower of the Main Building at Miami. Old Nancy came to report her damage to me and said her cow did not let down her milk as usual after the nerve-racking experience. When I asked how much she thought her cow had been damaged, she answered, "Well now, Mr. Hughes, I judge she's been damaged two dollars' worth." I paid the two dollars.

At Iowa State College, the discipline committee took action against a student for having liquor in his possession. He went to a lawyer, and we were shown that, while our evidence was convincing to us, it was not sufficient before the law. The lawyer did not wish to prosecute, and the student offered to withdraw the case if we would pay his lawyer's fee of $300. This I paid. It was my largest item of the kind.

At Iowa State College, with numerous small sales rooms operating all over the campus in the dairy, poultry farm, greenhouses, vegetable garden, and fruit farm, we suffered some small losses through theft. I paid these shortages as they turned up, dismissing the employee involved. I regarded them as due to poor administration under my direction. Later we improved our accounting system so that these shortages were stopped. I believe my way of handling these matters without reference to the board was sound. It saved me in worry more than it cost in cash. Every president thus has various expenses which a professor does not encounter.

There is one other major reason for a generous salary: Usually the term of a president's tenure is brief, more comparable to that of a football coach than a professor.

H.

Some Puzzling Problems

College administration is very different from the administration of a business. If a new president of a business or industry finds some high officials of the company unsuited to his policies, he can dismiss them. It is extremely difficult and usually highly inexpedient for a new president to dismiss promptly or retire to the ranks deans or department heads whom he may regard as unsatisfactory. In my own experience, I was perhaps too cautious in making changes. Both at Miami University and at Iowa State College I inherited some men and women in important positions whom I regarded as unsatisfactory. Some were lazy, some were maladroit in dealing with human beings within their jurisdiction, and some were too old for the job they held and lacked enthusiasm in their leadership.

While I had the satisfaction of turning these institutions over to my successors in distinctly better condition than I found them, there should have been even more improvement made. To meet the situation relative to the men who were too old, I introduced a regulation with the authority of the board that fixed the retirement age of all administrative officers at sixty-five years and for those then over sixty-five, at sixty-eight. This made certain improvements possible.

I am now convinced that all deans and department heads should be appointed for a fixed period — department heads probably for a four or five year term, and deans for eight or ten years. Further, I am now convinced that all these offices should be filled by the vote of the faculty members concerned. At the time I did not so believe. I made all these appointments after wide consultation, and felt fairly well satisfied with the result. Yet I am sure now that as good or better appointments would have been made by the faculty. Furthermore, if all these appointments had been made by the faculty members for fixed terms, poor appointments would have automatically terminated in due time.

I did retire and dismiss some full professors. My procedure was first to convince myself that the man in point was unsatisfactory. I then called him in to my office for an interview. I told him that he was as good as when he had been appointed but that he would undoubtedly fit better into some other faculty. I assured him he would not be dropped abruptly and urged him to secure another and if possible a better position. Two men who left the Miami faculty in this way distinctly bettered themselves.

The American Association of University Professors has intimidated many American college presidents by their searching investigations of many dismissals of professors. I am of the opinion now that if a president, confronted with the necessity of dismissing one or more men on permanent appointment, would ask that association to send a representative to confer about the situation before anything was done, an understanding would be reached. If through inadvertence an unsuitable man had been allowed to attain a permanent appointment status, I cannot believe the Association of University Professors would desire his retention. An unsatisfactory professor, at a $4,000 salary, would receive $60,000 in fifteen years for giving poor instruction to perhaps 1,500 students. Surely this is deplorable! I believe that with the help of the association a reasonable plan could be worked out that would correct such situations.

Able, enthusiastic and sympathetic leadership in a dean or department head is of the greatest importance! In a department with from ten to fifty or more instructors, the difference in the service rendered students under a thoroughly desirable man and one who is undesirable would be at least 10 per cent, and may easily be 20 or 25 per cent. Yet as one surveys the twenty to seventy-five department heads in his institution, how many possess this spark of enthusiastic, able and sympathetic leadership?

A department head can do a great deal to raise the teaching effectiveness of his staff. He can make very careful appointments, especially among positions on a lower level. He can see that every staff member with little teaching experience receives friendly criticism and help. He can see that every sarcastic, hard boiled teacher is speedily removed. It is possible to become so absorbed in the paper work of routine administration that no real leadership is given.

The president is usually the last person to learn of poor teaching situations. A rating of each instructor by other staff members and by students would be valuable in quickly pointing out the weak spots in the staff. Washington State College has instituted such a system.

For many years I prepared annually my own rating of the staff. So far as I could, I placed every person in one of the following four lists:

1. Those who could not be replaced. Men and women who had given themselves unreservedly to the institution, who were in every way satisfactory.
2. Those who could not be replaced by equally satisfactory men at the same salary.
3. Those who could be replaced by equally useful men at the same salary.
4. Those who could be replaced by better men for less salary. I always tried to reduce the number of those in group 4.

The appointment of the dean of the graduate school is one of peculiar importance. If he has been selected by the graduate school faculty, is generally trusted and is less than fifty-four years of age, he should be among those considered for the presidency when that office becomes vacant. The dean of the graduate school deals with all colleges and all departments. He should be a man whom all regard as honest, fair and capable.

Upon returning a dean or department head back to professorial status, his salary should not be cut heavily. In these positions the appointment is usually for twelve months with one month's vacation. If he were reduced to a nine month's basis, his salary would not be far out of line with that of other full professors. At Ohio State University, the normal professorial appointment is for three quarters or nine months. A department head receives the full professor's salary for twelve months. A department head upon relinquishing the headship will drop back to the nine month basis.

It is always advantageous, where possible, to promote a man already on the staff to be the head of a department, or dean. For one thing, it is cheaper, as the promotion will always be an advance. For another, he is already known; and if he is selected by a decided majority, he will rarely fail to make good. There should be in every department a man worthy of promotion to the headship. Occasionally there is no one regarded as suitable. In such a case a man must be brought in. At Iowa State College, one-third of those at the head of departments have been brought in from outside, while two-thirds have been promotions. The members of each group are about equally effective, roughly speaking: two-thirds good, and one-third only fair.

H.

Help From Outside Consultants

Bringing in individuals or committees from time to time from outside to report on certain aspects of an institution is usually stimulating.

I have had such external reports on our clerical staff, the catalog, the landscaping plan, and other phases of our work.

It is equally helpful to visit institutions you believe are doing some things better than your own and thus pick up ideas. Many improvements in methods and practices have been introduced in this way. The attitude that your institution is good enough is a dangerous one. It is almost certain that any one of one hundred similar institutions is each doing some one or more things better than you are.

Education is such a personal thing and is so complex that no good teacher or administrator should be satisfied with what he is doing. An ambitious, hard-working man in some institution has often developed the best way known in which to do some certain thing.

At Iowa State College, our former librarian, Dr. Charles H. Brown, was invited repeatedly to survey various college libraries and make recommendations. I know his work was valuable in every case.

H.

Public Addresses

No hard and fast formula can be applied to presidential speeches away from the campus. People want to see and hear a college president, and high school pupils often invite the president to deliver their commencement address. Various organizations call upon him for talks on different subjects. There is a limit of time that can be given to the making of speeches, but over a period of years some results can be observed.

I very soon concluded that I could give only so many talks and that those would best be arranged on the basis of first come, first served. This plan worked fairly well. One often received compliments from well wishers who had listened to a speech, but what others thought about it never came to his ears, or perhaps the number of speeches would have been considerably reduced. Many requests for talks were from student organizations and these were accepted.

To be good a talk requires preparation, and this in turn takes time. The president is invited to speak because the program makers want not only a speaker but a person of some prominence. It is a nice question whether or not it is worth while to accept some given invitation. A friend of mine, when he was elected president, gave out word that he would make no speeches the first year of his service. He made one during that year and many, many more after that.

In the course of my service as president, I inaugurated what was called "Between-Us Day" to give me an opportunity to know the problems of college students and also to comment on university policies and regulations. Without question these talks did considerable good. Also, one hour vesper service was held on Sunday afternoons at four o'clock. Eminent men from the various church denominations were asked to speak. The program was supplemented with music and scripture reading. The attendance was not large — some two or three hundred persons; the interest varied with the reputation of the speaker.

After a year's trial, the vesper service was given up due to the expense and the relatively small attendance. As a substitute, a Sunday concert series was arranged which has been going on now for twenty years. The attendance is large, made up of students and townspeople. The concerts are maintained by a grant, and the programs are given by professional musicians and university glee clubs, orchestra and bands, in successions.

M.

Public Addresses

Unless a college president is an effective speaker he accomplishes little by speaking on most occasions. Personally, I am a second-rate speaker and have avoided making public addresses outside the college, as far as possible.

I now believe that any college president should feel responsible for a certain amount of public leadership. This could best be accomplished by formulating one or two policies each year on which he has a firm belief and preparing carefully a few good short addresses on these subjects. He should then decide what audiences he can address most effectively. Two or three such addresses a year would be sufficient. If a man limits himself to this plan, he will have time to be a real president.

It is well to remember that there are usually several professors and deans who can speak as well or better than the president and who enjoy speaking. Send them.

The ineffective president often uses an invitation to speak as a means of escape from the campus.

H.

Responsibility for Leadership

Many men appointed to a college presidency from a deanship or professorship are so occupied with their new and demanding responsibilities that they give little thought to state or national education. Their leadership is needed in these fields as active members of the national educational associations and also as thinkers and writers.

Any person at the head of a college or university certainly should look over the entire field of education. He must relate his institution to the other colleges and universities in the state. He should sense that all of them together constitute the higher educational opportunities of the state. Their relation should be friendly and co-operative, although there may be frequent rivalry and friction. It is as each institution discovers its own peculiar field of service in the state and serves notably in that field that it makes its most valuable contribution.

The strength of institutions of higher learning depends directly on the quality of the work done by the grade schools and high schools of the state and their adequacy for service both in location and staff. In no state are our educational facilities ideal, and in every state each college president should feel a responsibility for strengthening the system throughout as well as in his own institution.

All education grows by imitation, by imitating the finest there is. One must view all education in the nation if one is to know the best. It grows toward perfection only as here and there an able and devoted man or woman is given the opportunity to work out his dream.

Years ago, Dean Carl E. Seashore of the Graduate School of the University of Iowa, while touring the country for the National Academy of Science, spoke in the chapel at Miami University. To encourage our students he called attention to the fact that when the automobile was first made commercially, the engine was underneath the body of the car. It took the engineering skill of the whole world twenty years to figure out how to bring it out of that awkward position and make it easily accessible up in front. So it is in education. We are usually following precedents and doing our work as it has been done. Changes come slowly.

The leadership of our 1,850 college and university presidents should contribute much toward speeding up progress in both state and nation.

H.

How Long Should a President Serve?

Years ago, Dr. William Allen made a survey of the University of Wisconsin. In the report on this survey, he expressed the opinion that the president of a state university should not serve more than eight years. He said that most men had made their main contribution to the institution in the eight years. Also, he thought there was a tendency for a president to build up a group of influential faculty men whom he had appointed, who became his personal supporters. He concluded that eight years is long enough.

My observation is that most men do make their peculiar contributions in eight or ten years. Also, during the first year or two everybody is friendly and hopeful for the success of the president. As time passes, inevitably a few staff members are offended by actions directed at them or by general policies which affect their departments. The offended professors gradually get together, and in a few years an opposition party is built up. The president's weaknesses become more apparent. It becomes more difficult for him to secure the support of trustees and faculty. Certainly eight or ten years is a better period of service than fifteen or tweny for 90 per cent of college presidents.

This has a bearing on the age of the man appointed, and on the appointee's plans. Assuming sixty-five to be the age of retirement, a man of fifty-three to fifty-six has only about ten years to serve. This may be a sound reason for appointing a man of this age.

On the other hand, a board often desires a younger man, one around forty-five years of age. In my judgment, when a man of that age accepts a presidency, he should plan to advance to another post after eight to twelve years. If he serves ably, he will have the opportunity to go elsewhere. Almost invariably his first ten years in any such post will be happier both for him and for the faculty than a second ten years. Furthermore, after ten years his service becomes more or less routine. A move to another post will pull him up on his toes again and will be stimulating.

H.

How Long Should a President Serve?

Hughes quotes Dr. William Allen as saying that eight years is long enough in which to make a contribution as a college president. To this contention, I am opposed. To begin with, it takes from two to three years to learn the ropes in an institution of even moderate size; in addition, a period of five years is required for a satisfactory acquaintanceship with the alumni, a knowledge of the area wherein the college is located and the men and women interested in the college. Another phase of this matter is the disturbing effect of change on a college organization. An institution may go along a year or more before a decision is made and a new president installed. Every change will cost the college a considerable sum in delay, in pension for the retiring president and in the renovation of the president's house.

Any plan that may be set up by the new administration cannot be completed in less than four years. The length of service should not be determined by an arbitrary term of years, but by the character and effectiveness of the administration.

M.

The Effect of an Old President on an Institution

As a man grows old, he dislikes more and more to face trouble. He becomes increasingly indisposed to hunt for trouble. Situations develop on a campus which could be checked at the start, but after a few years become difficult to correct. For this reason I strongly favor sixty-five as the retiring age for a college president. Seventy is too old and beyond seventy is terrible. Some of our greatest American university presidents served beyond the time of their greatest usefulness. The presidency of a college or university is a very hard job, and old age and weakness are no proper reasons for failure to serve effectively.

H.

How To Utilize a President Emeritus

Every president has developed policies and procedures which are dear to his heart, and it is difficult for him on retirement to hold his peace. He is greatly tempted to criticize his successor, who will invariably introduce new policies and ignore old ones. Yet the changes are usually good for the institution.

Either the president emeritus must be retired on a pension and encouraged to leave town, at least for a few years until the new incumbent is established, or he must be kept busy with new work. Perhaps every president emeritus should leave the college town for a year or two.

However, it seems inconceivable that a man who has served an institution usefully until retirement can become useless to the institution on attaining the age of sixty-five. There are several possible occupations which, depending on his abilities, might occupy the president emeritus usefully. For example: If he is a skillful money raiser, he might continue to head up that work. He knows the benefactors who have given to the institution during the past years and they know him. He should be able to render useful service in this field. If he has been well acquainted with the alumni, he could do much to serve them and strengthen the work of the alumni office. If he is a skillful teacher, he could well teach acceptably six or eight hours a week. Some men might serve usefully on the board of trustees for at least five years.

Undoubtedly a president emeritus could be a real curse to the president; this should not be permitted.

H.

The Attitude of the President Emeritus

The conditions under which the president retires from his post after a decade or more of service have much to do with his relation to the institution and to the new incumbent in the office. If, as an emeritus, he is expected to do some sort of work to justify the continuation of pay, he is still tied to the community and the institution.

I recall an instance where a president, after many years of distinguished service in a denominational college, was given the job of running a mimeograph machine at seventy-five dollars a month. In consequence, his feelings were hurt and his helpfulness reduced. This incident is perhaps a low in the relations of an emeritus officer and his college.

When a retirement allowance is free of restrictions, the emeritus president can choose his place of residence, but he will discover difficulty in making contacts and adjustments in another community. In fact, after a good many years of living in one place, he will find it hard at sixty-five or seventy to make the move. If he stays on in the college town, he can become a thorn in the side of the new president or he can be of considerable help through a tactful attitude of appreciation and understanding.

If all retired presidents were gentlemen, there would be no problem. Most of them are, but others have been willing to listen to talk, indulge in criticism of the new administration and to become the focal point of the opposition. Such men are a menace to good relations in the college community. Rules for the conduct of an emeritus president are easy to formulate; but after all, the relationship should be one based on understanding, friendliness, and a determination to help rather than hinder — qualities characteristic of all honorable men.

There are some suggestions that are quite obvious, but might be overlooked, so I list them for what they are worth: a president emeritus should not give advice unless asked for it; and if the facts are not clear, he should wait or decline to act. Under no circumstances should he listen to belittling gossip or questionable stories about the newcomer. The emeritus president should do all that he can to uphold the administration on the campus and in the community. In other words, he should act like a gentleman and remember to do unto others what he would have others do unto him.

M.

While a president is an adviser and a planner, he is, after all, an executive officer working under a board of trustees who are the ultimate authority. To know these members well is a matter of wisdom; for it is the president's place to instruct them in, and inspire them with, the purposes of the institution. This cannot be done in meetings alone; his efforts to develop and maintain friendly relations must go beyond such formal contacts.

2.
The President and the Trustees

McVey and the Trustees

When I joined the staff of the University of North Dakota in 1909, the board of trustees consisted of five members, two of whom were lawyers, one a banker, one a farmer, and one a businessman. On the whole they were an able board. None of them was an alumnus of the university, but they were interested in the stability of the institution, its buildings and finances. They were conservative in their attitudes and opposed to any show of radicalism among the student body. It was taken for granted that the faculty would stay in line.

On one occasion some student views were reported at a session of the board. I took occasion to say that students should show some interest in political, economic and religious controversies. "In fact," I said, "if you gentlemen were as conservative when you were young as you now are, no one knows how impervious to new ideas you would be today." They took my comment in their stride, but I had no way of discovering their inner feelings.

When a political revolution took place in North Dakota and the Non-Partisan League came into control, the party leaders wanted and got a central control board which had the direction of nine institutions — penal, charitable, and educational. The board met from time to time in the towns where the institutions were located. At these meetings each president was given about two hours to present the finances, policy, appointments and other matters of importance to the institution of which he was head. Many matters were left to the president, and he in turn had many decisions to make without the help of the board. It was an impossible situation and so recognized by the board and the president. After I left to go to the University of Kentucky, two boards were created, one for the educational institutions and another for the penal and charitable enterprises carried on by the state. Later, the legislature abolished the control board and placed the university under a single board, to the great relief of everyone interested in higher education. In the course of twenty years, North Dakota went through a series of experiences from single boards to a control board for all institutions; and then as a third step to a single board for the university, a board for the teachers colleges, and a board to care for the affairs of charitable institutions.

My conclusion is that there is no ideal system, since boards are no better than the men who comprise them. Centralization looks well on paper but has not turned out to be much of an improvement in managing state institutions. The University of Kentucky comprised all the departments usually associated with a central university. There was no competition with a separate agricultural and mechanical engineering college. The board consisted of three ex-officio members, three alumni, three members of the agricultural board and six citizens appointed by the governor — fifteen in all. The executive committee of five met monthly.

The appointment by the governor of board members to the managing body of a public institution made out quite well on the whole, but now and then there was a slip. On one occasion I asked the governor why he had appointed a certain man to the university board after a meeting attended by the new member. "Do you know," the governor said, "I never saw that fellow before. I evidently got him mixed up with somebody else." An excuse showing a lack of inquiry into the facts pertaining to an important matter.

When I was appointed president of the University of Kentucky in 1917, I stipulated that I should be present at all board meetings, without exception. As I was not a member of the board I held a position of neutrality. If I had had a vote on controversial matters, I would have been an advocate and a partisan. In my experience of many years, a half-dozen rejections of my recommendations would cover the differences of opinion. If there was marked opposition to an appointment, based on good reasons, I withdrew the recommendation and made another one. I have heard of presidents who stated that if their recommendations were not accepted by the board, they would resign. This is a quixotic attitude that overlooks the relation of board and president.

In a paper read at a meeting of the National Association of Universities, William Lowe Bryan said, "The president of a university can be compared with the prime minister and the House of Commons in the British system of government. If he cannot hold a majority of the Commons, he resigns his post." There is much to be said on this point, but the comparison does not cover all aspects of the problem. However, where important issues clearly separate the trustees and the president in matters of policy, the president should resign. His chances of winning out in a fight before the public are slim under our system of control. The president in such a case should make it clear to the public what the issues are and what his stand is on the questions that are before the board.

M.

Hughes and the Trustees

When I was acting president of Miami University in 1911, the board consisted of twenty-seven trustees (as it still does). Nine of these were appointed every three years by the governor. At that time nearly all trustees were alumni of the institution, and perhaps half of them were seriously interested in Miami.

50   The President and the Trustees

The entire board met once a year in June, with a few meetings of the executive committee during the year. During the preceding ten years Miami grew from an enrollment of one hundred to five hundred students, with corresponding increases in budget. During my administration, 1911-1927, the enrollment increased to fifteen hundred. During all this twenty-five year period, the labors of the trustees increased, and additional committees were appointed which carried on much of the business. During the presidency of the board by Walter H. Coles of Troy, Ohio (1930 to 1944), the committees were entirely reorganized, and the executive committee was made up of the chairmen of the several committees. While most of the committees are those common to other boards, two have proved useful and are somewhat unusual.

The Committee on Efficiency and Co-operation has had repeated meetings over the years with groups of faculty members, usually members from one or two departments at each meeting. This has gone far to increase confidence and understanding between the trustees and the faculty. The Committee on Student Affairs has brought a group of board members in contact with students and their problems and has proved to be valuable.

The entire board still meets once a year in June, but the great bulk of the work is done by various committees which convene when necessary and with the executive committee's meeting six or eight times a year.

About four-fifths of the present board are Miami graduates or former students. Frequent meetings of the various committees result in a larger proportion of the members becoming interested in the college. When organized into committees with authority, a large board can operate with efficiency. This board was concerned only with Miami University. It was a "Nourishing Board," keen to develop and strengthen Miami in any way it could.

All this was in marked contrast with the State Board of Education, under which I worked in Iowa. It was, in the language of Dr. Walter A. Jessup, then president of the State University of Iowa, a "Judicial Board." Under it were five institutions, including The State University of Iowa, The Iowa State College of

Agriculture and Mechanic Arts, and The Iowa State Teachers College. The board was concerned largely in seeing that each institution confined itself to its own major lines and did not unnecessarily duplicate work done elsewhere. It endeavored to see that each institution was adequately supported but that none held an undue advantage. It was a "Judicial Board."

This board consisted of nine members, three of whom were appointed every two years by the governor. The board held ten regular monthly meetings. It employed a finance committee of three full-time members who carried on the minor and detailed work of the board. This committee visited each of the five institutions monthly, and acted on all minor appointments and other routine matters. The board itself was thus left free to consider the more serious problems of the several institutions. The president of each institution attended all meetings of the board. He presented his own recommendations to the board in the presence of the other presidents.

Two things contributed much to the sound working of the board during my administration, 1927-1936. The president, Mr. George W. Baker, was always reluctant to accept any but a unanimous vote, so when an action was passed one realized it had the support of the entire board. This proved to be an excellent policy. If the board did not agree, the matter was put aside or postponed. Dr. W. R. Boyd was elected president of the finance committee when the State Board of Education was formed in 1909. He was deeply interested in education and in the welfare of Iowa. He was deferred to for his wisdom, his wide acquaintance among leading men in the educational world and his good judgment. In his forty years of service, while the personnel of the entire board and the other two members of the finance committee changed, Dr. Boyd remained a wise and stabilizing figure. He gave a continuity to the policies of the board it could not have had otherwise.

Dr. Boyd invited Dr. Henry Smith Pritchard, president of the Carnegie Foundation for the Advancement of Teaching, to meet with the new board of education shortly after its appointment and to discuss with them their duties and relations to the several institutions. The influence of these conferences undoubtedly prevented members of the board from meddling with the administration of the several institutions.

Dr. Boyd was active in securing the appointment of a survey commission in 1914, which spent several weeks at the various institutions under the board. This commission made a report which redirected the thinking of the board somewhat. Dr. Boyd later brought back the chairman of that commission, Dr. S. P. Capen, then president of the University of Buffalo, to resurvey the several institutions and to offer a final report.

Prior to the establishing of this board, the pressure of the several rival institutions upon the legislature had become so serious as to result in the establishment of the central state board. Not more than one alumnus of each of the three major institutions could serve at one time. The appointment of this board effectively stopped the rivalry of alumni for funds, and reduced duplication of work.

The three larger institutions today enroll more than 20,000 students. The university and the college together conferred 738 Doctor of Philosophy degrees during the five years 1937-1942, a record exceeded only by three other universities. In a state of two and one-half million population, with an income in proportion to population which places Iowa in the middle of the forty-eight states, these two accomplishments afford ample proof that such educational institutions under one board will thrive.

H.

The President and the Trustees

The following outline will give a starting point for this discussion:

The trustees of the college are responsible to:

The governor of the state — The trustees desire his good will and prefer that complaints about the college not be made to him.

The legislature — The trustees wish to be on friendly terms with the members; appropriations come from the legislature.

The people of the state — The trustees wish them to be

The President and the Trustees

informed about the college and its work; their taxes support the institution.

The parents of students — The trustees want them to be satisfied with what the college does for their children.

The faculty — The trustees expect the faculty to be contented and they do not want them criticized for radical statements or misconduct.

The students — The trustees desire them to be orderly, attentive to business and reasonably well satisfied.

The alumni — The trustees seek the confidence and approval of the alumni.

While the above applies to land-grant colleges and universities, slight modifications will make it apply to any specific college. The trustees look to the president more than they should to keep their relations with each of the above groups harmonious.

With what matters do the trustees concern themselves?

1. The President — The trustees select and elect the president of the college.

2. The Policies of the Institution — The trustees are responsible for their formulation and establishment. This should be their chief concern.

3. Finances — The endowment and all resources of the institution are in the charge of its trustees. A loss of endowment funds is perhaps the most unpardonable offense of which a board can be guilty. A board of trustees should be deeply concerned over the annual budget and earnestly desirous that estimates of income be conservative and that the total expenses do not exceed the total income.

4. Buildings — The board selects an architect, approves plans, lets contracts and supervises all building. The president should see that the plans embody the needs concerned so far as the funds permit. The board should insist that all buildings be kept in repair and painted. The latter is often overlooked.

5. Land — It is the business of the board to acquire adequate land. Often great effort by the president is required in order to give the trustees a true vision of the future.

6. Faculty — Usually the actual employment of the staff is

only technically a function of the board. As a matter of fact, in a large institution, the board should delegate this matter wholly to the president and hold him responsible. They are not sufficiently informed about each new candidate. (In one midwestern college, in 1949, a total of 777 people were newly employed to fill vacancies on the entire staff.) On the other hand, the board wishes to be proud of its faculty. Boards are made up chiefly of conservative men and women. They are sensitive to criticism regarding radical statements or actions by faculty members. The writer believes the able president will see that such persons are not appointed to his faculty. Also, such a president will protect faculty members unfairly accused of offensive radicalism from action by the board.

7. The Course of Study — While the trustees cannot well act on the details of any course of study, the authority to do so is often within their rights. They should certainly so define the policies of the institution that no new course of study obligating the college for additional expenditures can be adopted without their full approval. However, all detail in revising authorized courses of study should be in the hands of the faculty concerned.

8. Students — In some institutions the trustees have set a definite limit on the number of students who may be enrolled; this number is related to the endowment income. University trustees have been known to fix a limit on graduate student enrollment. In some institutions, on the recommendation of the president and faculty, standards for admission have been fixed by the board. Any board desires a large enough student body to justify the expenditures involved. On the matter of admission requirements there should be close co-operation between the board, the faculty and the president. It is fortunate when a board is able to set such limit on enrollment as to authorize the exclusion of unfit students.

H.

A New President's Opportunity

A new president entering on the complex duties of his office should certainly have in mind what he can contribute to the institution over which he presides. No man can hope to do all the things the trustees expect of him. He will be largely absorbed in routine work. If he is to leave the institution the better for his service after five or ten years, he must definitely determine what he can hope to do best with his abilities. It is well to recall that the average term of service of a college or university president is six or eight years and that very few serve fifteen or more years.

In general, five large fields of improvement are open to a new president. They include the student, faculty, finance, building and public relations areas.

In the *student* area, the president may raise the standards for admission and graduation in order to turn out a more select product. He may widen or restrict the college offerings of courses, as circumstances demand. He may resolve to see that the students are served as individuals, and he may determine to become acquainted with the members of the student body personally.

In the *faculty* area, he may hope for improvement through careful appointments. With an average turnover each year of something like 20 per cent of the teaching staff, any faculty can be strengthened if enough effort and intelligence is used each year in securing the very best men available at the salaries paid. A president can improve the faculty morale by a happy, cordial attitude on his part and by the development of social and professional co-operation within the faculty. He may reorganize the administration and so secure more effective service.

The *financial* field offers opportunities to secure a larger income from the legislature and from private gifts. Money may be raised for current income or endowment; or by concentrating on economy and careful spending, more ground can be covered within the normal income.

Buildings always seem to be needed on every campus. Some men are gifted with the ability to secure funds for the erection of new buildings and so leave a permanent monument to their efforts.

The *public relations* of an institution offer great opportunities for service. A gifted speaker can do much to create good will and to educate the people in regard to the value of their institution. This can be done through writing and publishing wisely. Also, by developing strong athletic teams. A president with certain gifts can make many friends among influential people who will be loyal to the college.

The college president, besides presiding over important meetings of the faculty and interpreting the college to the trustees and the trustees to the faculty, is expected to prove an inspiring leader in many areas of the college life. Where he leads, he must lead enthusiastically.

So far as possible the president must educate the trustees in the work, aims, teaching and research of their institution. He must acquaint them with the foremost men and women of the staff. I found a monthly letter to each trustee, covering current matters of interest, to be well worth while. Arranging for the trustees to meet the leading professors and their wives at dinner proved pleasant and advantageous.

I believe the president should use all his ingenuity to relieve the trustees of detail and to persuade them to delegate everything that can be properly delegated. Then, as time affords, he should focus their attention on the importance of defining proper policies. Sound policies, understood and unanimously approved by the trustees, will go far toward building a strong institution of both character and influence.

H.

The Size of the Board

In our American institutions, boards vary in size from three to one hundred. While, as has been said, a large board can operate efficiently if properly organized, it has little advantage. I believe that seven is the ideal membership for such a board, with one member appointed each year for a seven-year term.

Seven people will engage freely in a discussion. It seems to be the largest number of which this is true. The fewer the members, the greater the pressure for capable, worthy appointments. An increase beyond seven adds nothing to the strength of the board.

Fewer than seven scarcely give a wide enough spread of responsibility.

However, a board is extremely difficult to alter, regardless of size, once it is established.

In Ohio, with six state-supported educational institutions, each with a separate board of trustees, rivalry before the legislature has been very largely eliminated through the formation of a joint committee which presents the needs of the several institutions. The legislature finally appropriates a lump sum for salaries and operation which is then apportioned on the basis of enrollment.

H.

Relations With the Legislature

The matter of securing adequate funds for a satisfactory program must always remain a problem with every institution. My own experience has been confined to state institutions. Outside of these, I have been directly acquainted with only one private institution which had a sound and definite program for raising money. This was Oberlin College under President Henry C. King.

During Dr. King's administration, Oberlin had on its staff a very able and resourceful man, Mr. William Bohn, who was in charge of raising funds. He had carefully prepared a list of all possible donors to Oberlin and in his own way kept in contact with them. When one of his prospects would show a real interest in giving to the college, Mr. Bohn said to him, "Perhaps you would like to talk this over with President King. I can arrange to have him see you." Mr. Bohn did all the preliminary work, and when he had a really interested prospect, President King would meet and talk with the man. This proved a successful procedure.

In regard to the legislature, I have seen a tremendous change in attitude since 1905 when I made my first contact. I had accompanied President Guy Potter Benton, of Miami University, to the Ohio legislature that year. He had an appointment with the

Finance Committee of the House or Senate, and I remember when we were called in we were told very bluntly, "The Senate has little time. We can give you ten minutes." We were quickly hustled out when the ten minutes were up!

In recent years, both in Ohio and Iowa, I have been given considerate hearings before both Senate and House committees, and while the appropriations were never up to my hopes, they were reasonably good under all the circumstances.

As I am not a particularly impressive speaker, I always confined myself to the facts. I learned early in my administration, from President Hollis Godfrey of Drexel Institute, the great value of charts in making financial matters clear. I placed charts before the legislative committee showing what we had spent and what I regarded as needful, in as much detail as I could, considering the time I had at my disposal. I ran through the charts rapidly but covered all questions as well as I could. I felt that my presentation by charts gave a clearer idea of our condition and needs than could have been given in a speech.

At Miami, the business manager of the university, Mr. Wallace P. Roudebush, was of enormous help with the legislature. He followed the appropriations carefully and made friends with such senators and representatives as he could. I was always accompanied when going to a hearing by two or three trustees and by Mr. Roudebush. I made the main speech with my charts.

One of my associates in Iowa was Dr. Walter Jessup, then president of the State University of Iowa, who was certainly one of the most impressive speakers before a legislative committee I have ever heard. However, it is difficult to talk convincingly about three to five million dollars in twenty minutes. Usually I fared as well as Dr. Jessup.

In Iowa, we had one board for the three state educational institutions. The finance committee of this board occupied an office near the state house and kept in close touch with the legislature. A legislative committee of the board made up of men thought to be most influential with the legislature and usually including the president of the board was responsible for the presentation of askings for the appropriations. At hearings, the presidents of the three major institutions were always present and were carefully listened to. Aside from the regular hearings I had no contact with the legislature unless individual members called on me. In Iowa, the central board did away with all friction between the institutions in regard to appropriations.

The Iowa board has definitely stated that no member of the several faculties may go before the legislature or present any matter whatsoever to individuals in the legislature unless so authorized by the board. This is a good rule.

H.

Relations With the Legislature

An institution of higher education dependent for its income upon public taxation has a different financial problem from those of a private college. For instance, the trustees are appointed by the governor of a state or by the mayor of the municipality. Such appointments, by the nature of their selection, are apt to have a political tinge. Taken all in all, the appointments will run from average to high grade. The whole list of such appointments will range in the "B" class or better.

As a public institution, the college or university depends for support upon the governor and the legislature of the state in which it is located. The president and the board of trustees are faced with the responsibility of presenting the needs of the institution not only favorably, but effectively. Careful planning, able argument, and some political activity are required to obtain acceptable results. The first step is to learn and understand the political setup of the state government.

All the states but one, Nebraska, have bicameral legislatures. The house may have as few as one hundred members or it may consist of as many as three or four hundred; the senate will consist approximately of one-fourth as many members as the house of representatives. Both houses have presiding officers, and the work preliminary to the voting of budgets is done in committees. There are committees on budget and on education. The important one is the budget committee composed of from twelve to twenty members. Sometimes the budget committees of the two houses will meet together and make the same report to the house and senate. In the last twenty years, much of the work formerly done by these committees has been done through a budget commission composed of the governor, lieutenant governor, speaker of the house, and several members from the senate and house. This body meets a month or so before the date of the legislature session and is expected to have a bill fully prepared by the time of its opening. Prior to the first meeting of the budget commission, heads of public institutions and state departments are notified and asked to furnish information so the commission may act intelligently. In the course of the meetings, the presidents of public educational institutions are given the opportunity to present the needs of their institutions, together with the reasons for requests.

In compiling the institutional budget, much work will have been done on the campus in collecting, tabulating, and screening the requests and needs of the departments making up the institution. A mere guessing at needs is a dangerous procedure and should be regarded as a genuine breach of academic ethics.

When the institutional budget has been tentatively formed, the results are compared with possible income which must always be estimated conservatively. The president, accompanied by the comptroller and a dean or two, then goes before the commission. The facts and figures should be clearly presented with illustrations in graphic form. Long speeches should be avoided in this meeting and attention should be directed to the facts and reasons. Orations about education may be listened to; but the observation of President Arthur Hadley, referring to long sermons in the Yale college chapel on Sunday mornings, that "there are no conversions after the first twenty minutes," should be kept in mind.

Usually the budget bill is the first one presented to the legislature for consideration. Political strategy is employed to get the bill through and out of the way. The college president and his board may learn by the middle of the first month of the assembly meeting what provisions have been made for their needs, and so the president's sleep need not be disturbed by figures and statistical forms for another two years.

It is taken for granted that the president knows the members of his board and is on good terms with them. In addition, early and late he has given them a clear picture of the institution and has impressed them with the importance of the position they occupy. It is quite as necessary to know the leading men in the legislature and to acquaint them with the needs of the institution. To do this requires some travel and considerable visiting which will be of additional value to a college president by increasing his knowledge of the state he serves.

The alumni should be alerted so they will know something about the college beyond its record in the field of sports. To do this requires a good deal of effort by the college press and the public relations department. Alumni in each legislature and senatorial district should be asked to see and talk with prospective members of the assembly before election, not after! When the time comes for the vote on the budget bill, the institution has thus made some real friends who understand its needs.

Throughout this campaign, if it may be called such, there must be consistent fair dealing. The policy of padding budgets on the supposition that the legislature will inevitably cut down the appropriation, regardless of its validity, is a mistaken one. A reputation for making fair and reasonable requests will win the increased confidence of the legislature in the administration of a college.

On the whole, legislative members want to do the best they can. They have their own problems. Reduced income from taxes, changes in economic conditions as well as variances in the backing of the public, force them to give ground.

As I look back over fifteen legislative sessions that I have attended and before whose committees I have appeared, I realize that I was always treated with courtesy and consideration. Promises were not always kept, but in at least half of the sessions, larger support and more capital funds were appropriated for the institutions I represented.

M.

The President and the Trustees

Formulation of College and University Policy

While I was president of Miami University, I was annoyed by a joking remark often repeated by a trustee, "The trustees are again assembled to okay the recommendations of Raymond Hughes." As a matter of fact, that was largely what they did do and what I expected them to do. That is why the joke hurt.

As this situation continued to worry me, I finally realized that the trouble was due to the fact that the efforts of the trustees should have been devoted chiefly to the consideration of *policies*. Certain of the actions taken, such as appointments made during the year, did require formal approval and recording in the minutes of the board. This, however, could have been made a blanket approval of the action of the executive committee, or a general authorization of authority to the president. In any case, the time of the twenty-seven members of the board at the annual meeting should have been spent in the consideration and formulation of general policies that would control Miami University and within which the university's affairs would be operated by the president, the business manager and the staff.

When I assumed the presidency of Iowa State College, nine men and women constituted a board which controlled the five educational institutions of the state. Here, again, the time was spent at the monthly meetings of the board discussing and approving a long list of matters submitted by the several executives, so that at the end of the year, no advance had been made in formulating a clear-cut policy.

To me this procedure did not appear to be sound. I regret that only after twenty-five years' experience and ten years' contemplation has the matter become clear. I now see that the chief duty of a board is to formulate the controlling policies, with the guidance and assistance of the president, and to evaluate how well the current incumbent is operating the institution under those policies.

Every university that has operated successfully over several years is in fact controlled more or less by policies written or unwritten, and its presidents carry them through as best they

Formulation of College and University Policy 63

can. However, I am sure many presidents will bear me out when I say that during a good part of the time they have been in doubt as to what the policy was relative to many matters.

The board members assemble for meetings, whether monthly or yearly, for the most part with little consideration of the problems before them. They must depend largely upon the president and the business manager to present the business in hand. If matters of policy were regularly made a part of the responsibility of the board, and if such policies as were adopted were recorded and from time to time codified, a valuable document would result.

These policies would of course vary from one board to another and from institution to institution. They would inevitably deal, for example, with some of the following:

Selection of staff	Investments
Appointments	Incurring indebtedness
Dismissals	Financing buildings
Tenure	Dormitory facilities
Salary scale	Boarding facilities
Rating value of faculty members	Room and board rates
Admissions	Basis of estimate of income
Number of freshmen to be admitted	Preparation of budget of expenses
Selection of freshmen	Reserve
Ratio of men to women	Deficit
Scholarship standards	

If policies relative to these and other matters were regularly put in writing by the board, the president could be given authority to act within them.

Particularly in our larger institutions, it appears essential to depend more and more upon the president but to restrict him by fixed policies. Where exceptions are called for, reference should be made to the board.

In some cases the policy could be definite and fixed, as for example the maximum indebtedness which might be incurred in building dormitories to be amortized from total room rent. In other matters such as appointments, more flexibility would be necessary.

As one looks back over fifty or sixty years to the unimpressive size of colleges and universities then, it is clear that almost everything possible was brought to the board to justify its meeting. The entire annual income of Miami University from 1824 to 1873, a brilliant era in her history, never reached $20,000. The times have so changed that a very different policy is now called for if our institutions are to continue to move forward, or even to hold their present status.

H.

The President as Chairman of the Board

I have wondered how such a relation works out in practice. It seems to me that this method of organization is not in accord with the best type of procedure. In no instance, so far as I am aware, does a president of an educational institution supported by public funds act as chairman of the board; yet there are numerous instances where a president occupies the place of chairman on private college boards.

The objection to this practice is that the president is an executive officer, paid a salary, selected by the board, and subject to its rules and regulations. As chairman, he passes upon what he is to do as president. He could, in fact, vote on his retention in office, determine and raise the question of his own salary. As a gentleman, he would vacate the chair when such matters came before the board; otherwise he would be judge, a member of the jury and advocate before the court.

There is in this dual position much to be questioned. In fact, the responsibility for the welfare of the institution's progress rests too heavily upon one man. The board is, after all, a policy-making body and such policies are carried out by the president; in consequence, the responsibility for money raising, investments, construction of buildings, and many other important matters is placed on the shoulders of one man.

It is more responsibility than one individual should be asked to assume. It can be argued that the president runs the place, and knows more about it than the board can know; therefore, turn it over to him, and the members of the board can stand back of him. In the law, the board is responsible for the maintenance of property and the management of the institution. In case of trouble, the board would find itself in a questionable situation.

In another place, Hughes and I have written about the value of a wise counselor for the president, a need that exists even in the administration of a board. As an executive officer, a president must have advice and counsel. A board is supposed to bring to his help the experience of its members and their knowledge of conditions, business relations and trends.

When he is chairman, the president is in an anomalous position where he is the adviser, director and servant. The fact is that a rubber stamp board is not much help to a president and can't be because it is not independent. Where the members are free to discuss problems, the contributions made by the members to the welfare of the institution they serve are sure to bring better results than in the case where one man determines the course of the institution. It may be said that one man, even in the case cited, does not control the institution. To that my reply is that he can and often does.

M.

Assistants Whom the Trustees Should Provide for the President

I am convinced that the executive assistants provided for the president have not kept pace in recent years with the growth of colleges and with the increasing demands which are made on them by the public. While some presidents have the wisdom and courage to ask for adequate help, others, not fully realizing the burdens of the office, hesitate to ask for more aid than was provided for their predecessor. It seems appropriate to discuss this matter for the benefit of both presidents and trustees.

No two institutions are exactly alike and many differ enormously. Some are small and others are very large. Some devote their entire efforts to undergraduate instruction, and in others there are more graduate students than undergraduate. In some, practically no research is attempted while in others vast amounts of research are carried on in many fields. Some confine their work to the campus, while others have extension courses and correspondence courses. It is certainly difficult to lay down rules about the assistance the presidents of such varied institutions will need. However, some statements can be made.

One great reason for providing adequate assistance is the fact that the overworked president almost invariably neglects his most important duty. The quality and character of the members of the faculty are the president's responsibility. However, the initiative in these appointments usually rests with department heads and the college deans. When overpressed, the president is forced to approve these recommendations with little or no personal knowledge of the men appointed.

Furthermore, the attention of the dean and department head is strongly focused on the professional fitness in training, research and experience of the person appointed. The character, generosity of spirit, manners, integrity, and interest in students of the candidate are often not adequately canvassed. It is right here that the president's judgment is needed.

Let us first consider the needs of institutions based roughly on size and then consider the functions of some vice-presidents under consideration.

Roughly, in the staff from instructor to full professor there is a turnover of about 20 per cent a year. In colleges with less than 1,000 students, certainly a president with a competent financial officer should be fully able to deal with all matters and give full attention to the new appointments, which would not exceed from five to twenty a year.

With institutions enrolling from 1,000 to 2,500 and employing staffs of from one hundred to two hundred and fifty there would probably be from twenty to fifty appointments to be made each year. A competent vice-president in many of the larger of these institutions could easily earn his salary in securing abler, finer men for the staff. In some cases he would not be needed.

In institutions enrolling from 2,500 to 5,000, and employing from two hundred and fifty to five hundred teachers, there would be from fifty to one hundred staff appointments, and probably from ten to twenty-five graduate assistants to be appointed. It seems quite certain that a vice-president in charge of faculty and curriculum would be necessary.

In larger institutions engaged in much research and graduate work, more vice-presidents will be required but rarely more than five or six. Their functions and number will depend on the needs of each institution.

Some consideration of the function of the proposed vice-presidents will further explain their use.

Every institution must have a competent financial officer. In all the larger institutions he may properly be ranked as a vice-president in charge of business. In small institutions he is variously called bursar, treasurer or business manager, but in all cases he carries the financial responsibilities of the institution. He reports to the president. The work is variously divided in the larger institutions as follows:

Collections are under a cashier; accounts are under a chief accountant; purchasing is under a purchasing agent; buildings and grounds, under a superintendent; dormitories and boarding departments, under a director; erection of new buildings is under the architects' supervision; and all student activity accounts are under a supervisor. The payments of salaries and bills are made through the treasurer. The vice-president in charge of business retains no specific duties to himself. All the regular work of his office is dealt with by one or another subdivision. The vice-president consults with the president and is subject to call by him. He settles all problems that arise in his office. He prepares the financial reports for the trustees and has a large part in the preparation of the budget. He must see that no expenditure is made exceeding the amount appropriated for that purpose.

Evidently, with such a mass of business routine, efficient methods of handling it must be adopted. It is through the infringement of these routine methods by faculty members that most of the trouble arises with the faculty. A business manager who can get along amiably with the faculty members is a rare person.

While the president may be relieved of financial affairs under a vice-president, there remain burdensome faculty and

68 The President and the Trustees

curriculum problems with which to deal. Let us consider placing these, as well as the library, under another vice-president in charge of faculty and curriculum.

He might have under his charge from five to twelve colleges and easily from fifty to one hundred departments with a staff of from 500 to 2,000 persons. Theoretically, a department would fill a vacancy, subject to the approval of its dean. But deans and department heads will vary in their capacity to choose wisely and to search exhaustively for the best man available at the salary. A president does not dare to accept without question all recommendations that the deans may present. This whole matter could be turned over to a provost or to a vice-president in charge of faculty and curriculum who had the full confidence of the faculty. While the president should be kept informed of all major appointments, the vice-president would have power to act. This would save not only the president's time, but would largely remove his gravest source of anxiety, criticism by faculty members.

In order to more fully understand the importance of staff appointments, let us consider a large university with a faculty of 1,650:

Rank	Number	Appointed Each Year	Salary	Estimated Years of Service	Total Salary for Estimated Years of Service
Full Professor............	250	10–15	$8,000	20	$1,600,000
Associate Professor......	200	18–20	5,000	15	1,350,000
Assistant Professor.......	300	45–60	4,000	5	900,000
Instructor...............	400	100–150	3,000	3	900,000
Fellow and Graduate....	500	200	900	3	540,000
Total..............	1,650	....	....	....	$5,290,000

Assume that the total salaries of those employed each year, during the entire remaining years of service was $5,000,000. If an able man by careful supervision could improve the quality of appointments 10 per cent, it would be worth $500,000; if only 1 per cent, it would be worth $50,000 a year. Further, if he were able to improve the quality of appointments at the level of instructors and below, the fact that able young men were already on the staff would make possible the filling of nearly all vacancies of professional grade through promotion. If this were done, it would insure better appointments since such an appointee would be well known. Certainly the institution could afford to employ such a man.

The complete interlacing of loyalties in an educational institution often makes it very difficult to be frank. The department head must be loyal to his staff, to the dean and to the president. How can he recommend the discontinuance of some work in his department, regardless of how useless it is, when such a move will involve one or more staff members? He might talk this over with the vice-president in charge of faculty and curriculum.

A third vice-president should have charge of other activities including publicity, radio, athletics, alumni, infirmary, rooming and boarding departments, YMCA and YWCA, and student affairs.

A president should be able to find out what economies can be made. He needs a financial expert qualified to evaluate the expenditures of the university and to report his findings to the president. Such a man need not be a Ph.D. in education, although he might hold that degree. He should be a man the faculty members would trust, one to whom they would talk freely and honestly, realizing that he is working for the welfare of the university. He should report to the president, and his work should always be at the points of interest to the president.

There is increasing concern over public relations, and many feel that a man with the rank of vice-president should devote his time to this field. It is true that in a great university the complexity of the work and the diversity of the research carried on should be kept before the public. Also, the donors and members of the legislature should be kept informed and their questions should be answered. The wisdom of appointing a full-time man to this position and rank must be carefully considered.

With such a staff as has been recommended here, a president should be able to devote his time to the larger concerns of the university. He would work closely with his chief assistants. The knowledge which he acquired through them concerning the institution would be of great value in administering a ten or twenty million dollar a year enterprise, and the cost of such help would be small in proportion to the increased effectiveness of his work.

H.

The President's Need for a Wise Counselor

During the years I was president of Miami University, when any serious problem arose I went to Hamilton, a nearby town, and spent the evening in consultation with Mr. Walter L. Tobey, president of the board. Such conferences always cleared up my troubles to an astonishing degree, and I returned to Oxford with a sound idea of how I should proceed.

When I came to Iowa State College, I was already well acquainted with Dr. W. R. Boyd, president of the finance committee of the board. He came to the college once a month and usually spent a night with me at the president's home. I would go over my accumulation of problems with him then, to my great comfort and satisfaction.

A president cannot afford to develop an intimate relationship with any one faculty member. If one or more vice-presidents were on duty, the president could discuss the problems in their respective spheres with them. It has been suggested that a faculty committee advisory to the president might well serve as a consulting body. This idea may have merit, yet one would hesitate to discuss a very perplexing, serious situation with such a committee, some members of which might betray the confidence.

I believe, however, that a faculty-elected committee advisory to the president would be safer to consult with than any single member of the faculty who would soon come to be regarded as the president's confidant.

Of course, most problems would fall naturally within the province of a dean or a department head, and the president would naturally turn to him. Unfortunately, problems arise from time to time that cannot be cleared through a conference with another administrative officer. There should be some person on the board of trustees in whom the president can confide.

President Edward C. Elliott of Purdue was exceptionally fortunate in having as a trustee entirely devoted to that university, Mr. David E. Ross, who lived in Lafayette. He would often drop into Dr. Elliott's home or office, and the two would talk freely together.

I have been exceptionally fortunate in my own experience. Were I embarking again as a college president, I would try to consult with the president of the board; but if he were not readily accessible, I would try to select some chairman of a committee of the board who was truly devoted to the institution. If neither of these outlets were available, I would ask the faculty to elect a committee advisory to the president, and I would counsel with this committee, trusting its discretion.

I am convinced that a college or university president must have some person or persons whom he trusts and with whom he may consult confidentially.

H.

The President's Need for a Wise Counselor

Indeed, we all need a wise counselor, but where is such a one to be found? If he is from the faculty, there is a possibility the selection will be looked upon as showing favoritism, and the creation of a kitchen cabinet imminent. The counselor may be a member of the board of trustees or a man or woman interested in the college. Sometimes great comfort and help may come from a brother-in-arms who heads an institution not too far away. Wisdom is to be sought wherever it can be found.

In my own experience, I sometimes employed a method called "sending up a trial balloon" to encourage comment among board members, faculty, and alumni. This can be done by informal conversation, in small meetings or even in a newspaper interview. Still the wise counselor may not be clearly in evidence, and the resulting returns from the balloon test must be screened, weighed, and formulated. The wise counselor is greatly needed at this point.

The President and the Trustees

As the new president settles down in his office, he has time to look around and even to test some of the men and women close to the college for the purpose of choosing a wise counselor. If the goddess of luck supervenes, he may form a friendship that will be of the greatest value to him and the college. The wise counselor must have what is far too rare, a thing called wisdom, also discretion, the ability to weigh evidence, and all in all he must be able to see the problems realistically, free from personal bias. The president of the board of trustees is the logical candidate for the place of wise counselor, but many times he does not measure up to the requirements.

As Dr. Hughes writes in his comment on this topic, "A president must have some person or persons whom he can trust and with whom he may consult." I agree with this. Perhaps the president has in his own household such a wise counselor in the person of his wife. But in the world of affairs there are relations involving finance, administration, discernment, and a broad view point on educational problems; all so varied and complicated that the wise counselor should be a man of wide experience, of philosophical turn of mind, broad vision, and thoroughly honest in mind as well as in money matters. Given time, such a person, possibly several, may be found. Then the president is indeed blessed.

M.

The Age and Origin of Three Hundred Presidents on Election

A study published in *School and Society,* Vol. 51 (March 9, 1940), p. 317, gives the age of the 300 presidents then holding office, at the time they entered upon their duties. They are as follows:

Age	Number	Percentage	Age	Number	Percentage
30–34	31	10.1	50–54	48	15.6
35–39	52	16.9	55–59	21	6.8
40–44	67	21.8	60–64	11	3.6
45–49	73	23.8	65–68	4	1.3

Eighty per cent were between thirty-five and fifty-four years of age when appointed.

If sixty-five is fixed as the age at which a president retires, it is unwise to consider a man more than fifty-five or fifty-six, as an institution should be able to hope for eight or ten years of service.

On the other hand, if a man younger than forty-five years of age is appointed, he may desire to transfer, when opportunity offers, to a more attractive post.

The Previous Employment of Presidents

In the study quoted above, the positions held just prior to their appointment were tabulated for the 300 presidents studied:

	Number	Percentage
President of another institution	52	17.3
Dean: within the institution (51)	79	26.5
of another institution (28)		
Professor: within the institution (28)	68	22.5
of another institution (40)		
College executive other than above	18	6.0
Clergyman in active pastorate	27	9.0
Business executive	12	4.0
Executive in national post	13	4.3
Executive in minor public post	9	3.0
Superintendent of schools	12	4.0
Editor	4	1.3
Miscellaneous	6	2.0
Total	300	99.9

H.

The Selection of a President

Occasionally a retiring president is asked for aid in finding a successor, and more frequently he is asked to suggest a man to fill a vacancy in another institution. It is a matter of great interest as to how to select a college president. Some suggestions can be made.

It is important to secure a list of all men or women, so far as possible, who may be qualified for the post. It is a rather simple matter to eliminate undesirables from the list; but if the best man available is not on the list at all, he cannot be appointed. In an effort to assist a board of trustees in selecting a president, I once thoroughly canvassed the current "Who's Who in America." The biography of every college president and dean under fifty-four years of age was cut out; about five hundred names resulted. These clippings were pasted alphabetically on letter-sized sheets. All those born in the same year were placed on the same sheet or sheets.

From this collection I selected those who were most promising for the particular position, a list of thirty-three names. Twenty-three of these held more attractive posts than that under consideration. This left ten men in the preferred list.

Photostat copies were made of the entire list and copies were given to the committee of the board. While several men on the select list were not interested when approached, and while a number of men not on this list were also conferred with, no one was considered who had not the necessary qualifications.

I believe my list tended to keep the level of consideration high. The man finally selected was a dean fifty-five years of age and so was not on my list.

Of course, many men worthy of consideration are not employed in the academic field. However, about 70 to 75 per cent of appointments are made from this field. Usually many names from non-academic fields are suggested by alumni when asked for suggestions.

If the board would prepare a written statement of the qualifications it desires in a president, that would be of great help in finding the right man.

I am convinced that a faculty committee can make a valuable contribution to the trustees in the selection of a president. Such a committee should be elected by the faculty; it should be small.

Its contributions would be along several lines. It could nominate to the trustees names of several men worthy of consideration. When the trustees had acquired all the names they desired, the faculty committee could help in eliminating the less desirable ones. The faculty members would be able to get confidential estimates on any men in academic work.

Finally, when the board had narrowed down the men whom they regarded as most desirable to a list of five or ten, the committee could indicate which men would be most acceptable to the faculty. They could also get sound estimates from friends in colleges and universities where these men on the preferred list had served.

The faculty, more than any other group, would be continuously and seriously affected by the appointment, for good or ill. They would have more confidence in the final selection by the trustees, knowing that a faculty committee was working with the trustees throughout the search resulting in the final appointment.

One point voiced years ago by Dean Carl E. Seashore of the State University of Iowa is that you can never size up a man accurately as an administrator until he has done administrative work. You can judge how he will use power only when power is given to him. Especially in a large institution, the chances of a man's making good are far greater if he has exercised administrative responsibility and if he has been carefully investigated than are the chances of a man who does not thus qualify. Power often goes to a man's head and makes him a dictator. No dictator can succeed on a college campus.

H.

Evidence of a Good President

The trustees regard him as absolutely honest and frank. They trust him and accept his recommendations as being sincerely made after careful consideration. The president's success in satisfying the trustees will depend in large part on his unselfish devotion to the welfare of their institution, on his executive skill, on his honesty and courage and on the organization of the institution.

The faculty trusts him. They regard him as an honest, reliable man, interested in their work and their welfare. A university, in order to function properly, must be operated as far as possible on a democratic basis, not as a dictatorship with the president as dictator. The faculty believes the president desires the maximum individual and departmental freedom compatible with the proper control of the institution.

The students feel that he will safeguard their interests. If they present to him a matter of importance, they believe he will give it his careful consideration and will go as far as he can to satisfy all reasonable demands. They realize that he is trying to provide good teaching on the campus.

The college public respects him. They feel that he is a suitable man for the position. They are proud of him.

The alumni like him. If he is unable to provide winning athletic teams, they will be fairly well satisfied if the department from which they graduated is maintained at a high level. They want to be proud of their university, their college, their department. While many of the most outspoken alumni urgently demand a winning team, a great portion are deeply concerned for the standing of their university among comparable institutions.

In a relatively small college enrolling 1,000 or fewer students and employing 100 or fewer teachers, an honest, sympathetic man can by intelligent devotion to the institution and hard work attain good standing with these various groups.

However, as the size of an institution increases to 5,000, 10,000, 20,000 or even 40,000, this task is impossible for any one man to accomplish. The president's job must be shared by an increasing administrative staff. The logical thing is to provide a number of vice-presidents, each with authority in his own field. These men must be chosen with great care and must satisfy those with whom they deal by their honest fair-mindedness and concern for the right. Otherwise, everyone with matters which come under him will wish to consult directly with the president. If the wrong man is inadvertently appointed to one of these posts, he must be replaced promptly.

A university or college consists theoretically of a faculty of scholars and a body of students, all of whom are ladies and gentlemen. Together they seek truth. Any member of the group who is not a lady or gentleman may disturb the whole structure.

He does not belong. A gentleman is considerate of others; does his full duty; never takes personal advantage of a situation; is fair and just.

If faculty appointments were made more carefully, the men who are not gentlemen would be excluded, or if such a one were appointed, he would be removed promptly. As student bodies now stand, it must be the aim of a college to make ladies and gentlemen of them as far as possible during their four years' residence. However, I fear many are graduated who could scarcely be so ranked.

A good president, in order to satisfy those with whom he works, must have time free from fixed, demanding duties for the careful consideration of problems constantly arising. He is usually the authority of last resort, and his decisions must be just. The trustees should see that sufficient administrative assistance is provided to give the president this necessary free time.

The board should also insist that the president take from four to six weeks' vacation from all duties each year. His work is wearing, and he needs time free from all responsibility for rest and meditation and to give detached consideration to the problems of his office.

H.

Undesirable Presidents

At one of the meetings of the National Association of State Universities, President William Bryan of the University of Indiana said the mediocre president may be forced out of his job at the age of fifty-five. "There he is," said Dr. Bryan, "all dressed up with no place to go." Dr. Hughes feels that such a man should be able to find a position where he can make a living for himself and family. Maybe so, but the experience through which he has gone has done something to his spirit that leaves him depleted. He is never again the same man. It is easier to avoid appointment of an undesirable president than it is to get rid of one.

In selecting a president, it is essential that the faculty, trustees, and alumni should be satisfied. But the man who is selected should submit himself to real soul searching; he must take an inventory of his capacity and talents as he considers the job which he has been asked to assume. Perhaps this is too much to expect of any human being, for there are few men who are so intellectually honest that they will not rationalize such a situation. Many a good scholar has been lost and an excellent teacher blotted out by accepting a college presidency. Administrative officers are needed in our system of higher education; and consequently, selection becomes necessary, although a difficult and harassing task.

The very fact that so many presidencies are vacant each year raises the question in the mind of many a good man, why he should take on a job in which the tenure is uncertain. Yet he is attracted by the new prominence he will have and by the larger salary which a presidency will bring, as well as by the challenge of the service he can render. Here is presented a dilemma of considerable proportions that can be solved only by a more careful consideration of the problem.

As Dr. Hughes writes in his last paragraph, the fault may rest with boards of trustees and faculties. Neither group knows much about the problems and difficulties of the office. Many a president might be saved for a useful tenure if the board would talk frankly with him as problems and criticisms arose.

There is much dangerous gossip reaching boards that frank talk would eliminate. A kindly and helpful attitude on the part of all creates a wholesome atmosphere in an institution.

There is, however, no remedy other than change in the personnel of the office, if grandiose ideas and love of power get into the mental processes and individual attitudes of a president. He may be able because of toughness to hold on, but the institution will suffer in its morale under such circumstances.

Many a president has been faced with the "behind-the-scene method" sometimes used by board members to pump the faculty about the president's popularity; and in reverse order, some faculty members, not many surely, will go around the president to get the ear of the board of trustees, thus violating a fundamental principle of organization. When this is permitted, the president is placed in an impossible position. Many difficulties would not arise in college administration if the principles that go with the titles of lady and gentleman always guided the policies of a university. It may be quite as important to save a president as to fire him.

M.

How Can an Undesirable President Be Removed?

With 1,850 colleges and universities in the country, probably between two hundred and three hundred presidents are appointed each year. It is not possible that all of these appointments will be wise ones. In many cases, one trustee will press persistently for the selection of a certain man and will finally secure his election, rather than allow the whole board finally to unite on one man.

The position to be filled is so difficult and the qualifications desired so numerous that rarely is a man selected who is fully qualified. If he does fail, it is generally through his inability to work comfortably with the trustees or the faculty. If he is unable to win the confidence of the trustees and faculty, it is for the good of the institution that he be retired from office. The welfare of a college or university is far more important than the sensibilities of any one man.

However, over the thirty-five years during which I have followed the careers of college presidents, it has surprised me greatly to observe how reluctant boards of trustees are to remove a president. Many able men are kept far beyond their age of usefulness. Many more clearly prove their inability to serve acceptably within two or three years, yet are retained. Why is this?

I suppose boards dislike to admit they have made a mistake, for one thing. For another, as they are not professional educators, they hesitate to act on their own judgment. Also, they remember the labors involved in selecting the present incumbent, and are loath to undertake the quest again. In any case, trustees almost always set about making a change very reluctantly.

How serious a detriment to an institution is a president who lacks the confidence of trustees and faculty? Certainly he is a serious embarrassment that each year will grow more serious. If the institution includes in its administrative staff a vice-president who has the confidence of the faculty, considerable damage will be obviated. However, any board should promptly remove a president who is unsatisfactory. The question is, how may this be wisely accomplished?

I feel that several matters should be observed in such a case. The board should first learn the attitude of the faculty toward the president. This knowledge may best be obtained by consulting with a committee elected by the faculty. It would be undesirable to have a committee elected especially for such a purpose, but if there are faculty committees already elected, one such committee should be consulted.

Certainly, the president of the board should have a frank talk with the president of the college as soon as his failure to measure up to the board's requirements is evident. He should then be advised to find another berth within two years.

Depending upon the institution, its resources and the age of the president, suitable financial adjustment should be made. If he is given two years in which to secure another post, he should be told that at the end of the two years if he has not found a position, he will be granted a year's leave at full salary which will terminate his connection with the institution. Such treatment seems entirely fair to any man under fifty-five years of age. It must be remembered that regardless of his lack of suitability for a particular post, practically any man elected president of a college is outstanding in certain ways and can quite certainly secure another position if he tries.

For an older man who has served five years or more, the question of his employment by the institution in some other capacity or of his eligibility for a pension arises. His employment might be a definite handicap to his successor, and that possibility should be avoided. His pension may well be a matter of conference between him and a board committee. Any man under fifty-five years of age should be able through his friends to secure further employment. If so, no pension is necessary, or at any rate a small pension only. A man over fifty-five should have employment or a pension adequate at least for himself and his wife to live on modestly.

A president's post is precarious for many reasons and will always remain so. Many of the reasons arise from the character of the board itself and from that of the faculty. Just as a new president is largely an unknown quantity to the board and faculty, so are these bodies largely unknown to the president. If I were to live my life over again and undertook to serve either as a president or as a football coach, I would certainly put a certain percentage of my salary each year into an annuity. Regardless of the present wide promise of pensions, I should take steps at once to protect myself upon accepting such a precarious position.

H.

An administrator should have clear ideas of the purpose of the institution over which he presides. Constant study of the university is a large and important part of his duty. It is no easy matter to keep such an institution on an even keel. Integrity must prevail in all of his dealings, both personal and those pertaining to the office which he holds.

3.

Problems of Administration

The College and University Parliament

This is an important topic, since every college possesses a group of teachers that has developed through the years a legislative procedure of considerable power. This important body sets up rules for the admission of students; it prescribes their duties, establishes courses of studies, makes recommendations to the board of trustees, and in other ways touches upon and controls many of the college functions. At the same time, a board of trustees is provided in the articles of incorporation. Such a board has authority by law over finances, appointments, building programs and even educational policies.

Long ago, the teachers in an educational institution were the governing body and elected the rector, made the budget, determined courses of study and maintained police and courts of order (law which passed on the misbehavior and escapades of students). Later on, the church or the state was granted veto power over budgets and appointments, but the faculty continued as the local governing body. Within the memory of old timers, the faculty of a college would meet once a week to discuss students' work, misbehavior, and courses of study. It was, in fact, a kind of family gathering carried on quite informally. Yet this group had considerable power. In Timothy Dwight's time, 1830-1896, the Yale College faculty voted on appointments, passed on advancements, and laid a firm hand upon the curriculum of the college. Today, in the larger institutions, the power of appointment rests generally not with faculties, but with heads of departments, deans, vice-presidents and, finally, the president. The board of trustees receives their recommendations and usually approves them.

I have used the title, College and University Parliaments, because large faculties today cannot function effectively as did the smaller teaching bodies of earlier times, so a system of representation has developed to deal with the legislative matters of an institution. To a layman, the easy way to govern a college is to turn over all such matters to the president, to let the faculty teach and the students learn, a simple formula but a wholly unsatisfactory one as a governing procedure. A faculty must have something to say and the opportunity to formulate views about teaching, research, courses, budgets, and other matters that touch upon and mold the higher educational program. In consequence, a parliamentary system must exist in one form or another in all the colleges of the land, if the faculty is to be happy and contented.

Historically, the legislature of Great Britain consisted of these estates: the lords, spiritual and temporal, and the representatives of the country's cities, boroughs, and universities. The lords are now found in the House of Lords and the representatives, in the House of Commons.

In this country the parliament is made up of the Senate and the House of Representatives (a conference of representatives), which act on public and national affairs. In a college the faculty is the body specifically concerned; and, in consequence, the college parliament must be composed of all faculty members or of representatives elected by the membership of that group.

One plan or organization for this important agency is (1) a council, (2) the senate, and (3) the assembly. This may appear complicated and difficult to hold together, but I may say in passing it has worked! Although the senate may be too large for a deliberating body, membership in that group may be regulated in the constitution itself. I say "constitution" because that is what it is and should be. Once adopted by the faculty and approved by the board of trustees, this instrument, subject to change, is on a permanent basis.

Then the council is, in fact, an executive body which concerns itself with carrying out the legislative action of the senate. Usually it meets once a week. It is composed of the president, deans of colleges, the registrar and several elected members from the senate. Sometimes there may be one or two students chosen by the student body to sit on the council. If there are ten deans, four senate members and the president, the council may number as many as fifteen. This might be regarded as too large a body for good committee work, but the actual attendance will consist of no more than ten or twelve persons.

In some colleges the senate or the legislative body is composed of all who have a professorial status, including associates and assistant professors. Where there is a staff of several hundred in these categories, the senate would become too large, and "log rolling" and caucusing might creep in. In such an academic body where high standards of conduct are supposed to prevail, resort to political tricks is hardly considered good cricket. In fact, the decisions of the senate are supposedly based upon reason and the welfare of the institution; nevertheless, the ambitions of department heads may interfere with calmer judgments. Where the colleges composing a university are autonomous and therefore have almost complete control over courses of study, admission of students, and faculty assignments, the work of the senate will be greatly simplified. The monthly meeting can be reduced to a quarterly one, but those four meetings would be highly important. The president of the institution should always preside over this senate.

Reference has been made to a representative plan for membership. Each college elects members to the senate. The basis of such representation can be determined by the proportion of students registered in each college to the total student enrollment; thus the college which had one-fifth of the students enrolled in the university would elect one-fifth of the representatives in the senate. The term of service may be fixed at three years, with a limit on continued membership attained by restricting election to one or two terms. Once organized, the senate may create permanent committees that report their findings to that body. The registrar would make a good secretary because he knows the student body and has an office which can take care of typing records and other matters that need documenting.

The last division of the governing formula presented above is the assembly. The idea behind this part of the plan is to bring every officer, teacher, assistant, clerk, craftsman, janitor, and other worker into meetings held once or twice a year, a great democratic gathering of the institutional staff. It may be said that the assembly, definitely a part of the legislative organization, does give a feeling, a sense of belonging, to all university persons. In the assembly meetings a member may present any subject that he thinks worthy of consideration. Questions, too, should be encouraged, and frank and honest answers given to all questions put to the chair. The president of the institution presides over the meetings and may use the opportunity to talk about some of the important matters relating to the operation of the college.

The effectiveness of the assembly was demonstrated to me in the depression of the thirties when many financial questions came from the floor. It was then that reduction in salaries was necessitated by the fall in annual income. The assembly was a natural agency for the consideration of problems arising in the minds of many concerning reductions in salary. Under normal conditions, the assembly considered insurance plans and pension procedure. The work of both council and senate was satisfactory and worth while.

M.

The College and University Parliament

While McVey has chosen what at first glance seems an awkward title, I can think of nothing better which would include all I have in mind.

With the enormous growth of institutions during the past fifty years, the problem of organizing this phase of authority has grown difficult. We must manage our colleges and universities so that each person on the staff feels he is a part of the great whole and has a share in its control. The organization should be such that the least possible amount of faculty time is wasted. Long debates over inconsequential details must be avoided, while important matters should be discussed freely, the majority opinion prevailing.

The inclusion of these several ends has resulted in the type of organization Dr. McVey has described.

I agree that one or possibly two meetings of an assembly each year is desirable. During my own administration I had one such meeting prior to the opening of college in the fall. I then read a printed address which was distributed to all present. McVey followed his address by a period in which he answered questions. I am sure this is sound, and I regret that I did not follow that plan.

At Iowa State College my address preceded meetings of the six faculties, the Experiment Station staff and all the different department staffs. Each group was addressed by the executive head of that group, who set forth the past progress and the plans for current progress.

What McVey designates as the senate consisted at Miami and at Iowa State College of the entire teaching staff, including assistant professors. This was quite all right in my day at Miami where the faculty was small. At Iowa State College, with its subsequent growth, the senate was limited to professors and associate professors, a group of about 460. This group is too large for useful discussion. I am inclined to believe it should not exceed 100 and that these should be elected, as suggested by McVey, for three-year terms.

It is essential at Iowa State College for this group to meet five times a year to vote degrees. However, if the approval of the several college faculties were accepted as final, the responsibility of voting the degrees would be lifted from the senate.

It is essential that certain powers be retained by the senate.

These usually include (1) standards of admission, (2) curriculum questions, (3) standards of scholarship requirements, (4) requirements for graduation, and (5) voting on honorary degrees (all degrees, unless the approval of individual colleges is accepted as final).

Through its committees and the approval of their reports, the senate would exercise considerable control over the entire institution, faculty and students. If it relaxes this authority, it loses command. Where the senate retains and exercises its authority most wisely and energetically, the democratic spirit of the institution flourishes. While I appointed all senate committees in my day, I now believe that committees should be elected by the senate itself. I also believe one committee should be "Advisory to the President." To this committee, any member of the staff should feel free to bring any matter he desires brought to the president's attention.

The council, an executive body meeting once a week under the chairmanship of the president of the institution, seems essential. It is important that this body not encroach on the authority of the senate, but limit itself to the execution of the senate regulations, referring matters back to the senate when necessary.

While the above organization would seem to cover the needs of the institution as a whole, each college should also have its faculty organized under its dean with necessary committees.

As stated elsewhere, I regard it as sound democratic procedure for each faculty to elect its dean for a period of eight or ten years. Such elections should be held after due consideration by a committee and should be subject to veto by the president or his representative. This veto certainly should be exercised through the elimination of names on the list to be submitted to the faculty by the committee, and not after a vote is taken.

H.

The Chief Financial Officer

The "money man" was the cognomen given by Costain to Beaumarchais, who served King Louis XVI of France as finance officer. On Beaumarchais fell all the problems of keeping the king and his extravagant consort in funds. Similarly the comptroller of today fills the place of "money man" in the college kingdom.

The university finance officer, often called comptroller, has become increasingly important with responsibilities added to those of the bookkeeper who managed the money of the small college a half century ago. The spread of higher education on immense campuses, huge student bodies, and extended activities has increased the duties of the finance officer. He sometimes has a staff of from 10 to 130 persons who use machines to expedite the accounting and purchasing records. This staff keeps up department accounts, figures obsolescence, cost of materials and insurance policies, maintains inventories of building contents and department equipment, as well as reports the income and expenditures at least each month. The comptroller has a job and an important one.

The accountant, once a bookkeeper, now sits at the head table with the administrative officers. His ideas have great weight in the business field, and his importance in educational administration has grown enormously; he can and does enter into policy making. In addition, by the setting up of accounting regulations he may affect departmental expenditures. As a matter of fact, checks and counterchecks can alter and even hinder the educational purpose. This is not a superficial conclusion reached through hearsay, but a fact well known to the college president. The comptroller is not an educational officer and should not attempt to impose his accounting methods upon the educational functions of the institution beyond the requirements of his office. The point is brought out in the comment of a campus repair man when he said, "This would be an all-right job if it weren't for the students and professors."

Financial support for, and the maintenance of, higher education in this country face a difficult future with declining income and an increasing student body. Endowments earn less than they did. With the refinancing of bonds on lower interest rates, the returns have dropped. Meantime prices, salaries and wages have gone up in contrast to stationary or declining incomes. Obsolescence of buildings and equipment go on steadily through the weeks and years, a process of deterioration that occasions great concern for the efficiency of the plant and the investment of the college. All these are problems threatening to future education.

To meet this serious situation resting so heavily upon all thoughtful minds, several solutions have been offered. The most evident is a proposal to raise student fees, and it may be said that the raising of student fees presents several aspects. In public institutions today fees are comparatively low, although the out-of-state student is charged more for his education. In the better private colleges the fees are too high, thus largely excluding all but the well-to-do and wealthy classes. This is unfortunate, but the situation is improved by scholarship grants.

Another proposed solution regarded as having possibilities is that of securing federal aid for higher education, both public and private, by grants from the treasury of the United States. Friends of this proposal usually support a scholarship scheme to be administered through the state to individual students who may select any accredited college, public or private.

In the application of this method a good deal is being said about the relation of church and state, but the need can become so great that this principle long held sacred may be violated. And finally institutions of learning may take stock of the situation facing them and so set themselves the task of administering their affairs on a realistic basis involving economy and co-operation. Undoubtedly most colleges and universities could economize to the extent of 10 per cent of their income without serious injury to the program. The comptroller's office could furnish valuable data for a study in cost reduction.

Anyone who studies a catalog — and it's a rather dreary pursuit — will note the number of courses printed therein. Undoubtedly many of these could be eliminated, while other courses having been unduly extended might well be reduced in time requirements. Several institutions might co-operate in unifying specific fields of study, thus saving costs while strengthening the program.

Professor Hiram M. Perkins taught mathematics when I was a student at Ohio Wesleyan University. He possessed an ardent interest in astronomy and had mounted a small tripod telescope in a little tower on the top of his house. When he died he left a considerable estate to Ohio Wesleyan with which to build and endow an observatory. The university erected a good sized building and equipped it with a telescope of sixty-nine inches in diameter and with additional instruments. When the building was completed, only a small sum remained for carrying on the project. After a futile struggle to finance its operation, those in charge arranged with Ohio State University, twenty-eight miles away, to co-operate in developing a good astronomical organization. Ohio Wesleyan furnished the building and the equipment; the state university provided the funds with which to carry on the work of the observatory. In one field or another, institutions might find opportunities for a co-operation that would yield better facilities than either could provide alone. Libraries furnish another example of the need for co-operation in times when money is hard to come by. Vanderbilt University and Peabody Teachers College use a joint library with a large saving.

The comptroller is a kind of weather bureau. He should be able to foresee the drift in expenditures and to keep administrative officers informed of the school's financial status. This discussion on the comptroller has shown certain methods of meeting the financial situation which faces educational institutions. More might be added, but would require an expert study of accounting methods. However, another important problem should be mentioned. I have reference to the strict accounting and use of funds designated for specific purposes.

It is disheartening to have to report the dispersion of funds given to an institution for a specific end and the failure, in other instances, to keep funds in separate accounts so they may be readily identified. When hard pressed for money, a board of trustees will sometimes borrow from endowment funds or actually use them for capital expenditures. This is an unfair practice. In fact, there have actually been cases where endowments have been used to meet payrolls! The justification has been the issue between the life or death of the institution. Even in such a crisis, the observance of law and honesty should be followed. The end of such methods is never justified, since the collapse of the institution is not far distant. A competent, honest, and understanding finance officer with the backing of the president may prevent disaster, if both are imbued with the high purposes and integrity that should prevail in the administration of an educational institution.

M.

The Chief Financial Officer

The title of this office is quite undetermined. As McVey says, it is in some places comptroller, in others business manager, business manager and comptroller, bursar, bursar and business manager, or treasurer. It appears to me the title will tend more generally to become vice-president in charge of business.

In sound organizations, this officer should report to the president and not to the board of trustees directly. While the president cannot pretend to be acquainted with the details of business, he should see that the business of the institution serves the interest of education and research in the fullest way.

One of the important agents of the vice-president in charge of business should be the department of buildings and grounds. This department should be directly responsible to the business office, not to the president.

The treasurer should also properly report to the business office. That is to say, the officer who collects all money due the college or university should so report. If the treasurer is in charge of investments, he may report to the trustees or their finance committee.

One important duty of the business officer should be to publish a complete and easily understandable financial report each year. At Iowa State College, the former business manager, Mr. H. C. Gregg, who had made an extensive study of the reports and financial affairs of 100 or more institutions, set up our annual financial report. It has proved so satisfactory that the same form has been continued since he left to enter upon similar duties at Syracuse University.

Briefly, the duties of the chief business officer include: receiving all money, paying all bills, accounting, purchasing, making contracts, selling products, auditing student accounts, making an annual report, supervising buildings and grounds, new building and all other business. The office is very important and calls for a superior man.

H.

A Provost, or a Vice-President of Faculty and Curriculum

Within the past ten or twelve years quite a number of our large institutions have appointed vice-presidents to relieve the presidents of academic management. Of course this academic management of a college or university is vital; in fact, it is the most important aspect of all executive work. However, as our institutions have grown larger, many other important and demanding aspects of administration have developed. As the president's time has been increasingly called upon for other matters, he has been obliged more and more to allow the academic management to rest with the deans of the colleges. In many cases, it has passed largely out of the president's hands. This would be satisfactory if all the deans were thoroughly competent and attentive to faculty matters. Unfortunately, such is not the case.

Furthermore, it is necessary to maintain harmony among the various colleges and to maintain a certain uniformity in salary policies. Someone must keep in close touch with all faculty and curriculum matters, if the best interests of an institution are to be protected.

There is another reason for appointing a vice-president in charge of faculty and curriculum. If a college president is to be responsible for all faculty and curriculum matters, he must be selected from among men familiar with these matters; he must be a faculty man with experience and training. If, on the other hand, a vice-president thoroughly competent to deal with faculty matters is a part of the executive staff, the president may be selected from among men with other backgrounds.

The appointment of General Dwight D. Eisenhower as president of Columbia University is a case in point. As an executive and as a man among men, General Eisenhower had perhaps no superior. He was eminently well prepared to deal with a great segment of Columbia's important affairs. On the other hand, he was inexperienced in all matters connected with the faculty and curricula. This was fully covered at Columbia by the appointment of Dr. Grayson Kirk as Provost in Charge of Faculty and Curricula.

It is essential that such a provost or vice-president shall have the full confidence of the faculty. Usually this will mean that he must be selected from among present or former members.

There are now many universities and colleges large enough, and with such diverse and important interests, that their best welfare would materially profit from such a vice-president.

Many years ago, an executive officer was generally appointed to handle all business matters, relieving the president of this burden, for which he was often unfit. The time has now come when this further relief is called for in many institutions.

H.

College Deans — Appointment and Contributions

The elimination of deans is an interesting factor in the organization of the Japanese Christian University near Tokyo. This action is called by the American president of the Japanese Foundation "a genuinely new approach to university administration." In the place of deans, five vice-presidents function, and these form the president's cabinet. In the different categories, the vice-presidents administer: (1) instruction and the academic program; (2) campus religious life; (3) student relations; (4) business affairs; (5) public relations.

All of these activities are taken care of in American colleges through one department or another. With the possible exception of business and religious relations, a dean or department head administers and directs the work to be done. In institutions on private foundations, religious matters are guided by a chaplain; in public institutions, organizations such as the YMCA, YWCA, Newman Clubs, and church societies are concerned with the religious life of the students. If the Japanese university develops professional schools, there must be some overhead direction there, whatever the officer may be called. One vice-president could head all instruction activities and with the assistance of second or third vice-presidents, could carry the increasing load of administering instruction. There is, in this Japanese university plan, a possibility of uniform and co-operative development that does not often prevail under a college dean system. I have reference here to instruction which in the American system is combined by departments and colleges; but there is a growing movement to integrate departments. For example, the departments of economics, sociology, anthropology, political science, and history are grouped in a division usually called the social sciences. The student under the division system is free to make choices without too much department restriction.

Why is the elimination of deans from a university organization regarded as a genuinely new approach to university administration? Is it because the dean of a college becomes a partisan who fights for student enrollments, higher budgets, larger staffs and greater public recognition as against the needs of other colleges in the university? As institutions of higher education drift more and more into professional and vocational types of training, the divisions between colleges in a university are quite likely to build academic fences that set them off from each other. Science, however, moves steadily toward integration as seen in the increasing co-operation of such sciences as physics, chemistry, and mathematics, as well as the breakdown between the traditional courses in the engineering field.

In defense of the tightly bound college in a university system, the dean and faculty will point to the increasing requirements made by present day technology for the training of qualified men and women. More time is needed in which to give the foundation and the application of the principles taught, if the student is to have the best training; as a consequence, the specialized colleges tend to go their own way. In the Japanese university plan, the vice-presidents might well develop little kingdoms of their own and so pull the institution in this or that direction. After all, a scheme of organization is no better than the men and women who direct it. The emphasis in this plan, or any other, must be upon the man, his character, training, and experience.

A dean has been called many things and given various characterizations by students and faculty. Among these is the much quoted remark that a dean is a man not smart enough to be a professor and too smart to be president. The fact is that a man chosen as a dean possesses outstanding qualities, or he would not have been selected for the post. But too often he does not have a wide knowledge and understanding of the larger problems in education; and in consequence, at the meetings of administrative groups he will support the vocational trend of the college. If this point of view were followed by the majority, the university would lose unity and become a collection of educational kingdoms. The selection of a dean determines the trend and development of not only the college, but of the larger institution of which it is a part.

I am quite of the opinion that a dean should be given a limited appointment of five or ten years. In this view I am in accord with my colleague. The faculty of a college should have the opportunity to express its views on the selection of a dean. The use of a majority vote in a faculty meeting to recommend an appointment is in accord with democratic procedure, but it often produces a division that may cause friction in the college.

When President Herman Lee Donovan of the University of Kentucky entered upon his duties in 1941, he was confronted with the selection of deans for four colleges. This unusual situation was due to retirement age and death. To avoid the electioneering and the campaigning for candidates, the president sent letters to all the faculty members asking them to name their choices for the post of dean then vacant in the college. The faculty members were invited to comment, and if they wished, to sign their nominations. There was no compulsion about the procedure, and the purpose and fairness of the president, recognized by the faculties, brought an unusual number of replies. A careful study of the returns gave the president a fund of information that proved valuable, as shown in the appointments made and the satisfaction with which they were received.

This way of meeting a difficult situation has much to commend it, but faculty members are quite sure to support some member for whom they have affection and to overlook the need for new blood in the college administration. Bringing new deans into an institution delays the development of the school or college, because it takes two or three years for a new officer to learn what the situation is and to know the faculty and the type of teaching done. However, there are instances when the future of a college depends upon new leadership, and it is then that the president must go beyond the faculty lists in search of a dean.

In looking for the head of a college, a president may very well consider the option between specialization and leadership. The latter may be the more important of the two. The decision must depend upon the situation in the college. An example of action in such a case is to be found in President Edmund Day's selection of Sarah Gibson Blanding as dean of the New York State College of Home Economics. At the time she was dean of women and associate professor of political science in the University of Kentucky. The training and experience of Miss Blanding were entirely outside the curriculum and activities of the college, but she brought to her new duties leadership, enthusiasm, and administrative ability. The faculty of the college accepted the dean from another field of education, and co-operated fully as her views and plans unfolded. Here is an example, and a very successful one, of the wider view brought in contact with the ingrown curriculum and methods that had prevailed in the college. Now and then, emphasis upon the essentials of leadership, character, vision, judgment, and a co-operative spirit yields large dividends in the field of education.

M.

College Deans

My ideal dean of years ago was Frederic C. Ferry, of Williams College, 1902-1917, later president of Hamilton College. Dr. Ferry understood college students. He spent a great deal of time with them. When he told a student that he was suspended or expelled he did it so graciously and courteously that the student thanked him and only came to a full realization of the significance of the interview after he had left the office. Ferry knew, loved and understood students. They were his main concern.

Such deans are rare now. The pressure of administration has forced the students into the background. Human interest, while still important, receives less consideration than is either reasonable or right. Especially is this true in our larger institutions where colleges have budgets that run into the millions and faculties numbered in hundreds. It is true, also, where the personnel office, the testing bureau and the admissions office have taken over part of the dean's former work.

A dean today, especially in our larger institutions, is far busier with administrative duties, exclusive of students, than most college presidents of thirty or forty years ago. In fact, many deans of today rarely see the students. They and their problems are in the hands of assistant deans or counselors.

All of this is written, not to minimize the importance of the dean, but rather to emphasize the change in his position. He once was a kindly but shrewd man who knew all his students, who held the wayward in line and at work or sent them home. Today, he is an administrator of college affairs, only slightly less important than the president, also of vital importance to the president and to the success and effectiveness of the institution.

The last year I served as dean at Miami, about three hundred students were under my care. I had no other duties as dean but continued to teach. I knew all the students fairly well, and those who were for any reason prominent or who needed my supervision I knew well. It occurs to me that the old title of dean is now a misnomer in all but our really small colleges.

A dean in any one of fifty or one hundred institutions is really a vice-president and might be so called. Under each vice-president, a dean of students might supervise the students in each large department or two or three smaller departments. Department heads are almost entirely administrative officers and are so occupied with matters other than students that it is impossible for them to give much time to students. In the electrical engineering department of an engineering college, a dean of students who dealt only with students, besides having to do some teaching, could know his students and mean something to them.

We now try to do this through counselors, young men and women who for a few years give part of their time to groups of students more or less effectively. I am increasingly convinced that a dean should really be a very human person who cares little for administrative work but who knows and works intimately with students.

Today, deans of colleges, as has been said, are of concern to all professors and instructors in their colleges. They play a vital part in selecting new staff members. When you consider that the turnover in most institutions is 20 per cent a year, the task of filling twenty vacancies a year in a college with one hundred staff members, even with the able help of department heads, is a big and vital undertaking if well done. *

The initiation of these twenty new teachers into effective work in his college is a serious matter, and the dean should so consider it. His follow-up on the work of these twenty new teachers, along with that of the other eighty, could occupy a great deal of time.

The direction and review of research work, the checking up on the needs for repairs and alterations in the equipment and supplies of all departments are very much worth while. The making of a college budget and all that its preparation implies in securing the best value for the money and in doing justice to each staff member is a laborious job. Also, the dean will be

---

* See "The Technique of Making University Appointments," by Dean Ralph C. Epstein, Bulletin American Association of University Professors, Vol. 35, p. 349.

obliged to attend national and state meetings of various sorts. He will have speeches to make and committees on which he must serve. He is vitally important.

As I see it, he should be first a man of unquestioned integrity, and that is a very difficult status to maintain. Everyone who questions him will listen attentively to what he says. If he makes any promise, it is never forgotten by the one to whom it is made. He must remember that promise and make it good if he is to retain the confidence of his staff. Furthermore, he must use his language carefully and with unmistakable exactness lest any halfway promise be accepted as a definite pledge.

He should be a shrewd judge of men and have a considerate, sympathetic method in dealing with them. It is his job, among many, to keep his staff happy and contented. He must have the confidence of the members of his staff.

The election of its dean by each faculty, as practiced at Ohio State University, is a sound, democratic procedure. Of course, the dean must be satisfactory to the president, but it is quite as important, or more important, that he be satisfactory to the members of his faculty.

In American colleges and universities over the past fifty years, there has been an almost complete change in the function of all officers. The institution is no longer a cloistered retreat. All the people of the state come to the campus for help and advice. The president has almost more duties off the campus than on. The business manager deals with millions instead of thousands of dollars. The dean now is absorbed in problems which used to belong to the president.

H.

Dean of Women

Many presidents object to the use of the title *dean* when applied to supervisors of students and their activities. The reason for this opposition is based on the idea that a dean is a director of course instruction. In fact, the title of dean when given to the advisers of men and women students raises the office into the upper brackets of the administration hierarchy. Here you have a division on what constitutes education. In these days of large student bodies, it is highly necessary to have an officer who can advise, help and co-operate with students. This is distinctly important, for good deans of men and women can save a president many headaches. What these officers are called is an academic question, but the term *dean* is used in most institutions today.

Why not one dean as a general adviser and instructor to all students? There is much to be said for this proposal, but if the one dean is a man, he would be forced by the circumstances existing to have a woman as an assistant dean. In such a case, objection would then be made that the girls' problems were subordinated to those of the men students. That would undoubtedly be the case where the combined plan was used. Hence we have deans of women in the colleges today.

In an earlier period, a kindly woman with little academic training but who had been a wife and mother was regarded as fitted to fill the post. A good deal more is demanded of a dean of women today. The requirements for that office are now exacting. Excellent health is a first consideration. Then there follow such matters as a good appearance, intelligence, courtesy, tact, patience, and firmness. The ability to make a good speech is a helpful accomplishment for a dean of women. That is by no means all that comes within the scope of this office. Her training is important, so one of the requirements is a bachelor's degree gained by good work in college; and better still, an additional year of graduate work in the field of administration and psychology. Her age at the time of appointment may be from thirty to thirty-five. During her college course it would be well if she had served an apprenticeship in the registrar's or dean's office and then had taught for a time in a college or good secondary school. Added together, these requirements are considerable.

What are the duties of the office of dean of women? It is necessary for her to know as many of the young women as possible and to gain their confidence. In this relationship cases of discipline will occur from time to time. A student court, if well organized and carefully selected, can be of assistance. A vacillating dean can confuse the issue. Firmness and justice, tempered by understanding, are necessary. The housing of women students is an important responsibility. The dean, therefore, should control the placing of the girls in their quarters and also should have an advisory and control authority over the dining halls. Thus she will appoint house directors, sorority house mothers, and dietitians with, of course, the approval of the president. She will make out the budget for her office as well as for the dormitories and so enters into many business matters involving considerable sums of money.

The social activities of a college, especially in coeducational institutions, are important. These affairs must be organized and placed in the date book, and rules must be made for their conduct. With the help of a student social committee, the dean has a controlling hand over such extracurricular activities. And I may add that as a final duty she plays the part of buffer between parent and student, between parent and college, and between student groups. It is then an interesting post to fill, important and helpful, but difficult. The dean of women should have and is entitled to have the sympathetic co-operation of the president. If he knows his job there will be no barriers between the two.

M.

Dean of Women

Formerly the dean of women held a definite part in every college attended by women. She still holds her old place in most smaller colleges. However, she is more or less handicapped in rendering her most valuable services by her reputation for being the disciplinary officer of women. Discipline is less of a problem in many ways than it was formerly. When a girl becomes liable to discipline in a serious way, I believe her case should be dealt with by the discipline committee. So it is conceivable that the dean of women might be relieved of all disciplinary responsibilities.

As enrollment has increased, and the various duties usually carried by the dean of women have increased, certain responsibilities have been taken from the dean and assigned to an assistant or to a separate officer in many cases.

Some of the dean's advisory duties are now taken over by the testing bureau. Room assignments, supervision of dormitories and appointment of hall directors are often in the hands of the director of dormitories and boarding. The control of social affairs is frequently in the hands of a social director. The peculiar subdivision of the dean's work best adapted to the institution will depend on the local problems.

At Miami University our dean of women, Miss Elizabeth Hamilton, was an irreplaceable person, comparable to Miss Sarah Gibson Blanding, who served as dean of women under Dr. McVey. When such women can be found, they are wonderful. They certainly should be provided with the assistance they ask for, and given full authority.

When I went to Iowa State College, the dean of women was an elderly woman who carried her burdens well. On her death, shortly after my arrival, it seemed wise to divide the work somewhat as outlined above.

One of our most successful appointments as social director was Mrs. Iza Merchant. There is great advantage in employing as social director an attractive person whom the students will like to consult. All of their social enterprises involve problems on which they want advice. If they enjoy consulting the social director as a person, they will go to her to talk over their plans and make it easily possible for her to eliminate undesirable features. The girls will quickly realize that she only wants their parties to be pleasant and successful. Her interest and theirs are identical. Her wider experience and knowledge make it possible for her to help them. Her duties are almost entirely advisory and hardly at all disciplinary.

I should like to relate one experience of our social director which gave me much satisfaction.

At Iowa State College we had (and have) a definite rule against drinking alcoholic liquor, and it was difficult to deal with this problem in the fraternity houses until we developed the following technique:

Where the social director was satisfied there was drinking going on, a representative of the fraternity was called in after the party and told that there had been evidence of drinking at their party, that the college could not allow girls to attend parties where there was drinking, and that therefore they could have no more parties.

Since the chapter had just had a party, they did not want another one then and perhaps nothing further was said at the time. However, in a few months they did want a party, and an officer of the fraternity called on the social director to inquire about it. He was told that they could not have another party where drinking was permitted. The chapter then asked what they should do about it. The social director said that was not her business and turned the whole responsibility over to the fraternity.

Usually after the chapter had discussed the matter thoroughly for a few months and had returned repeatedly to the social director for counsel, they would finally work out some plan that would insure a dry party for students and alumni. This policy worked surprisingly well.

H.

Dean of Men

Just when the office of dean of men first appeared in college administration, I do not know. However, there was no considerable demand for qualified men to fill the office before 1915. The post of dean of women was recognized in coeducational institutions long before that date, but under a less dignified name, such as matron, principal, adviser of women and director of student houses. The growth in numbers plus increasing campus activities had laid burdens upon the president which he was unable to meet. At first the head of the college would follow the usual method of naming a committee on student affairs and designating a professor who had some qualifications as chairman. In time the problems, activities and social affairs, in addition to such important matters as student government, loans, and assistance, proved too much for the committee. Often enough, discipline alone took a good deal of the committee's time from teaching. As a result, the office of dean of men came into existence.

This new officer at first had to find his way around. He had to work out new techniques of approach to student problems before his office would justify the expense of maintaining it. This man still continued to give part of his time to teaching, but not for long, since he became more and more occupied with a great variety of problems and demands. The president's office dumped on the new incumbent student matters that had been regarded for years as distinctly presidential functions as far back as the establishment of the institution.

In the early stages of development, the dean of men may have been a YMCA secretary, a successful high school principal or a young minister who had come into notice as the spark plug of boys' organizations in some church. These men did very well with group activities, but they were not especially trained to handle matters of discipline, to advise students and to anticipate the questions and difficulties that might arise, or to meet problems before they reached the acute or breaking stage. It was found to be necessary that the occupant of this new office should have a good college training with possibly a master's degree in education. This was a highly important standard. The incumbent should understand the purpose and meaning of education, because he came in contact with students where he saw the educational process at work. He was sure to notice the effects, results and failures of education in his college. Since it was not his function to act as a critic, but as a friend of students, he must have faith in and an understanding of the purpose of education.

As a friend of boys, a dean of men exerts great influence as he meets them in his official position and as a man. His attitude is very important. This job is no place for a cynic, but calls rather for a gentleman of courage, resourcefulness, tact, understanding, friendliness and courtesy. If I were trying to find someone to fill this post, I should look for a young man in his middle thirties, of good health and married to a fine and tactful woman. In addition to his educational qualifications, I should want to know about the jobs he had had. If he had been a coach of athletics or a good football player, I think it would be to his advantage. A man who has been a coach over a long period of years, however, is likely to overstress the importance of athletics and underestimate the real purpose of a college. So coaching experience is to be regarded as a help in dealing with boys and not to be regarded as a *sine qua non*. I might add that intellectual honesty, frankness and a sense of humor are necessary to this post, also administrative ability and a canny knowledge of the college male.

One might say only the angel Gabriel could meet such requirements, for such a person is a *rara avis*. However, I am sure that there are men who can meet these standards. The fundamental requirements are character and an agreeable personality. Moreover, under proper guidance the new incumbent can learn. He will succeed if given support and if the authorities believe the dean of men is an important officer, not merely a policeman. He must not be a spy, but an honest inquirer into all matters, especially cases of discipline.

I see the dean of men as an adviser, as liaison officer, administrator, and a friend of students in the meetings of the college hierarchy. In the first of these important functions he is called upon to advise individual students about finances, jobs, housing, and personal matters. The present day college usually develops some form of student government, and in his advisory capacity the dean of men must keep this on a useful basis. The same is true of social affairs. One of his important responsibilities is to develop good relations between student groups and the college administration. In adition, he has charge of dormitories and men's fraternity houses and serves as chairman of student loans when these are administered by a committee. He is the disciplinary officer of the college and must temper justice with wisdom. Even violations of parking rules are left to him to enforce. This dean is an important officer whose good work keeps an institution on an even keel.

M.

Department Heads

The chairman of a department may be regarded as the presiding officer at department meetings who is held responsible for routine business. On the other hand, the head of a department is usually regarded as the leader of the department, the man who sets the pace and maintains the standards. When department chairmen are elected, occasionally an associate and sometimes an assistant professor is chosen. Where department heads are appointed or elected, it is exceptional for any other than a full professor to be chosen.

In some institutions, old in years, where each department has several full professors and the prestige of the institution is fully established, the chairmanship plan works well. Where the situation is less stable and fixed, where progress and leadership is definitely desired, the policy of having department heads is better.

The work involved varies greatly, depending on the size of the department staff. Where that is small, few new appointments are made; the division of the work of the department is simple; few changes occur in the catalog, and the teaching load may be light. Where the department is large, employing from fifteen to fifty individuals or more, the responsibility of the department head is much greater, naturally. Often ten to fifteen new appointments are made each year. The scheduling of classes and sections, arranging teacher programs, getting grades in to the registrar and filling out requisitions all involve considerable labor.

In such cases, the question arises whether to appoint as head of the department its most distinguished member, or someone of less distinction who will do the routine work. If a distinguished scholar is selected as head, it is almost certain that he will cease to be highly valuable in teaching or research. Too much of his time will be taken up by his new duties. However, he may give the department as a whole a stimulus which will make up for the loss of his personal contribution as a scholar. On the other hand, if a man of less ability is made the head, he may do the routine work well, but he cannot be expected to give the department the vision and inspiration it needs.

I have found this to be a difficult problem. Without doubt, when a brilliant teacher or research man is appointed, an exceptionally able secretary should be provided to carry the routine work. Where the position carries an increase in salary, it seems unjust to withhold the appointment from the ablest and most distinguished man on the staff. If this recognition is not given to him, he may become deeply offended and discouraged. It has happened.

Not infrequently a man who has been a productive scholar from his thirtieth to his fiftieth year will tire of this work and become much less inspiring as a teacher and much less productive in research. Certainly, no harm would come from making such a man head of the department, if he is still vital enough to keep the department on its toes.

At Iowa State College, there are more than fifty departments, about one-third of which are large. It is striking how the tempo of a department can change with the head. I would estimate that a first-class department head can increase the efficiency of a department from ten to twenty per cent or even more. Where the department elects its own head for a four or five year period, fewer mistakes will be be made than where the head is appointed by the dean or president to serve until he is sixty-five years of age.

H.

The Registrar and His Functions

The registrar stands as a kind of outguard between secondary and higher education. He has had an extensive development in the last fifteen years: he has moved from a bookkeeper and a guardian of records and grades to an officer who is really interested in educational procedure. He has more material in his possession for study of academic processes than has any other agency or group in that field.

What shall be done with this material? How can it be put to use?

The tendency must be more and more, I believe, toward

The Registrar and His Functions 109

applying these records and documents to the purposes of research. The office of registrar should have among its personnel a research man, associated possibly with the college of education, who can make a helpful and constructive study of the material too often locked away. The record books contain the story of what is actually happening in the field of higher education; therefore, intensive attention must be given continually to the data in the registrar's office, if we are to know what to do, where we are going, and when we may hope to arrive.

Problems are apparent in the field of secondary education itself, and problems are present in the relations between the secondary schools and the colleges and universities in the matter of certification and admission of students. An enormous expansion of subject matter has developed in the high schools. In some degree the schools have copied the college courses, often making it embarrassing for the colleges to build or to modify their procedure in the fields in which secondary education has already given superficial previews.

There must be a restatement of these courses, not on the basis of college needs or necessities, but rather on the basis of the problem which faces the secondary school. The reselling of the secondary school to the public becomes a necessity because of loss of confidence in it. You have seen the attacks upon the high school, emphasizing the fads that have been developed. After all, a presentation of the content of secondary education will have to be made from the point of view of the group with which it deals and of the part which it plays in the social order.

Pedagogues are noted for being able to tell the world that it ought to be reformed, but less known for explaining how this may be done. Secondary education as it stands today occupies an important position in the whole field of education; it must rest upon the idea of doing a particular thing for the youth at that particular time, in a new environment, and under new conditions. The expansion which is taking place, it seems to me, must be checked, and emphasis must be placed upon the fundamental courses.

The handling of students in the secondary field who are entering colleges brings additional problems. The registrars of our country have set up a system of admitting students and of recording their grades in the college archives. It is a very neat system, there is no question about that, and it works well from the viewpoint of accounting. But a registrar who is alive to his opportunities will not abide by any procedure just because it is convenient. He must adapt himself to the current trends. One pattern stresses the admission of students into college on the basis of ability to do the work. Such a basis of admission means that a lot of the things which have been required in the way of English and mathematics, social science and other courses are put aside; instead, students are accepted on the basis of their abilities and interests.

I think a new criterion for college admission will soon come into favor. Under the old plan, applicants are admitted with fifteen units, the old Carnegie Units. We are finding, however, that these unit requirements do not really bring out the abilities that we want in college students. The tendency must be more and more toward asking the high schools to co-operate in selecting the best students in their graduating classes for college, not on the theory that these students have completed a certain number of units, but rather on the ground of their ability and interest in college work.

There is very little use in sending a boy to college simply because he wants to go—if he has no literary or scientific interests of any kind and if he is not concerned with books or learning. The lengthening of adolescence by four years is a delightful thing; but from the point of view of the college and of the student himself, the question of ability and interest should come first.

Under the procedure proposed as an alternative, the high school would send the student's record to the college. This record would indicate not only the kind of work which he had done, but also his scholarship, his attitude and his activities.

His scholarship would include, then, his interests and abilities. His activities would show his relationship to his fellow students and his co-operation, his integrity and good sportsmanship, and his honesty of mind and of purpose. The student, therefore, instead of coming to college with a record showing that he has done *this*, *that* and *the other thing* in special topics, would come to college with a record that would show his abilities, his interests, his activities, and his relationships to his fellow students. When he is admitted to college on such a basis, the interest that would be aroused in that student would have a very beneficial effect upon him.

Now what is the relationship of the registrar to all of this? I would say that he can stand in the way of such a procedure by insisting upon the old type of record and admission, and that he can hamper the movement very considerably by his attitude. When the members of a faculty determine on a mode of conduct, necessarily the registrar will have to comply with it; on the other hand, you will always find in a faculty certain conservatives who, strengthened by the office of records, can make impossible any such reform.

The registrar's office, then, must necessarily move in the direction of a more exacting study of the records with which it is dealing. It must formulate from the study of those records new policies, since the administrative officer of an institution, because of the multiplicity of his duties, must rely upon the work which is done by his colleagues in the study of educational problems. If the registrar's office has a trained research man or woman in its organization studying the problem from the point of view of the institution and of the high school, it can make a great contribution.

In this epoch education must adjust itself to the changing forms of government, of political organization, and of social life. To arrive at even a fair solution of these problems, constant study is necessary. Nobody knows the drift, and nobody can see the shore toward which we are going. The only way we can keep up with present day tendencies is through constant study; the agency through which that study can best be done is the registrar's office.

The registrar who is equal to this opportunity and who has sufficient knowledge of statistics and educational policy to make the needed contribution will occupy a much larger place in the future than he has in the past. The marked change and increased scholarship in the registrar's field will bring added importance to that office.

In commenting on the above discussion of the registrar's functions, my colleague has written, "It seems to me one of the handicaps of the registrar is that he has no authority except to collect, record and report grades. Also, any authority conferred on him is likely to conflict with the authority of the deans, and so make trouble. What authority could he be given? It must be authority derived from the president and not from the deans. As I conceive it, many presidents confer their authority for appointments, promotions, and dismissals of faculty members upon a vice-president in charge of such matters, who could confer such authority as he has over the field, upon the registrar.

"But what authority along this line does he have? It occurs to me that you might wish to pursue this matter through another chapter." The following is my reply to Hughes' suggestion:

The granting of authority to a registrar that his ideas, reports and recommendations may have some standing appears a logical procedure, but in the final analysis that officer must have the knowledge, understanding, and capacity to make his work authoritative. Just how far he can go in placing his stamp upon the educational process depends upon the registrar's understanding of the problems involved. In most colleges, the registrar is a young man or woman who has gained some knowledge of administrative matters while serving as a principal in a secondary school or even as a superintendent of schools. Sometimes the registrar is a former member of the faculty who has shown an interest in the problems of college entrance. This will explain in part why the registrar does not count for more in the academic organization. Then, too, if a president does not see the office of the registrar as an important part of the educational setup, he is not likely to enlarge the staff and increase the budget.

Authority is granted to extend activities when there is a clear idea of what can be done. The history of college education is filled with examples where departments have been extended because someone in the department had vision. The results of one man's work have been brought to the attention of an administration by arguments based on facts, and requests have been made for funds to carry on an enlarged department. The fact is that registrars have not regarded the material in their offices as a valuable source of information about education and have had little interest in doing anything with it. What is needed in the registrar's office is leadership based on training, experience and vision. Such a man would win a hearing that would result in authority.

Under the American system of college administration, the faculty passes upon rules and regulations. In building the courses of study a good deal of log rolling may take place, and committees will bring in a report for the consideration of the legislative body which, if accepted, becomes the law of the college. In many faculties the registrar has no membership in such a body, but he should have, and upon the same basis as a department head. If such were his position, an able registrar would be a potent and helpful influence in forming college educational policy. He could secure a hearing and become a strong influence in the building of better courses of study. It would be necessary for this registrar to have a small staff to work up the material which will form the basis for the recommendations he must make. He will become then a university policy maker depended upon by the deans of colleges to help solve the curricular and student problems confronting them.

M.

Importance of an Able Admissions Officer

Many of our American colleges and universities are too careless about admissions; and after students are admitted, small effort is made to become really acquainted with their abilities, aims and ambitions.

This is due in part to an attitude of Americans that all people should be treated alike, that no discrimination should be made. It is also due in many places to the overwhelming number of students. Furthermore, in small colleges students are often a financial asset and so accepted without special regard to their fitness.

Institutions which have a definite limit on their enrollment fixed by trustee action, or by housing shortage have a great advantage. Under these conditions the best applicants are selected, and the minimum level of admission steadily rises.

The value and cost of a student can be estimated on various bases. Many who enter college are of relatively small value as students. Their ability, interest, ambition and determination to work are on a low level. On the other hand, a few students are outstanding in ability, hard work and personality. These go on after leaving college to lives of invaluable service. They are worth to the nation from $500,000 to $10,000,000 or more. How can we select these choice students? I contend that we should, by repeated resurveys of a class, be able to uncover the leading 3 to 5 per cent that will make up the 90 per cent of the ablest men. This 3 or 5 per cent should receive the finest service the college or university can give, the best in teachers, in inspiration, in counsel and advice. If any in this group are short of money, the college should provide necessary funds.

What does the instruction of one student cost each year? I should say between $300 and $1,000, depending on the institution. In some cases, the cost may be less than $300, and in others, it may exceed $1,000. However, in no case do the student fees pay the full cost. Should we spend the excess of cost over fees on students whom we know will not profit from it? Education is a privilege, not a right. A student should prove by the quality of his work in the secondary school that he is worthy of a college education.

It is the prime business of the admissions officer to cull out the weak applicants, and deny them the privilege of admission so far as the rules of the trustees will permit.

There is another responsibility of the college which is more often ignored than discharged. Each student has a record of past achievement; he has ambitions and an objective. These should be inquired into and evaluated. If the student is able and has done first-class work, nothing could be more stultifying to him than requiring him to repeat the work in a similar course, just because it is a required freshman subject. For his best development, he must face a real challenge.

Is his objective sound? Conversation with him may throw doubt on this. Much can be learned from vocational aptitude tests, and they should be given. It is most important that the student of unusual promise be challenged by his work, that his teachers be able and inspiring and that he be given every assistance in selecting the best field in which to work.

The mediocre or average student faces the same problems, but the loss is not so great if he does not get the very best the institution can offer. Many such students need vocational aptitude tests and careful advice about their objectives and their courses.

From my own observations, I conclude that over half of our ablest students fail to do their best work and so drop to the ranks of the mediocre. Most of this deterioration occurs in the high school years, and the colleges can rarely correct it. However, the high schools and homes are not wholly to blame. Where these students are not challenged intellectually by able and inspiring teachers whom they respect, they usually turn to student activities and neglect their studies. Often they continue to make good grades, but their intellectual effort is not first class.

Surely American colleges and universities have a heavy responsibility to do their best for these few highly gifted students.

Much of the above is a reflection on the admissions officer. If he does a routine job, he simply admits all who meet the entrance requirements and have fifteen acceptable units. If he is an able, conscientious officer, he forms a surprisingly accurate estimate of each student and follows each one through to see that he is given the necessary tests and meets the person with whom he should confer. Later, college records should be checked to determine whether or not such a student is fulfilling his promise.

An able, conscientious admissions officer is an invaluable member of the registrar's staff.

H.

Problems of Administration

The Maintenance of the Plant

The professionalizing of college staffs goes on apace. Not so long ago a clever young woman looked after student records, a professor gave part of his time to the library, laboratories were just exhibit places, the college doctor and nurses were unknown, and the business office received fees and endowment income and spent the money by order from the president. Now purchasing is a difficult and special task, and accounting has become a guiding agency for the administration of the college. Along with these developments, which indicate the progress made in educational facilities, the superintendent of buildings and grounds has come into his own and is rapidly reaching a professional status.

The office of superintendent of buildings and grounds has grown in the last twenty years from janitor, gardener, and man of all work to a position of major importance. The old college plant needed little attention, comparatively speaking, aside from the cleaning and maintenance of buildings and campus lawn. The remarkable advance in college architecture, the improvements in sanitary arrangements, the enlargement of heating and lighting facilities, with their possible breakdowns and constant repairs, demand a trained and experienced man to look after the institution's physical equipment.

In my college days, the student body was allowed to shift for itself both on and off the campus. There may have been advantages in such a regime; however, illness, cold recitation rooms, draughts, and the closing of the college in periods of heavy weather were of frequent occurrence. Moreover, the modern requirements for the comfort and the equipment of libraries, offices, rest rooms, dispensaries, living rooms, swimming pools and laboratories with many kinds of machines and motors have complicated the maintenance of a college plant and have made that operation a business in itself. This fact is gradually being recognized by college boards and executive officers, along with other officers of health and administration. The result is that the superintendent of buildings and grounds is being given his rightful place on the university staff.

What does the superintendent of buildings and grounds do? The answer to this question will throw some light on the duties of this department in the college organization and will also give a basis for the discussion. The list cannot be complete, nor is it given in the order of importance. A list of active verbs will afford an idea of the responsibilities of this officer and his organization: employs, cleans, gardens, repairs, paints, mends, builds, estimates, selects, plans, draws, disciplines, watches, observes, listens, transports, confers, records, orders, collects, catalogs, inventories, analyzes, experiments. The list might go on indefinitely, but the main activities are there.

What has the institution in the way of grounds, buildings, and equipment? Where are the roads, telephone wires, sewers, water connections, and heat lines? Even today few institutions have data covering these matters. The superintendent of buildings and grounds starts his office with a campus map showing topography, location of buildings, roads and all service connections. Such a map cannot be made overnight, for it requires accurate data on all the locations.

Campus planning is superficial indeed unless the data on these matters can be supplied by the institution when the plan is made. Quite often the board of managers forgets the cost of service line connections and the money for building is exceeded because the service connections have been overlooked. In this respect the superintendent of buildings and grounds supplements the work of the architect and is a potent factor in making the building a going and habitable structure.

Following the mapping of campus and grounds, the superintendent has the problem of inventory. In some institutions this falls upon the business officer, but it might well be one of the duties of the superintendent because he is in close contact with buildings and their contents. At any rate, he must keep an inventory of supplies for janitors, building materials, lamps, towels, and the like. He must watch the market for these materials so that purchases may be made advantageously.

As a purchasing agent, the superintendent must keep on hand catalogs of all the manufacturing and jobbing concerns that deal

118   Problems of Administration

in the materials required. Such a catalog collection to be of any use must be systemized and kept up to date. His office is visited constantly by agents and representatives of business concerns far and wide, who take much of his time and an infinite amount of patience. His real problem is the conservation of his time; otherwise he is harassed and hindered in his daily duties. The study of catalogs is a matter of importance to the institution since a careful and keen superintendent can save money for his university or college by watching the changes not only in prices, but in the type and character of materials.

The buying of coal is an example of this. To most people coal is merely coal. As a matter of fact, coal varies greatly, and the buying of it scientifically by tests not only saves wear on furnaces, but lowers costs of transportation, reduces ash handling, and produces more heat units. The superintendent of buildings and grounds, therefore, should have the help of the chemistry department in analyzing the coal. His records, moreover, should show what every furnace is doing and who are the most efficient firemen. Of course, he knows how many square feet of radiation he has to heat, and he learns where the careless professors are who open windows and leave lights on. His records must show the costs of operation and be comparable from year to year so that he may know the expense of heating each building.

Staffs come and go, though some that should go stay on and become college characters! The success of a department of buildings and grounds depends upon the reliability, honesty, intelligence, and industry of its staff. Besides the superintendent, the staff for an institution of average size would consist of an assistant, a clerk, a night watchman, a plumber, a boss carpenter, an electrician, a gardener, janitors, and laborers. These men and women should be selected with great care, and emphasis should be placed upon intelligence, honesty, and physical fitness. The institution should provide liability insurance, grant a vacation of at least two week's each year, make provision for illness, pay a living wage, and retire the worker at the age of sixty-five on a small pension. In the office of the superintendent should be kept a record card for every employee on which are listed name, age,

The Maintenance of the Plant 119

nationality, color, job, residence, wage, and length and effectiveness of service.

The wise superintendent will bring his staff together several times a year to talk with them not only about their work but also about possible accidents, about methods of cleaning, about guarding the property of the institution, about the reports they should make, and even about the purposes of the college. Problems of discipline will arise now and then. These vary from carelessness to drunkenness and theft. The atmosphere of the institution will permeate the staff in time; and, as the staff gathers morale, such lapses will become less frequent. Patience and understanding accompanied by firmness and clear, definite instructions create loyalty and good will. Many a superintendent has failed because he is hazy and indefinite in his orders. Written orders posted on bulletin boards meet this difficulty in part. A booklet containing general instructions and stating the obligations of employees would stop a good deal of friction because the employee would then know what his duties were and what he could rely upon.

In the early days very few institutions had night watchmen, and none of them had a police system. The automobile, together with the increasing size of student bodies, larger campuses, and buildings has turned what was once a minor problem into a very difficult situation. Watchmen must be chosen after much thought, given clocks, and required to cover certain stations and to make a daily report on temperatures, on open windows, on unlocked doors, and on other matters seemingly unimportant but nevertheless indicative of what is going on during the dark hours.

In the daytime, the grounds police have to deal with traffic and parking. There are strangers to be directed with courteous comment. Meantime the superintendent must study his road and walk scheme, hoping that he can make improvements that will reduce the noise or traffic and keep motor cars concentrated at two or three points. The faculty may rule that students are not to have automobiles, but this law seldom solves the traffic problem. The superintendent has the traffic question before him all of the time. One campus differs from another so that the solution in an individual case does not help much in solving the problem elsewhere. To expect a seventy-five dollar a month man to be a good night watchman and the ordinary laborer to become a day policeman is to expect the impossible. Modern living conditions have loaded a police problem on the college; and the wise superintendent recognizes it as such, trusting that his president may understand and make suitable provision in the budget.

Fire protection has advanced considerably under the pressure of insurance companies and the advantages of co-insurance. Not only must the buildings have water connections in case of fire, but apparatus must be able to approach buildings on hard roads. The superintendent who would be *persona grata* with the local fire department must furnish the chief with a map of grounds and plans of buildings.

Like all other campus dwellers, the superintendent of buildings and grounds is beset by the temptation to organize a staff that will do everything, that can be housed compactly, and that will enable him to cover the obligations he hopes to take on. What shops ought his department to have and how far should they be expanded in making furniture, setting up boilers, steam fitting and plumbing, painting, grading, carrying on construction and architectural planning? I do not know that anyone can say offhand just how far these activities should be engaged in by the superintendent of buildings and grounds and his staff. A warning should be given that a drifting policy regarding these things may prove to be very expensive to the college. The reason is to be found in several facts: first, an organization may be too large for the college and may maintain a staff that cannot be profitably employed; second, the supervision of many activities may be more than the superintendent and his office can take care of; third, the cost of production may be larger than careful buying and effective contracting can meet. The result depends upon local conditions and the size of the institution.

It is doubtful that the buildings and grounds organization should attempt to do architectural work in the planning of buildings. The training of the superintendent hardly fits him to undertake such work, and the high grade professional architect can produce better looking and more convenient buildings than can any department of buildings and grounds. The employment of a permanent architect who shares an office with the superintendent is seldom satisfactory. However, the superintendent of buildings and grounds, especially if he is a good engineer, should be in constant communication with the architect, keeping him in line with the problems of the institution as a whole.

It is quite desirable that the superintendent's office should supervise construction, taking over this function from the architect. The average building supervisor employed by the architect is apt to let construction proceed and then report on the defects after the mischief has been done. The superintendent of buildings and grounds, as the direct representative of the owner, has a greater responsibility and far more pride in the excellence of the construction. His relations with the contractor are on a solid basis since he is the owner's representative.

When students are housed in residence halls, the college will undertake the responsibility of earning an income on endowment, or more often, to provide better housing facilities than can be had in the town. Whatever the purpose, the erection and management of student halls add to the burden of the institutional administration. Sometimes the men's residence halls are placed under the military department, if there is one connected with the institution. More often they are managed by a separate staff under the dean of men, supposedly independent of, but always falling back on, the superintendent of buildings and grounds, who in any event must look after the heating, lighting, and care of lawns.

The cleaning of the buildings is placed in some colleges upon the superintendent's organization, and he may be called upon to hold down the lid when the populace that inhabits them gets out of hand. Should the matrons of halls be under his organization since they are primarily engaged in keeping the buildings clean and well directed? Or should the whole matter of discipline and care of buildings be located with the deans of men and women? If the purpose of a buildings and grounds organization is taken into account as it must be, then discipline and everyday management should be left to the deans' offices, and the superintendent of buildings and grounds should be given the responsibility of keeping up heat, light, lawns and repairs. In any case, the line must be clearly drawn to avoid constant confusion and to prevent much going back and forth to settle problems over which no one seems to have any authority.

Colleges as a general rule pride themselves on the appearance of their campuses. The lawns and ivy covered buildings inspire many a poem dedicated to alma mater. Chance does not make beautiful campuses. It is true that some campuses have more natural beauty than others, but all of them must be planned, thought about, worked over and loved, if the grounds are to continue attractive. A first-class landscape architect can lay out the grading and planting scheme and can do the initial work; the institution itself must go on with the ideas in connection with its own general plan. On the staff of the superintendent should be a gardener, and the superintendent himself ought to know that round flower beds or star-shaped embellishments have no place in campus landscape plans. Adherence to the planting design is fundamental, and diversion from it by occupants of some of the buildings who have planting ideas or by the superintendent himself brings confusion and ugliness. If the campus is large enough, the college may undertake the maintenance of a small nursery where may be grown the larger portion of the shrubbery for building and walk landscaping. The laying out of walks and roads is a problem that may well test the wisdom of Solomon in these days of traffic. There is no rule except to hold the number down and to make them as broad and as convenient as possible.

Among the important things that the superintendent of buildings and grounds must analyze and must show in his records as the result of experimentation are the cost and reliability of various kinds of coal, paints, plasters, roofing and material of all types as well as methods of cleaning. The cost of cleaning is an increasingly expensive item in budgets. To hold this sum down and yet obtain efficiency requires great vigilance and the careful selection of the staff, with the use of the best soaps, cleaners and scrubbing machines.

The records must show the cost per square foot of floor space and the various uses to which buildings are put. Comparisons from year to year will yield valuable information as a guide for the best results. Although creditable manufacturers are usually careful about the claims they make for their products, still the use of them under different circumstances shows a variety of performance that requires close inspection and study, if the institution is to get the most for its money. Paint must be weather-tested. Radiator valves, steam pipe coverings, gaskets, and all the long list of technical materials should be under constant observation. The results must be tabulated and the records kept, if accuracy is to be obtained.

The budget question looms large in the problem of the office. It requires much bookkeeping to make it clear to the buildings and grounds department as well as to every other department in the institution. General repairs on buildings are chargeable to the budget of the building. This appears to be understood by all concerned, but the various changes and repairs for departments may be charged to the budget of the superintendent or may be chalked up against the department. In addition, unexpected expenditures, often small but necessary, leave the businessman of the institution wondering what to do about them. Bickerings over matters of this kind can consume the time of highly paid officers. The main thing is to know what the plan is. The budgets of departments may carry repairs within the habitation of the department, or the changes may be charged to the building. Perhaps it is fairer to charge such costs to the departments because comparison of expenses from year to year will then include all the items of departmental costs. The budget of the superintendent of buildings and grounds, therefore, should include the main items of repairs but not the small expenses of the departments. If such is the plan, the office of the superintendent must have a copy of the budgets for all departments in which such allowances have been made.

The patience of Job has been regarded as the acme of human endurance. The superintendent of buildings and grounds has need of this attribute. He is called on to do almost everything from the trivial to the important. His telephone rings constantly carrying requests and complaints from every part of the campus. These matters must be attended to promptly and good-naturedly if the campus is to be a happy place. So equanimity of mind and heart is an essential quality. Honesty is a fundamental requirement. The office is subject to many temptations and is in a position to secure commissions and gratuities from salesmen and contractors, if it is in the mind of the superintendent to take them. Such a course is desastrous to any officer who allows himself to go in that direction and will sooner or later bring disgrace upon him and break his professional career. Seldom does this happen, and it is an honor to the professional standing of the superintendents of buildings and grounds that such is the case.

Many are the burdens and long are the hours that the superintendent carries in his daily routine. A weak man, physically, is not equal to the calls made upon the holder of the office. Good health is essential.

Sympathy for his staff and his colleagues, comprehension of the goals of the university, understanding of men and a sense of humor are all necessary for the person who would fill adequately this important position.

Professional training is essential. The old-fashioned superintendent of buildings and grounds could hardly cope with eccentricities of motors, machines, valves, meters, contours, balances, and mathematical calculations of stresses and pressures. This new calling requires the trained engineer who has had experience in the practice of his profession. Modern plants of colleges and universities are complicated and intricate. The demands of the students, the professors and the public grow every day. The sanitation of buildings, the heating and lighting of rooms, offices and laboratories, the protection of property, the maintenance of structures against wear and decay, the care and beautifying of grounds—all rest upon this officer, who should be accorded an honorable place in the staff of an institution of higher education.

M.

Clerical Services — A Stenographic Bureau

The cost of clerical and stenographic service for a large college or university is surprisingly large. Whether it is worth what it costs is a question. In 1937, I visited the Agricultural Department of Cambridge University, England. It occupied one large building in which, I would judge, fifty professors and research workers might be accommodated. I was obliged to wait some time before I could see the director. While waiting, I observed the lack of telephones and clerical staff. In my conversation with the director, I inquired about the number of telephones in the building. He said there were only two, one in his office and one at the information desk. In reply to a question about the clerical staff, he said they employed two or three clerks and stenographers and an errand boy. It was his opinion that telephones and clerks took the minds of workers off their work and were a source of unnecessary interruption. Also it required some effort to keep a secretary busy. I am sure he was right, and yet in this country we are committed to a large staff of clerks and stenographers and many telephones. In fact, a professor generally feels embarrassed if he does not have a telephone and at least one stenographer. At one institution, a clerical staff of 362 was employed to serve 566 teaching and research professors. Their salaries totaled close to half a million dollars, roughly 10 per cent of the total salary item. Did they increase the value of the professors' output 10 per cent?

Of course, the employment of a large percentage of this clerical force is essential. But is it not excessive? Fifteen years ago, I employed a Chicago firm to study our clerical staff at Iowa State and to suggest means of saving money. The study cost $5,000, and I believe it enabled us to save $5,000 a year; but while it recommended much larger economies, I was not able to carry out all the recommendations. Aside from numerous details, the report stated that many men on the staff had heavy peak loads at certain times in the year and undoubtedly needed considerable clerical help at that peak. However, the professors were strongly inclined to insist on a regular clerical staff adequate to provide for the peak load, even though there was not work to keep them busy throughout the year. To take care of this situation, the report advised setting up a number of stenographic bureaus or pools to serve certain groups, allowing for a minimum of individual secretaries and stenographers. The report was sound and would have saved quite a sum if followed in full, but the anguish of removing secretaries and stenographers from our older staff members was too much for me. We did cut department staffs as low as I thought practical and set up stenographic pools to serve the staffs of three divisions and to meet peak loads. The survey paid for itself.

I am inclined to think that in a large institution no personal secretaries or stenographers should be employed unless the need warrants a college graduate at a salary that will secure and hold her. Such a person could materially increase the value of a dean or professor. A cheap clerk or stenographer with only high school training usually only obeys orders, relieving the staffmen of certain routine duties, but does not materially increase his value. It is rare to find a college professor who works at top speed eight hours a day. Some routine work would serve as a time filler; lower salaried girls could well be employed as members of stenographic pools. I personally had a perfect secretary for sixteen years who greatly increased my efficiency. The others, and there were several, did merely routine work.

At Iowa State College we have maintained a service known as the Printing Department, although the name describes only part of its work. This department does all types of duplicating and has the latest equipment. It also does typing, folding, has addressograph equipment, prepares material for mailing, does blueprinting work and binds mimeographed material. Since its services are used by all departments of the college, it handles much work and employs 25 to 30 full-time people.

While a small college would not need as large or expensive a department, I am much impressed by the great service such a centralized department could render any college.

H.

Making Use of the Inventory Clerk's Records

Shortly after coming to Iowa State College I met the inventory clerk, Mr. A. A. Smith. From him I learned that the college had a complete inventory of all furniture and equipment, which was kept up-to-date. Some time later, he suggested to me that his salary was low. I inquired what work he did, and after hearing his explanation I told him that I could not see that his work was of any special value to the college. However, I said, if he would use his inventory as a basis for collecting unused equipment and furniture and supplying the needs of other departments from his store of surplus, he might expect a raise.

His contribution to the economy of the college since then has been considerable, as he has saved, by moving equipment, from $5,000 to $10,000 a year. Every requisition for new equipment or furniture passes through his hands, and if he can supply the needed item he does so.

Today we could not get along without an inventory clerk.

H.

The Budget

The preparation of the annual budget seems to me to be the most important single administrative job of the year. In it must appear every salary paid and every appropriation made, for whatever purpose. If these are fair and just, if every reasonable demand is met as far as the funds permit, it will go far toward securing a successful and profitable year. It is also the time one can practice wise economy.

I think now that I took an unnecessarily heavy burden upon myself in this budget making. Our procedure was as follows: The business manager and I worked over every possible source of income and arrived at a close estimate of the total income for the coming year. I then advised each dean how much he might expand or must contract his budget. The deans asked each department head to submit his proposed budget for the coming

128   Problems of Administration

year and then endeavored to bring the totals as close as possible to the figure I had named. When all the deans' budgets and the business manager's budget were in my hands I totaled them to see how much must be cut out. Then came many conferences and discussions until we had worked out the best budget we could within the income. I was always thankful the state laws forbade spending beyond the income in a state institution.

The detailed form of the budget was a great help. The total income was detailed on one page; the total expenditures were detailed by chief objectives on one page. Then the total expenditures of each college were listed on one page by departments, followed by each department in detail.

The president of one of our greatest universities told me that he had entered on his copy of the budget the age of every faculty member opposite his salary. This would prove valuable.

Many other procedures are followed in preparing a college or university budget. At Oberlin College under President Henry C. King, the budget was prepared by a faculty committee under the chairmanship of the librarian, Dr. A. S. Root. President King, of course, had a part in the work.

In some institutions, the business manager prepares the budget. I do not believe this to be wise. A college is an educational institution, not a business. I feel that many important educational values will not be properly conserved by a business manager. While buildings and grounds must be kept up, salaries, books, equipment and supplies are very important to the faculty and students and must have first consideration. In my day, I felt that these values should have full consideration; so I made up the budget myself with the assistance indicated above. I am now inclined to think that an elected faculty committee with a strong chairman could do as well and might satisfy the faculty better.

I had an interesting experience twice. Both at Miami and at Iowa State the first budget I submitted to the trustees was given their closest attention. All income and outgo figures were minutely questioned. After that first budget was approved, all other budgets were passed quickly with but few questions. A president certainly ought to prepare his first budget wisely.

One budgetary practice I copied from Mr. Carl E. Steebe, then the business manager of Ohio State University. He had a book in which all budget changes, decreases and increases were entered. At Iowa State College, our coal bill was large and difficult to estimate. I always tried to include enough under the item "Coal" to be fully prepared for the coldest winter. Then as each month passed, at our monthly budget conference, the business manager stated how we came out on the cost of coal consumed compared with our quota for that month. Any balance — and there nearly always was a balance — was credited to surplus. Also, as the year progressed, income from fees, sales, and other sources were checked against estimates and our actual status fixed. Any vacancies that occurred had the unexpended salaries credited to surplus, as were all other savings. At the same time, any expenditures not included in the budget were charged to "New Expenditures," as were salaries of all new employees, whether substitutes for men who resigned or new positions. Of course, all these changes were reported to the board. Each month I knew exactly where we stood financially, and I never incurred a deficit.

H.

Surveys of Colleges and Universities

Iowa State College, in common with the other two institutions under the state board of education, has been surveyed three times. The first was in 1915, by a commission under Dr. S. P. Capen, then Specialist in Higher Education in the United States Bureau of Education. The second survey was a follow-up of the first, by Dr. Capen alone. The third, in 1950, was made by a commission under Dr. George B. Strayer of Columbia University. Each of these surveys presented valuable criticisms and constructive recommendations.

I have served on three survey commissions — on the three

Iowa institutions under Dr. Capen, on Western Reserve University, and on the several public institutions of higher learning in Oklahoma. I found these experiences both interesting and stimulating.

The first reaction of a faculty to a survey is usually opposition with an attempt to discredit it. A survey suggests that something is wrong with the institution and such an idea is hardly popular with the faculty. As time passes, various items in a survey report are considered and usually adopted by the trustees.

I am satisfied that a survey made by a wisely selected group of men and women from outside the institution and usually from outside the state itself is fully worth its cost. Especially is this true where several institutions are under one board and all are included in the survey. Probably a survey repeated at ten year intervals would be rewarding. The difficulty in most surveys is that the time is limited both by the amount of money available and by hardship of securing an able commission to serve. This makes it almost impossible to carry on a thorough investigation.

Surveys are almost always brought about by the action of the trustees, and the report is made to the trustees. It would be very enlightening to them if they were to make it a matter of serious study and discussion over a sufficient period. So far as I have been able to observe, trustees rarely give such reports adequate consideration.

Where several different institutions share a field of work among themselves, as do the public institutions in Iowa and Oklahoma, a survey of all the institutions involved by the same commission can have much value. Such a survey brings out duplication of work where it exists and tends to discourage and reduce that condition.

The Iowa survey of 1915 developed the idea of major and service lines of work. They urged that no identical major lines be developed at any two institutions, at least not in identical fields. Bacteriology, for example, had to be emphasized at the postgraduate level at both the State University of Iowa and at Iowa State College; at the university, along lines to serve the medical school; at the college, to serve dairy industry, agronomy, sanitary engineering, and veterinary medicine. While major lines should not be duplicated, the commission recognized the necessity of duplication in the lower classes of minor lines such as English and mathematics. This distinction of major and service lines was accepted by the trustees and thus objectionable duplication has been avoided since the survey in 1915.

Members of the Strayer Commission were on the grounds in 1950 for four months. Their report covered quite fully the four subjects in which the board of education indicated chief interest. These fields were:

I. The state board of education, its organization and operation.
II. Coordination of the educational programs.
III. The internal organization and administration of the institutions of higher education.
IV. Financing the future programs of higher education in the state of Iowa.

A survey of some particular phase of the work of an institution can also be of real value, provided one of the ablest men in the field is called in. The library, the registrar's office, the business office and the heating plant might each profit greatly through an external survey conducted by able men.

H.

Surveys of Colleges and Universities

My colleague's experience with surveys is similar to my own. Over a period of years I have served on five state-wide educational surveys and four institutional ones. From these I learned much about the techniques and the effects of surveys upon the state and institutional administration of education. The states were awakened, for a time, and enacted new school laws and often increased appropriations for support. Some real progress was made. The institutional surveys were involved in such matters as faculty ratings, teaching efficiency, adequate financing, condition of plant, future plans, and administration. The impression that I have is that the state surveys were taken more seriously by the school interests and the people than by the trustees and faculties.

When I came to the University of Kentucky in the fall of 1917, a survey by Dean K. C. Babcock and Registrar C. M. McConn, of the University of Illinois, and President T. F. Kane, of Olivet College, had just been completed and placed in the hands of the board of trustees. The commission offered eighty-five recommendations that, in their judgment, should be earnestly considered. In the course of the next five years, all but two of the recommendations were carried out. This was a helpful piece of work that gave the University of Kentucky a clear picture of what it should do. I expect this survey ranks near the top in accomplishment. The situation was on the desperate side; and since the board of trustees instituted the survey, the members were committed to do something about the findings.

One of the reasons faculties are opposed to surveys is that they are seldom consulted about the survey until it is actually under way. The board of trustees accepts a president's request for a survey and passes a resolution authorizing the study of the institution; then only does the staff learn about the proposal. The members of the commission arrive and questionnaires are distributed; reports are collected. The commission visits, talks with the staff, studies the questionnaires, and returns to some pleasant hotel nearby to discuss the material they have collected. It formulates a report and makes recommendations for the benefit of the institution.

The report and the recommendations are both valuable and worth-while, but the commission has not reached the real heart of the institution, which, after all, is a vital matter. Lack of time, insufficient money and an inadequate typing and analyzing staff are obstacles in the way of a better report. The commission has done its best under the circumstances, but the implementing of the report now rests on the trustees, the president of the college, and the faculty. Here tact, understanding, patience, and time are required to produce results. I am quite sure that the final effect, let us say after three years' time, is not remarkable. The staff grows weary of the numerous meetings and the failure to get agreement, yet some good things are accomplished through the survey.

It is certain that the study of an institution is a matter of great importance to its future welfare. Since that is true, what is termed a self-survey should be set up by the institution with the approval of the board of trustees and the active participation of the faculty. These surveys would undoubtedly fall into groups such as the study of graduate work, the examination of departments, their co-operation, and the part that they play in the growth of the institution. In addition, there are problems of student housing, the future plant, activities of student organizations, public relations, and many other important phases of the institution's purpose. An example of the procedures followed in such studies is to be found in two that were made in the University of Kentucky.

One of these two is a study of graduate work; the other, an examination of the purposes and activities of the university press. The management of a press is a complicated task requiring wide knowledge of editing, manufacture, and sale of books. For this a general committee consisting of eight members was appointed and that committee set up several categories for study and selected committees from the faculty members to study them. In all, there were six subcommittees with chairmen from the over-all committee, so no great burden was laid upon the shoulders of any one committee member. A schedule of reporting was agreed upon. I was surprised by the amount of material and the adequacy of the reports that were brought in to the general committee. The compilation of information and the committee recommendations stated the press problems and opened a clear way for future action and growth. What was accomplished by this committee can be done in the study of other institutional problems.

The self-survey has merit, and when used with judgment and purpose it can be a real substitute for the commission type of survey. In the long run, an institution gains by the knowledge which comes to its faculty through a survey made by the campus dwellers.

M.

College Catalogs

College catalogs appear to be a necessary evil. Almost no one can understand them. Each differs largely in form and content from all the others. Much faculty time is spent in revising them from year to year. Yet we must have catalogs.

Some things can be done to make them less objectionable, however. If catalog changes in courses were permitted only once in two or three years, instead of every year, considerable faculty time would be saved without any loss in efficiency.

Again, far too many advanced courses are advertised that are never given. Dean Carl Seashore of the State University of Iowa insisted that this could be avoided by offering one catalog number under each department which could be used to designate any one of a variety of possible advanced courses. The number could be printed in the catalog with a brief explanation. Then the department, upon learning what unadvertised advanced course would appeal to the largest number of upper class or graduate students, would arrange for such a course to be given. This plan seems entirely sound to me.

When more advanced courses are offered than it is possible for the department with its listed staff to give, doubt is thrown upon the integrity of the department. Such advanced courses creep into the catalog and, once in, they are hard to get out, no matter how dead they are.

One year at Miami we sent our catalog to be read and criticized by a competent expert. One of his suggestions was that the list of the staff, which usually appeared in the front pages, was of small interest to prospective students. He suggested that we move this list to the end of the catalog and open with material of special concern to students. So we began with admission requirements, expenses and like information. I believe this was a decided improvement.

One thing which I introduced in the Miami catalog was a statement of the income of the college. This, with the enrollment, gave a basis for appraising the ability of the college to offer good educational facilities. While I have no idea how many read this page intelligently, I still think it worth the space it occupied.

The clarity of the catalog is important. This publication should certainly be edited carefully each year with a view to (1) making it as understandable as possible, (2) cutting out all material that can be spared, (3) placing the essential contents of interest to prospective students where it can be found easily, and (4) stating clearly the courses offered by each department.

The catalog is an essential publication of a college. It certainly should be prepared with the utmost care.

H.

College and University Advertising

True scholarship and the rewards of learning are difficult to advertise. The prowess of the football team, the pleasant activities outside of classes may be so presented as to attract inferior students, but will seldom draw the able, hard-working type. Increased numbers of students quite certainly may be secured by skillful advertising, but the scholarly standards of the institution usually suffer, directly or indirectly.

I have always felt that a college can count on an adequate growth if it has skillful, inspiring teachers, and if it trains its undergraduates effectively for the work they prepare to do, sending them out with respect and affection for their alma mater.

I believe the same is true of the graduate school, perhaps even more so. A great teacher attracts graduate students from all over the world. A mediocre man cannot be made to appear attractive through any kind of advertising.

Our educational institutions are becoming too deeply inoculated with the methods of business. Advertising is usually in the hands of a publicity man or public relations man. One wonders why any such men are needed by a college or a university. "By their fruits ye shall know them."

H.

A Twenty Year Plan

After I had been at Iowa State College a few years, I proposed to the faculty that we prepare a twenty year plan for the college. While my idea did not meet with enthusiasm it was accepted and we went to work.

Department heads held conferences with their staffs and finally turned in their ideas for the development of their departments over the next twenty years. These reports covered an estimate of students and graduates, staff, curriculum, research in general, graduate work, supplies, equipment and buildings. Some of the departmental plans were excellent, very suggestive and informing; some were absurdly grandiose; some, very timid. On the whole, they were quite worth the effort spent.

The deans and directors made plans based in part on those from the departments already submitted to them and partly from an administrative viewpoint. The personnel director, dormitory director, social director, librarian, superintendent of buildings and grounds, and many others prepared plans. The business manager and the president did likewise.

Since I had taken the idea from the Russian five-year plan, queries came in as to whether or not I had communistic leanings; but no embarrassment resulted.

Finally, copies of all the plans were bound in typewritten form and deposited in the library. In a sense that was the end of the matter.

However, everyone had been compelled to look ahead and think. The whole effort tended to correct the usual hand-to-mouth attitude. The deans, directors, and the president got an over-all view of the thinking on the campus which certainly influenced them and the appropriations they made.

A few years later, this plan was revised and strengthened at its weak spots. How profitable the preparation of successive plans would be over the years is uncertain. It is true that college instructors work very much in the present and allow current changes in circumstances to control their plans too much. In any institution there are gradual shifts in emphasis which are proper and well warranted. Perhaps a recurrent look into the future would draw attention to their changes and bring them more forcibly to the notice of the administration officers.

H.

Attendance at Professional Meetings

It is stimulating for young staff members to attend the meetings of their professional societies. While the senior members of the staff are usually able to finance such trips, many of the junior members are not able to meet this expense. It would be valuable to any institution if it had some funds available to assist some of the young professors to attend these meetings. For example, an institution might cover transportation costs for men and women on salaries below $4,000 who were on the program of their national society. This would seem to me to be a minimum approach.

It is desirable for each department in a college to be represented at national meetings of professional societies at least once every two or three years. Of course every department of a university would be represented regularly.

I found it well worth while to pay the expenses of department heads occasionally to visit a few of the strongest departments in their field in other institutions. They always gained valuable ideas from the trip, and these usually led to the strengthening of their own departments.

I believe it is desirable and stimulating to have an approximate idea of where an educational unit ranks among its peers. This is true of colleges and universities. At the time I left Miami University, I estimated that the educational impact of eighty to ninety institutions in the country was greater than that of Miami, which ranked perhaps eightieth. While I was president of Iowa State College, I felt that not more than twenty or twenty-two institutions outranked Iowa State in educational importance.

In the same way, I attempted to estimate the rank of our several divisions or colleges, Agriculture, Engineering, Home Economics, Science, and Veterinary Medicine, and of our stronger departments.

It is certainly stimulating to deans and department heads to visit those institutions which are stronger than theirs and to size up their strong points. On return from such a trip, the competent men will see that certain advances can be made, and are made, in their own colleges and departments.

It was my practice at Iowa State College to attend as few meetings as possible but to send others to represent the institution. I may have gone too far in this matter. However, certainly, many of the men I sent accomplished more and learned more than I could have. The idea that the president should represent the institution is overstressed. Deans and department heads are more permanent members of the staff than the president and over the years can build up many useful acquaintances in the bureaus at Washington and elsewhere. Also, there is such a thing as a president's being away too much.

H.

Public Relations

During my years as a college president I regarded public relations as a matter of doing a good job at the college. I maintained that if the teaching was carefully done and the students were satisfied the news would spread. Of course this is true.

However, with the increase in the accent on higher education, the growth of our institutions, the rising importance of research to the nation and the great increase in the expenses of operating a college, more attention must be given to what is generally known as public relations.

With changes in the administrative organization, different institutions handle this problem in different ways. Where the president has been selected because of his skill and experience in public relations he will probably direct this work himself. In other places a vice-president has been appointed to have charge of public relations. In any institution the most suitable person available should give all or part-time attention to this matter. It is still true that the quality of the college itself and the character of the staff are fundamental to sound public relations.

This is borne out by the excellent article by Professor Scott

M. Curtlip in the *Bulletin of American Association of University Professors,* Volume 36, page 646. In answer to the question, "What is Public Relations?" he says, "In simple terms public relations is any situation, act, word which influences people favorably or unfavorably. The public relations of a college, then, is the sum total of all the impressions it makes, good or bad. These impressions are made by an institution's policies, its performance, its people, and its publicity. The last is least important. The nub of sound public relations is good performance that is understood and appreciated."

Today much college teaching is wide open to criticism of students and parents. Many students are allowed to remain in college after they have fully demonstrated their lack of interest, inability or unfitness for college training. Publicity, no matter how good, cannot alter these facts if they exist in the college, nor can publicity maintain the college's good name.

I am inclined to think that the innumerable relations of institutions with the public have gone beyond the development of the administrative staff to meet them. Men as presidents or deans or department heads are expected to do what men in their positions formerly did satisfactorily. But the jobs have changed. Many department heads have more complex demands on them than the deans had a few decades ago. Many deans have many more duties than presidents formerly had. Many presidents are wholly swamped with demands on their time. In these circumstances inadequate attention is often given to individual students. Unsuitable teachers are employed. Many matters deserving careful attention are overlooked, due to stressing more or less outside matters.

Costs of college operation have gone up quite as much as other costs. Expenditures have greatly increased in recent years, but not in proportion to reasonable demands. To increase the income for higher education as it must be increased, public relations should be looked after more carefully. This is a matter which must receive the closest attention of the president and the trustees.

H.

With the need for enlargement, an ever-present possibility, long-time plans for buildings should be worked out with care. Fundamental to such forward looking views is the maintenance of good records and maps of the campus.

4.
The Campus, Buildings and Plans

Campus Sites

Now and then, but not oftener than the appearance of a blue moon in the sky, does a college president have a chance to develop a new campus site. The board of trustees makes the final choice, but the president may have the opportunity to determine the bases of the decision. Very few educational institutions have adequate campus sites in this country, or anywhere else for that matter. Often the beginnings are laid in the middle of a small town, which later may become industrialized, with the result that the college is crowded into narrow quarters and cannot expand its campus except at high cost for the additional real estate. The usual procedure when the situation becomes desperate is to buy new acreage at some distance from the birthplace of the college. There are a few instances where institutions have moved to another town, as Yale did in its early history, or have given up their old campuses and purchased larger acreage on the edge of the city.

How many acres should a college campus contain? In the words of the old farmer the answer would be, "All the land contiguous to the original site." The expansion of college activities, along with recreation facilities, student housing and faculty needs requires a large area. Even a small college ought to have a campus of 160 acres; and when it comes to a large state university, the combined campuses will run into several thousand acres.

To illustrate this, I offer a list of items comprising a college plant which is to house, teach and direct a thousand students. Let us begin with the buildings which contain the library, recreation rooms, and science activities; add to these the other areas needed for the care and recreation of students, and so set up a standard for the institution:

		Acres	
1. *Buildings*:	Teaching area needed	20	
	Recreation buildings	5	
	Housing—dormitories	20	
	Faculty residences	20	
	Service buildings and garages for trucks, and the like	2	
	President's house and grounds	2	
			69 acres
2. *Grounds*:	Athletic and play. Football gridiron with stadium	6	
	Football practice field	3	
	Baseball and diamonds	3	
	Track	3	
	Tennis courts (20)	3	
	Golf course	40	
			58 acres
3. *Walks, roads, and parking space*		25	
			25 acres
4. *Campus adornment*:	Shrubs, flower beds, trees, gardens	8	
			8 acres
	TOTAL ACREAGE	160	

Naturally, this classification and the assignment of space will be open to criticism on liberal grants of land for purposes of education. Yet I am certain that the development of such an institution will require that much land, although it may be allocated differently. If we go into the requirements of larger institutions, principally those engaged in research and experiment stations, the land areas mentioned in the illustration are inadequate. An agricultural experiment station can use with benefit several thousands of acres. Again, the work of an engineering experiment station might easily need considerable amounts of land, as in the instance of aeronautical engineering, which requires a landing field of at least twenty-five acres. The time is now here when college administrators will travel by air; athletic teams are already flying by plane. The land question may thus become another "Sinbad and the Old Man of the Sea" for the college president.

The problems contained in finding a site and developing a plant are so numerous and so tied up with technical matters that no one man has the time or the knowledge to work them out. "The man who is his own lawyer has a fool for a client." The same may be said of any president who tries to carry the whole load. The wise man will seek the best architect, the most experienced engineer, the most honest and highly gifted builders. Even then, the result is largely in the lap of the gods.

M.

A Landscape Architect Should Plan the Campus

The employment of a landscape architect to plan the campus layout and locate new sites has become as general as the employment of an architect to plan a building. However, it has not been long since the chairman of the building committee or the president of the board, looking over the campus, would finally stick his cane in the ground at some preferred place and say, "We will locate the building here." And there it was built.

Not only is a first campus plan made, but over the years as building after building is erected, it is enlarged until another plan is set up modifying the original to suit the growth and change, yet retaining the desired symmetry.

It is only as a competent landscape architect, experienced in campus planning, struggles with the many campus problems from year to year that these various demanding problems are solved. How much parking space is needed here and how much there? How wide should each road and walk be? How will the buildings differ in size? Which of the prevailing types of architecture should be finally adopted?

It has been impossible for anyone to anticipate the growth of our colleges and universities. Those now enrolling more than 20,000 enrolled only about 5,000 from 1890 to 1900.

A competent landscape architect can no more anticipate the future size of an institution than can anyone else; but he may observe certain laws of balance, keep certain vistas, and group buildings together that serve related subjects, modifying the plans from time to time so that there is harmony and unity throughout.

A landscape architect should be selected who has had experience with college and university campuses. Such a man will possess valuable knowledge and understanding of the problem. It is helpful to visit some of the college campuses he has planned. The college administration should select a man in whom they have large confidence, then keep him over the years. He should collaborate with the college architect. They should work together toward the desired goal. It is easier to draw a horizontal line on a drawing board and design a building on that line than to get the exact grade of the land at the location and design a building to fit into the site. I still remember with pleasure a building on the Smith College campus which I saw forty years ago. It fitted perfectly into a slightly rolling location and seemed to grow right out of the ground. A good landscape architect can add greatly to the beauty of a university and to the joy of its occupants.

One other matter related to landscape architecture may properly be mentioned here. There is always a violent protest when trees are cut down on a college campus, yet trees must be removed when buildings, walks and drives are to be built.

The best way to counter criticism for cutting down trees is to plant trees and shrubs systematically each year. An annual appropriation must be made for the purchase. It is surprising what a showing this continuous planting will make on a campus over ten years' time.

H.

Preparing Building Plans in Advance of Need

During the depression years of 1930 to 1934, there was no chance at all of securing funds for the erection of buildings at Iowa State College. At the same time, there were several buildings we needed badly: a veterinary clinic, science building, an addition to the library, a men's dormitory, and a women's dormitory. Each of these buildings called for extensive planning. An arrangement was made to secure the help of an able graduate in architecture to work on plans under the supervision of Prof. A. H. Kimball, then head of architectural engineering. Faculty committees were set up which prepared a statement of the needs of each building. Our young architect drew up plans embodying the requirements outlined. Various arrangements were tried, and over the three or four years a final agreement was reached on floor plans for several buildings; rough estimates were made of cost.

The first building for which money was secured was the Veterinary Clinic Building, in 1937. The appropriation was too small to erect the building that had originally been planned. However, it was a rather simple matter to remodel the plans so that they came within the appropriation.

As each building became a possibility through an appropriation, our plans prepared years in advance were very largely followed, because they embodied the best thought of those who would use the building.

One of the difficulties in erecting a college building is to secure adequate time to consider all the requirements of the departments concerned. The architect wants to push his work to completion. Professors are slow to embody intelligently their real needs in an architect's plan. This deliberate consideration at a time when no money for building was available finally resulted in more usable buildings than hurriedly drawn plans could possibly have produced.

Iowa State College was fortunate in having a department of architectural engineering and a capable young graduate architect glad to work during the depression on our plans. However, any college could enter into an arrangement with the college architect to draw up plans under similar conditions without extra cost beyond the architect's regular charges for each building.

I am convinced that it is good economy for a college or university to prepare plans for four or five buildings in advance of having the funds with which to build them.

H.

Architecture Is Important

In earlier days of higher education, the buildings which housed the academic activities were bare, unattractive and inexpensive. A square or oblong, two- or three-story building with little or no pretense of beauty was the rule. Money was scarce, and architects none too skillful. Examples of this condition are to be found in the early buildings erected on the campuses of land-grant colleges. A few of them still may be seen, however, on campuses of many other institutions. Now and then exceptions are to be found as in the central building of the College of William and Mary, but the main building at Vassar with its mansard roof is an example of an early architecture. Now that the institutions of higher education have come into funds through gifts or tax appropriations, the architectural appearance of their buildings has greatly improved.

Three types of architecture and their variations cover the

offerings of architects for college structures. These are Georgian, Gothic, and Modern. The first two, in the main, place the emphasis upon exterior appearance rather than upon the functional purpose. Both Gothic and Georgian are noble styles of architecture, but neither is well adapted to college use. The Gothic in particular hinders proper lighting; and while the same is true of the Georgian in a lesser degree, it cannot be regarded as the best exterior for a university building. The modern architecture emphasizes the functional purposes of a building and lays special stress upon lighting. A building used for teaching and research must have as its main purpose carefully developed employment of space and light. Anyone who has seen the Gothic structures on some of the campuses of this country is impressed with the monumental beauty of the exterior but appalled by the absence of good planning and lighting in the interior.

There is considerable prejudice against modern architecture, based on preconceived notions. Such buildings look too much like factories, it is said, and are therefore unsatisfactory, especially on a college campus. However, modern architecture is in reality based upon classic principles. When employed by skilled artists, the results are highly gratifying. More and more modern architecture is coming into use, especially in England and the northwestern areas of this country. It is so well adapted to the needs of education that it cannot be denied a place on the campus. Harvard University, long an adherent of the old Colonial and Georgian architectures, has built a large structure planned and decorated by modern and forward looking architects. A notable example of the change that is taking place is to be seen in the buildings on the campus of Miami University, in Florida. Here site, climatic conditions and needs have been skillfully considered, resulting in a remarkably beautiful campus. Why should educational institutions lag behind the development in architecture any more than they should sit back and refuse to teach the modern phases of physics and chemistry?

M.

Faculty Housing as a University Project

While my experience with providing homes for the faculty has been very limited, I believe it will throw some light on the problem.

Inasmuch as the institution has large resources, there is a tendency on the part of the faculty member to expect the rent to be low and generous funds available for decorating and repairs. Faculty housing by a college or university appears to me to be a greater source of annoyance than of satisfaction. However, under certain conditions, faculty housing has been forced upon some institutions.

It is better to have a business agency of the institution handle the project rather than the institution itself; for example, the alumni trustees, if such are organized. Also, a committee elected by the faculty might be very helpful in determining rentals and in setting up regulations relative to repairs, rights of occupancy and like problems. If this faculty committee had had a part in the original arrangements for securing the building funds, meeting the interest and paying the principal cost of repairs, insurance and upkeep, they would prove more intelligent in dealing with the situation.

If such a project were to stand wholly on its own feet, or with a definite amount of subsidy, it would be easier for a faculty member to understand, especially when handled by some subsidiary organization as suggested.

Personally, I oppose a rent-free house for a faculty member as a part of his salary. The professor tends to forget that his house is a part of his salary. Unless the size of the institution is rigidly fixed, any amount of growth will call for more houses, or for some of the faculty to live in college buildings and some, in private homes. I believe it is wiser to rent the houses or apartments to the faculty members outright.

This matter is further complicated by the fact that the need for housing is usually greatest among the lower ranks of the faculty where salaries are smaller and the ability to pay rent, less.

In any town of reasonable size, it would seem possible for an institution to work in co-operation with the chamber of commerce or some specially organized group to insure reasonable housing for the faculty, except in times of emergency, such as 1945-1947.

In my opinion faculty housing is an enterprise upon which any institution should enter with extreme caution.

H.

It is important for a president and a dean to know their staff members and to understand their problems, for faculty morale is of vital importance. Through informal discussions, the faculty may gain an understanding of the institution with its problems of the present and its hopes for the future.

5.

The President and the Faculty

The President Should Know His Staff

At Miami University I knew almost every staff member by sight and name. This was possible because the college was not a large one. I made a practice of visiting each building on the campus to see what was going on. These trips about the campus with Mr. Wallace P. Roudebush, the business manager, were a real pleasure to me. Certainly, as far as possible, a president should know all persons who are on the staff of his college. Where the enrollment does not exceed 1,000 to 1,200 students this can be done. At Iowa State College, the numbers were so large it was impossible to know everyone, especially for a man coming in from the outside. One advantage of appointing a man already on the staff as president is that he already knows many of his associates. During my first year at Iowa State I invited the faculty, department by department, to lunch in one of the college dining rooms, on which occasion I asked the department head to introduce each member of his staff to me. I discussed the problems of the department and asked questions. I encouraged any who cared to do so to visit me in my office. These luncheon meetings proved to be well worth while for all of us.

Although I had many duties and a large and changing staff, I tried to know all the professors and associate professors, and of course others, though not many. A man more gifted in remembering people would have done much better.

I found it pleasant and interesting to walk over the grounds and meet the men who maintained the heating plant, carpenter shop, sewage disposal plant, college greenhouses, the many barns, the storerooms, the laundry, and all the rest. These men interested me, and for many I formed a high regard.

One matter troubled me and still does, and that was how to make each member of a department feel free to come to see me if and when he desired. Theoretically the approach was through the department head and the dean. Occasionally it was desirable for members of a department to come to me, but it was difficult to use the information they brought without hurting them with the department head and the dean. In a large institution such interviews would be impossible; in a small one they offer no problem, but in a moderate-sized college where the dean and department heads fully realized their authority and were inclined to maintain the situation, it did not encourage such interviews.

On one point I am not certain whether I was right or wrong. I spent no money at all on my own office. There was a hole in the carpet in front of my desk where some wires had once come through. I cherished that hole. We had little money from '30 to '36, and I gave no one a chance to say I could find money to maintain my office in style but could not get needed equipment for his department. That may have been wise or it may have been foolish. I was indifferent to my immediate surroundings and felt that the important thing was to maintain good, friendly relations with the members of the staff.

H.

Recruiting New Faculty Members

The heart of this problem is to get the largest possible list of persons available for each position. Discarding the less desirable is comparatively easy, but if a desirable person is not on the list, he certainly will not be employed.

When I was able to give adequate time to recruiting the staff, I found it helpful to write out the qualifications which were needed for the position. I included age, sex, academic training, teaching experience, marital status, children, church relationship, and such other items as seemed pertinent.

My experience with teacher agencies was disappointing. While I often consulted them, I rarely secured a staff member through their service. My usual procedure was to get all the names I could from members of the staff and to write the deans of the most likely graduate schools.

When I had eight to ten possible candidates, I submitted the list, my specifications, and probable salary to everyone who I knew might have a candidate. I inquired whether he had anyone to recommend and asked his opinion of the ones on my list. This seemed to be the most challenging approach I could make, and it usually drew an enlightening reply.

After striking the names off the total list, so far as my information warranted, some staff member whose judgment I trusted or I myself would interview the remaining men. This activity usually reduced the prospects to two or three persons who were thereupon invited to the campus to look us over and to meet the men with whom they would work. This visit always resulted in a unanimous decision.

At one time, while Dr. S. P. Capen was director of the American Council on Education, an effort was made to prepare and maintain a card catalog of all teachers in American colleges, with considerable data, including that of salaries, I found this list of enormous value. Strange to say, it was little used and was discontinued after a few years. The men I got track of through this catalog proved excellent material. All were in good positions; none were seeking other appointments, and it is improbable that I could have secured their names by other means.

I felt that this academic list would prove valuable to those seeking good men, and would secure a recognition for alert teachers. I regret that it is not now maintained. When you consider that there are from 50 to 5,000 or more men and women teaching in each of our 75 to 125 fields of knowledge, it is easy to see how difficult it would be to get the names of all who were interested at a particular salary, say $4,500. Not only are the best men who might be interested usually happy and contented where they are, but most of the names submitted are of those who need a job, recent graduates or persons holding inferior posts. It certainly would be a great boon to higher education if a complete roster were maintained, open to all, of men receiving salaries above $3,000.

One modest appointment I made long ago has interested me very much. At the time we badly needed an instructor in physics at Miami; money was scarce, and I could not provide a salary of more than $800. Knowing that a man holding a Master's degree who would accept such a salary would be undesirable, I wrote to the head of the department at Haverford College stating my needs. I asked if he could suggest a man with an A. B. degree and a desirable personality who might be interested in gaining experience as a teacher under an exceptionally able professor. Richard Sutton, the young man who was recommended and who accepted the job, proved eminently satisfactory. He later went on for his doctorate at California Institute of Technology, and Dr. Sutton is now head of the physics department at his alma mater, Haverford.

I cite this example to illustrate the fact that no college can hope to secure a good man for less than a fair salary for the level of education and experience desired. An excellent man with a master's degree is better than an inferior man with a doctor's degree. The former may obtain his doctor's degree and real distinction later; the latter will never shine in an academic way.

From one-half to two-thirds of the higher posts in a faculty will usually be filled through promotions. The more ably the minor staff positions are filled, the more promotions there will be. However, it inevitably happens that men must be found outside the staff for some important posts.

There is one area from which excellent teachers could be recruited which has largely been overlooked. I refer to able young high school teachers. Perhaps there are not a great many suitable for college positions, but there are some, and many a college and university would be strengthened by the addition of able teachers with an experience in high school teaching. Such men are most likely to be found in large city high schools.

H.

Interviewing Prospective Staff Members

Everyone will agree that it is desirable to see and talk with prospective staff members; the only objection is the cost this involves. If a man is asked to come to the college, his expenses must be paid. Where a number of men and women are brought in, this expense will probably average sixty dollars at least.

Usually the president, a dean or a department head will visit a number of institutions and interview a number of candidates. From among those seen, only two or three will prove worthy of serious consideration. These should be brought to the campus, especially if they are being considered for full or associate professorships. It can be safely estimated that from 5 to 10 per cent of all full and associate professorships will have to be filled each year either by promotion or from the outside. Perhaps from a quarter to one-half will come from outside. The abler the men are who fill the junior positions, the fewer appointments from outside will have to be made.

If one regards the relatively high salary paid these men, their length of service, usually twenty years, and the extreme difficulty of getting rid of them after appointment, it is certainly worth $200 or $300 to bring the best available men to the campus before reaching a decision.

When we drop to the grade of assistant professor and instructor, the salary is not so high, nor is the length of service necessarily so long. From this viewpoint the expense of a campus interview may not be warranted. But these men will spend most of their time in teaching. They should therefore be persons acceptable to the students. Since their academic history would be brief, it is difficult to get a true picture through correspondence. Can money spent on a personal meeting with the man be better used in any other way?

The number of vacancies on a faculty of 100 or more, including graduate assistants and fellows, will run in the neighborhood of 20 per cent. Perhaps one-fourth to three-fourths will be filled by promotion. To interview the men to be appointed yearly to a faculty of 100, including the men seen but not appointed, would probably cost $1,000 or more. By having a faculty representative visit a number of institutions, this cost might be cut down somewhat. The expense in any case would be well worth incurring.

The number of additions to a staff each year are greater than one realizes—about 20 per cent a year. At Iowa State College, in 1948-49, with a staff of 1,045 ranking from professor through instructor, 199 men and women were added for replacements and 78 to fill new positions. This is 19 per cent replacement, which is about normal. At Miami, when I was there in the 1920's, with a very much smaller faculty, the turnover was about 20 per cent. To look up all such people is an expensive procedure. However, when one considers that a professor at $7,500 for twenty years will cost $150,000, an associate professor at $4,500 for twenty years will cost $90,000 an assistant professor at $3,000 for three years will cost $9,000, an instructor at $2,500 for two years will cost $5,000, a graduate assistant or fellow at $600 to $1,000 for one year will cost $800, it is certainly important to be sure that each man is worthy of his hire.

One appointment may raise or lower the service and standing of a college. Nothing is more important than the individual men on the staff. While poor appointments are easy to make and extremely hard to unmake, a good appointment will remain good and will elevate the standing of the college.

H.

Judging the Value of Faculty Members

No college can be stronger than its faculty. The scholarship, enthusiasm for learning and research, interest in student progress and welfare, and loyal support of the college by the faculty are the qualities that make a college strong.

Judging Faculty Members

Faculty members are recruited one by one, largely through bringing in men from other institutions. Every president has a limit on the salaries it is possible to offer. His problem is to recruit new men fully as good or better than those already on the faculty.

Of course, the ideal professor improves with time. As he becomes acquainted with the college and the town, he builds himself into the fabric of the institution, and becomes irreplaceable. Such a man may be developed over the years, but he cannot be brought in from another institution. Unfortunately, there are not many such professors.

One of the most important problems confronting a president is the formulation of trustworthy rating standards for the faculty. I attempted at Miami and at Iowa State College to make such a classification by dividing all teaching members into the following groups:

Irreplaceable	Cannot be replaced at any salary
Very good	Cannot be replaced at present salary
Satisfactory	Can be replaced but only at present salary
Poor	Can be replaced for less salary
Impossible	Must be removed

It is illuminating for a president to make such a classification each year. He will find many, if the faculty is large, whom he cannot evaluate accurately. Such a list, however, prepared with the aid of a dean and considered by several deans separately, can be of value in determining promotions, salary increases, and dismissals.

President Wilson Compton, of Washington State College, developed a more elaborate and valuable method of rating faculty members. It is based on a detailed and intelligently prepared rating scale to be filled out by each of six colleagues who know the individual well. There is also a second rating scale to be filled out by students who have studied under the professor who is being rated. These several reports are collected and filed in the personnel record folder of the individual. On these, in part, are based promotions and salary increases. If such scales are in use over the next twenty years at Washington State College, I predict that the institution will become one of the strongest separate land-grant colleges in the country.

When I was a student at Miami University, 1889-93, Presidents E. D. Warfield and W. O. Thompson had a faculty of about twelve men. Of course they knew them well and saw them almost daily. Today, with a staff of 300 to 400 members, the only way such a faculty can be dealt with effectively is through a vice-president who can devote his time to their work and proper promotion and replacement. While there is certainly a shortage of able college teachers, any college may recruit a strong faculty if sufficient effort is put forth.

Members of college faculties usually resent class visitations. Yet how anyone can really estimate a professor's work without observing his teaching methods, I don't understand. I am convinced some arrangement should be made for each newly employed teacher to be so observed. The best plan is to have each department head request the new staff member to select, after a few weeks, some member of his department with whom he can consult on the practices in vogue at the college. The new instructor and his mentor will then arrange to visit each other's classes and discuss teaching methods. Thus the department head will get a line on the new man's qualifications and attitudes through someone who really knows of his work.

H.

Pensions

In the past decade the people of the United States have become pension-minded. Security for old age is no longer a phrase heard now and then, but a demand rising from nearly every phase of life today.

The insurance companies print elaborate advertising on how to retire on two hundred dollars a month; the trade unions insist on pensions for workers over sixty-five years of age, and the government has established a plan for social security. Such is now the pattern. The colleges and universities have long been familiar with the problem, but as yet many of them have no definite plan of retirement for staff members. Many colleges continue the older members of the faculty on the payroll as long as they can, but the feeling of anxiety is there.

Some colleges have contracted with the Teachers Insurance and Annuity Association, sponsored by the Carnegie Foundation for the Advancement of Teaching. Under this plan the institution agrees to pay 5 per cent of the total of its annual payroll and the teacher agrees to contribute 5 per cent of his salary. Over a period of twenty years there is thus accumulated a considerable capital fund which is used to buy an annuity upon the policy holder's retirement. As interest rates are low, the annual payment to the retired member is not large. It is usually inadequate, and he should supplement it by saving to meet the cost of living.

Other colleges have contracted with insurance companies on much the same basis. The workings of such a retirement plan require a college to pay out annually 5 per cent of its teaching payroll. If this sum were $750,000, the institution would have in its budget a fixed charge of $37,500 which might be difficult to meet in days of tight budgets and small surpluses over expenditures.

Here was a serious situation which faced the University of Kentucky in the early nineteen twenties. The budget could not stand an annual cost of $50,000 a year for pension funds. Members of the staff who had reached the age of seventy were carried on part pay or on full pay. The whole situation was one of uncertainty, and it was necessary to face it.

A committee of five had studied for two years the pension problem as it concerned the university. The elements involved were the cost to the institution, the cost to the individual and the security and practical working features of a pension plan. From the first the cost to the university seemed prohibitive, and the cost to the individual member of the staff might better be used to pay premiums on personal insurance. With these arguments in mind the committee reported a plan that has been in effect twenty-five years without a breakdown.

The plan was called "A Change of Work Program." At the age of seventy, a member of the staff was placed on a retired basis with certain work assigned to him by an agreement between him, his department and the president. As a basis of payment, he was given 20 per cent of his salary and 1 per cent additional for each year of service. Thus a professor who had served thirty years would receive one-half of the average salary he had received during the last five years of his tenure.

This is a good pension as shown in comparison with the retirement provisions used in other places. The amount of work the recipient was expected to do was reasonable and usually in the field in which he was interested. During the time that the plan has been in effect some good research has been done; considerable editorial supervision by retired persons has been helpful to the institution. The list of accomplishments is quite impressive.

In addition, it should be remembered that most men are glad to have an agreeable task to perform after their retirement. The payment ceases upon the death of the recipient, and no provision is made under this plan for the widow or children. The institution provided for a retirement plan for the staff members and expected them in turn to secure insurance for the protection of their families. However, a group life insurance plan was set up for the whole staff, giving the heirs of those who died a specific amount of insurance, to be paid on the death of the staff member. This insurance was supplemented by a group health insurance plan. The provisions for retirement and protection in case of sickness or death now consist of the following:

1. The Change of Work Program.
2. Insurance against death up to $3,000.
3. Health and hospital insurance under a group plan.

The group insurance costs are paid by the staff members. The combined plan thus includes monthly payments to retired persons from the age of seventy until death; insurance paid at death (this sum could provide for funeral expenses and other expenses resulting from sickness) ; and, finally, hospital and health insurance for staff members.

There is one criticism of the system used by the University of Kentucky. It is this: The plan has no financial basis; it rests upon the promises of the board of trustees. That such promises may be violated is true, but pension plans based upon elaborate financial support have broken down in the past and left in their wake a group of disappointed and embarrassed persons.

While twenty-five years is a short time, it is still a long enough period to test the value and results of any one plan.

M.

Pensions

I believe thoroughly in the plan outlined by McVey for the care of the faculty in old age. However, my observation leads me to think that it would be stronger if a pension without work could be provided at the age of seventy-five. Not many men can work usefully beyond that period, and they often become a real burden to the department if work must be assigned to them.

Inasmuch as the number who reach seventy-five would not be large, and as the average number of years they would live beyond that would not be many, this contributary system should not be costly. It also appears desirable that only associate and full professors contribute to it.

I fully agree with Dr. McVey that most professors would prefer a part-time appointment from seventy to seventy-five years of age rather than a straight pension.

H.

Sabbatical Leave

There is no question but that a sabbatical leave is a great privilege and that it is highly prized by those who enjoy it. It is also of real benefit to a college or university if carefully administered. Furthermore, it can be set up in an economical way so that, while valuable to the faculty, it will be inexpensive for the college.

Sabbatical leave at Miami was instituted around 1905 on the basis of one semester's absence at full salary or a year's leave on half salary. Usually a substitute teacher could be employed for half salary. At that, only one person might be absent at a time. While the faculty was small, leaves did not occur every seven years but every eight or ten years. However, they proved to be a valuable experience to those so privileged. I enjoyed only one sabbatical leave, in 1910-11, during my thirty-one years at Miami. I visited over eighty schools, colleges, and universities in the eastern half of the United States and throughout England and Scotland during that period. I formed many useful and stimulating acquaintances and learned many things new to me about colleges and universities, and thereafter could cite a precedent for any change that might be contemplated at Miami.

I heard of one abuse of the sabbatical leave on this trip: A professor simply dropped his classes, remained at home, played golf, and jeered at his fellow professors, who were hard at work. As a result of this unhappy example, I instituted the custom at Miami of requiring the professor who was eligible for leave to file an application setting forth his plans for study or observation, which information I presented to the trustees.

At the time sabbatical leave was established at Miami, with a student body of 500, there were about thirty-five members of the faculty eligible for the privilege. When I left Miami, with an enrollment of 1,500 students, there were about seventy faculty members qualified for leave. Two members were granted their sabbatical at one time. Since then a larger number has been on leave each year.

Some type of sabbatical leave, even if it were available to only a small portion of the faculty, would be better than none. For example, even if leave were afforded only to full professors who had held that rank for ten years, it would have a stimulating effect.

In a great university with 15,000 students and a teaching staff of 1,500, any type of sabbatical leave might prove so expensive as to be prohibitive. The sabbatical or seven year idea might well be eliminated. A man who reached the rank of associate professor at thirty-five or forty years of age and continued in the institution until he was sixty-five or seventy should certainly deserve one, and, if possible, two years of leave on pay sometime during the last thirty years of his service. Possibly one year might be arranged as an exchange with a professor from another institution and one could be straight leave on full pay.

It would be wise to place this matter in charge of some person who had the time and wisdom for the job. He could consider all requests of eligible professors and work out the best possible arrangement of leaves within the appropriation allowed for that purpose.

Any arrangement other than an automatic rule applied in rotation would result in charges of unfairness and injustice. The members of college faculties are prone to make such charges. It will hardly be possible for the majority of colleges and universities to operate an automatic system in rotation, but any charge of unfairness should not be allowed to stop leaves of absence on pay.

H.

Teaching and Research

As we have endeavored to improve the training of college teachers, it has become more and more necessary for them to hold the doctor of philosophy degree in order to be eligible for a desirable college position. Today it is the exception for a man without the doctorate to be appointed to a full professorship.

The increasing emphasis on the doctorate has so stressed research that most faculty members now firmly believe that only in research lies the path to advancement.

Among the men and women who hold the doctorate, not many really have great talent for research; but under the compulsion of a popular idea, they devote a considerable amount of their time and attention to such work regardless of their ability in this field. Young persons, instead of doing their utmost to become able, inspiring teachers, often look down on teaching as being second in importance to research.

A study I made a few years ago at Iowa State College showed that the ten ablest research men were receiving on the average about $200 more salary than the ten ablest teachers whose research was inconsiderable. This seems to indicate that research is not paid for at a much higher rate than able teaching.

While the demand for good research persons is steadily increasing, both in our universities and in industry, the number of really capable persons fitted to direct research in our universities is not large. Industry, with large research staffs, can use numerous men of secondary ability, trained in the technique of research, working under able directors. Universities require research persons who are fertile in ideas, productive scholars who can direct research work at the doctorate level. Persons of mediocre research ability have small value in research in a university.

Those with the doctor's degree cannot look forward to any considerable preferment in a university on the basis of research unless their research ability and productiveness are noteworthy.

On the other hand, there is a very real demand for inspiring teachers. Of our 1,850 colleges and universities, only about 100 confer the doctorate. Among these 100 universities, candidates for the doctorate compose only a small percentage of the students. Even here strong teachers are badly needed for nine-tenths of the work.

Unfortunately, the present stress on research is becoming a menace to good teaching. How can this situation be remedied? It appears to me that the only effective remedy lies in limiting the teaching of persons recognized for research to graduate courses and junior and senior courses, excluding them rigorously from freshmen and sophomore teaching and from all beginning studies offered in the junior year.*

Steady pressure should be exerted to secure efficient teachers by offering them good salaries and good professional standing. Undoubtedly such a policy would increase the expenses of the university. Some of this expense might be met by limiting the doctoral training to departments employing only distinguished research professors. How else to place teaching in a position

---

* Professor J. H. Hildebrand, of the University of California, has an able article on the other side of this question in the *Journal of Chemical Education*, Vol. 26, p. 450.

comparable with its importance, I do not know. All colleges that ignore research and stress good teaching are free from the research handicap, but often the salaries offered are too low to be attractive. Therein lies the main trouble.

There is a large group of institutions — on the borderline between the avowed colleges and the universities conferring the doctorate — which offers training and the universities conferring the influence of research is felt and may be injurious. These institutions include many of our strongest colleges, paying good salaries. If the leading positions are filled by research persons catering to the small group seeking the master's degree, the impression is likely to spread that only through research can promotion be won.

There is one field in which research and experiment are always appropriate—the field of good teaching. No one who has taught has been satisfied with his own work. Always it seems as if sounder procedures would have brought greater results. The striving for better methods is worth while and wholly commendable, for such striving improves teaching. Research in this field does not impede good instruction.

In spite of enormous enrollments and much sophistry attempting to prove that large classes are as good as small classes, the simple truth is that a keen teacher leading and directing a lively discussion with a group of fifteen to thirty eager students remains the ideal situation for developing young minds.

The handicaps to good teaching are innumerable: big classes with a mixture of able with dull students, much formal imparting of facts, lectures containing no new or especially interesting material, students who have no desire to learn outnumbering the ambitious—all result in an instructor who finds his enthusiasm smothered and his teaching sterile. Research and experimentation on how to avoid such conditions will always be welcome.

In talking with students one occasionally hears praise for the inspiration certain professors have given them. It is not a common experience. One wonders why more professors are not inspiring. Perhaps we too often select them for their degrees, for research ability, and for distinction among their colleagues. Certainly every student should confidently expect to enjoy some inspiring teachers during his college course.

H.

Guilds Control Higher Education

Danger ahead is the warning signal to be seen by observant men on the college level of education. The budget, the staff, and the courses of study are being threatened by the demands upon them made through various educational groups. In the not-too-distant future, education on the higher levels will be controlled by guilds and the rules they set up. This trend is apparent to many administrators in the college field. To a considerable degree these men are helpless, for faculty members will join the supervising agencies without taking under consideration the results that are sure to follow.

The aim is to better instruction, but the requirements set up by these agencies go much farther than that. Colleges of a certain enrollment must pay designated salaries, employ persons with given degrees, impose standards of equipment and living facilities; they must offer required courses of study and limit the number of students in these courses. All this sounds reasonable enough, but the procedures and rules are made by committees and employed without the knowledge of those responsible for the maintenance of the institutions. In the long run, applying a yardstick to universities and colleges will result in a prescribed type of institution and a mediocre form of education. The deans of colleges will say we cannot do this and we must do that because the association has said so, all of which has the effect of binding the institution in fetters.

What is so disturbing about this important matter is the blindness of faculty members to a dangerous trend. The institution's policies are not determined by those responsible, but by a dozen agencies which do not work together. Thus, engineering societies will declare that if the institutions want recognition, they must meet their particular standards. Students in schools outside the favored group cannot be accredited and so are left to struggle along under a handicap. Employers come to recognize these arbitrary standards and in turn choose their employees from certain prescribed institutions. The choice is no longer determined by ability and personality, but by the college the student comes from. When a faculty member is to be selected, the standards set up by an association limit the choice to those who belong. So a fixed salary, a given number of books and periodicals, laboratories that provide so many square feet per student, equipment of this and that, courses of a certain type, and buildings of a given design are all in the code.

What can the harassed president do? He can instruct deans and professors to remember that they cannot commit the institution to rules and standards without the consent of governing boards. But these standards are set up without the knowledge of administrators, and their first contact may be on the day that the committee of the associations comes to the campus to inspect the college. In the long run, the heads of institutions must demand recognition and have a part in the formation of such codes. Would it not be better to permit education to work out its own destiny without the domination of these new guilds?

M.

Democracy in College Administration

Oberlin College, the University of Wisconsin, and Yale have been spoken of as notably democratic in their administration. Ohio State University also has claims to this distinction. As colleges and universities have grown enormously, it has become increasingly difficult for them to operate in a democratic manner. Probably the only sound criterion of democracy in a college is the amount of control on policies that is exercised by the faculty.

In the old days, the small faculty met weekly; the president presiding, they enacted all rules and regulations. As the faculty grew, it was divided into colleges, each college faculty largely controlling its own affairs, and the general faculty dealing with over-all matters. Coincident with this change, many young assistant professors and instructors were added. The general faculty now numbers 1,500 or more in some institutions. It is difficult to enact a regulation subject to faculty debate where the faculty exceeds one hundred members. What is the answer, if democracy in control is desired?

One thing is certain, the general faculty should supervise the appointment of all committees. Probably a committee on nominations would have to be elected, and the nominations of this committee submitted to the general faculty for approval. The same procedure should be followed by each college of the university.

The selection of department heads and deans should also be controlled through the faculty, subject only to veto by the president. Each institution would have certain policies of its own relative to tenure of deans and department heads. In my judgment, all such terms should be limited.

At Ohio State University, the department heads are elected for four year terms. At the end of this period, the head may withdraw, he may be re-elected for another four years, or he may be replaced. There can be little argument in favor of a department head holding a permanent appointment terminated only by the incumbent's having reached sixty-five or seventy years of age.

The head of a department has a great influence upon the character, effectiveness and happiness of the members of his department. So long as the department flourishes under his leadership, it will want to continue him. At Wisconsin, where the term of a department head is one year, some men have been re-elected for twenty years. It is difficult for a man to keep on his toes as head of a department for many years. To maintain all appointments in a large staff at the highest levels, to see that the teaching of each new staff member is well done, to give adequate assistance to the less capable, to keep in close touch with all staff members, and to afford inspiration and encouragement to each is a heavy responsibility. I favor a four or five year term, with re-election possible.

In an institution striving for democracy in administration, it is my opinion that the dean of the college should be elected by the departments of that college for a term of six to ten years. The selection of the dean should be made by the college committee, or by a committee of the department heads, under the chairmanship and subject to the approval of the president or the vice-president in control of the faculty.

If the deans, department heads and committees are selected by the faculty, the control certainly lies with the faculty. It is impossible in large faculties for the whole body to debate and vote on all matters of policy and make all decisions. If these problems were solved by men of their selection, the faculty would be allowed fair expression.

It is certainly true that increased democracy in administration makes decisions slower. However, it is hard to see how we can develop a democracy, if colleges and universities are to be operated autocratically.

These ideas did not appeal to me while I was serving as president. I did consult freely and widely with the faculty, but I must admit I made most of the decisions myself. I sincerely believed my decisions were supported by the best faculty opinion and were both wise and just; nevertheless, they were in reality largely mine. I now see that this was wrong and that the control should rest with the faculty.

It also appears desirable that a faculty committee should be consulted by the trustees in the appointment of a president. One method which has proved satisfactory is to have the trustees collect the names of all men available for the post and submit this list to the faculty committee for their consideration and advice. From this list, the trustees would select a small group of five or six preferred men. The new list would, in turn, be presented again to the faculty committee for their opinion. The trustees would finally select for president a man approved by the faculty committee and endorsed by the trustees.

One cannot leave a discussion of committees without expressing regret at the amount of valuable time they consume in proportion to the importance of the work they do. Some method should be devised to reduce this waste. One great time-consumer is the catalog committee, which has charge of all changes in the catalog. I arbitrarily ruled that all changes in the catalog be made every second year, thus cutting the work in half. No one expressed dissatisfaction. It even seems possible that catalog changes might be made only once in three years.

Where committees are appointed to conduct examinations of candidates for the master's and doctor's degrees, much of the time of the ablest men on the staff is consumed. I see no way to avoid this.

Most of the work in a committee is done by the chairman. Often, through a sense of delicacy, he insists upon a full discussion of every point by the full committee. I suggest that the committee discuss the whole matter, whereupon the chairman would write up the consensus of the meeting and submit the written report to each member for alterations and suggestions. The report should then be rewritten with the suggestions embodied within it. A final meeting should be sufficient to approve the report or settle the disputed points. Usually the chairman does 90 per cent of the work anyway.

Another embarrassment in committee work is that too large a share of it falls upon a small proportion of the ablest senior men. More younger men should carry this burden than is usually the case.

H.

Two Faculty Committees

The committee system is a part of the democratic procedure by which a meeting of minds results, and thus wisdom is attained. This is the theory; but in point of fact, a committee decision does not always attain the height of wisdom. The committee method, whatever its merits, consumes the time of a considerable number of persons throughout the course of an academic year. The tendency in making up committee membership is to keep able members of the faculty as chairmen over long periods of time, until they become tired and bored with the assignments. In cases where the president appoints the committees, he turns to men or women who have demonstrated their ability along certain lines;

in consequence, the committees are continued with much the same membership from year to year. This method has the advantage of a smooth procedure but the disadvantage of creating a *status quo* in the operation of the institution. The junior members of the staff, on the other hand, feel that they will never have a chance to try their wings but will remain grounded in an academic hangar.

From several standpoints this is an unfortunate situation which, in the long run, may develop into a kind of dull routine. One way to break it up is to ask the faculty to appoint a nominating body to prepare a list of possible nominees for the various standing committees. From the lists so made up, the president would appoint the members of the standing committees. In this way the faculty will come to feel that it has a real part in the government of the institution. It is doubtful that the work of these committees will be any better than those selected by the president, but this nominating committee plan certainly would help the general morale.

The budget-making procedure in most institutions runs along in a rather set pattern as follows:

(1) Call for departmental statements on appointments, salaries, equipment purchases, and incidental expenses.
(2) Discussion among departmental staff members of the needs of the department, and new appointments. In most instances the head of a department regards this information as a private matter, though he may discuss the salary question with individuals.
(3) The material, information, and estimates now go to the deans of the colleges who may make up the budgets to fit the general income situation. The deans will, undoubtedly, talk with many persons about expenditures, but in time they must present college budgets to the president's office.
(4) Conferences with deans, librarians, and other department heads in the president's office. To the best of his knowledge and ability the president will tentatively approve the budgets, but the matching of expenditures with income is yet to be made.

172   The President and the Faculty

(5) In the business office, a detailed statement of income is compiled from carefully considered estimates. The guide to this procedure is found in the maxim: "Underestimate income; overestimate expenditures." This wisdom is appropriate in days of high prices. The businessman of the institution then brings his study of income to the president; after several conferences, it is modified and set up as a tentative sum.

(6) The expenditures prepared by the college deans and the various agencies are placed side by side with the estimated income. Seldom is the estimated income greater than the proposed expenditures, so a cutting down process must be followed. Shall the expenditures be reduced by a flat percentage across the board, or shall the reduction be made by a re-study of the expense of operation and instruction? Repairs and maintenance can be reduced in most institutions, and some cutting of instruction cost may be made, but usually not much. Even salaries may be reduced by a flat percentage, but this is a dangerous procedure and should be resorted to only under extreme circumstances.

(7) With the two sides of the budget now in balance, the margin between income and expenditures should be carefully reviewed. In my own experience, I regarded 5 per cent as the minimum buffer between the income and costs of operation. The next step in this long and arduous task is to type the whole budget with all the details, so the board may have a clear picture of the situation.

(8) Adoption by the board of trustees is the final step. This may require a long session which is determined, in the main, by the care with which the budget has been made. If the financial guide for the next year is vague and uncertain, the president may find himself in hot water.

In this process of budget making, should a faculty committee have a part? Certainly the members of the staff are personally interested, but too often do not have an opportunity to express themselves. In many institutions, deans see only their own college budget; also, heads of departments know only their particular department expenditures. In consequence there is talk, some of it charging that favoritism has been shown in the budget as adopted by the board of trustees.

I am of the opinion that well selected committees, appointed by staff action, would be of assistance in budget making. I doubt that it is wise for such a committee to take over the whole supervision of the budget as it passes through the different stages of its formation. At the fourth stage, the faculty committee might well come in as a reviewing body. Then the committee would be aware of the problems from an institutional point of view. The process of changing the budget would be by way of recommendation; the final decision should rest with the president. Again at stage seven, the committee is given a full statement of the tentative budget and the opportunity to make changes is presented.

Objections to the committee's supervision or advice will center around delay and the development of controversy. While there may be annoyances, in the long run there will come into the process of budget making a greater understanding, an institutional way of looking at finances, and a co-operative spirit.

Such a change in institutional budget making is quite at the opposite end of the methods now pursued; consequently, it should be adopted gradually and only after frequent discussion. As this goes on, the college or the university can open the way to fuller co-operation. I am sure the institution will be the richer by the uncovering of new talent valuable to the life of the college. This procedure is well worth trying.

M.

The Salary of the Football Coach

This is a subject that troubles almost every college president. In America, where the coach largely plays the game from the side line, directing the players, his skill is very important. The alumni are vociferous in urging the employment of an able coach regardless of the salary cost.

I could never justify the idea of paying a coach more than

our ablest full professor. Yet in several well known colleges, the coach has been paid more than the president. In such a case the president is an unnecessary expense. If football is the main concern of the college, it is logical to make the coach its president and so organize the college that it may revolve around football and allied interests.

With a coach receiving an absurdly high salary, it becomes obligatory on the part of the college to hire the ablest players available, so that he can maintain his reputation. Even a highly priced coach cannot win his games with inferior players.

The problem of honest amateur football is a very difficult one to solve with gate receipts ranging from $35,000 to $500,000 or more. Since the University of Chicago has dropped out of the Big Ten and operates its football on a truly amateur level, I have observed no loss of standing in that institution.

Football serves as a great pageant for a college. The crowds, the band, the organized cheering all make a football game a gay and notable occasion on the campus. It is an excellent diversion and an outlet for the spirits and energy of the students. Up to that point, it serves a useful purpose. Football should be played on an amateur basis. The coach should not be permitted to direct the plays; the game should be played by the team. How to accomplish these ideals today I am unable to explain. I did my best to promote intramural athletics; I opposed in every way I could professional football. I believed ours was always an amateur team, and it seemed to be defeated often enough to prove my point.

H.

The College Teacher Has a Good Life

A great many young people do not believe that a college teacher has a good life. One main objection is that the dweller in an ivory tower has to get along on meager rations, in the opinion of the young men who are satisfied with an undergraduate degree and who look to business as an outlet for their ambitions. Another view is that a professor leads a narrow life and travels with his head in the clouds. The young men say they want action, success, money; the professorial job appears to them to lack excitement. These young men expect to reach a good executive position in business; and in their rosy dreams, they overlook the millions who never get above routine and treadmill conditions.

To manufacture things, especially useful and needed products, is a good service, but too often the business is one that brings little return to those who buy, and a lifetime employment in such a field yields but small satisfaction in the days of retirement. The pace in business is very fast; the toll is heavy. As recorded in the daily press, men at middle age drop by the wayside or come to their end through the strain of competition in the modern business world.

Of course, education as an employment has its limitations, but it is a highly necessary and important function. Man does not live by bread alone, nor do pleasure and recreation constitute the true aims of life. Many successful businessmen know that, and the little man in his everyday fight for a living is sure of it. He dreams of success, but he ends in trying to keep going as the main purpose of his life. It seems to me, after a half century of work in higher education, that it is a good life productive of many satisfactions.

My own experience may be divided into three periods: First, that of a student; the second, that of a teacher; and the third, that of an administrative officer. I propose to write briefly about the types of men and women under whom and with whom I worked as a student, teacher, and president. My college days were spent in a denominational college and later in the graduate department of a famous university. The college faculty numbered about twenty; of this number, ten had been preachers in their earlier days. A missionary spirit prevailed in the group, for the members believed wholeheartedly in what they were doing. At least seven of the twenty were outstanding teachers; another half dozen were good; and the remainder, mediocre or poor. The men probably received a top salary of $1,500 to $1,800. They had their own homes and reared children who did well, judging by the standards of those times. These men were looked up to in the community. They possessed wisdom as I remember them and attempt to rate them as citizens and teachers.

In the university graduate school, the men were more aggressive; all were excellent teachers, co-operating with the graduate students. They, too, lived well and dwelt in good houses. Often they were called upon, even in those days, to advise in public and private business. Some of their affluence came through inheritance or marriage.

The scene changed when I spent a year in New York City and later became a teacher in a Midwestern state university. The staff was younger, highly ambitious. It contained men who reached considerable reputation, three of whom were later appointed as presidents of large universities. The salaries extended from $1,200 for instructors to the top payment of $4,000 for full professors. Morale was good, salaries, fair. The community was a pleasant place in which to live. I got on comfortably; but when children came, the going was difficult, and debts hard to pay. That situation is a general one for a man of thirty-five with a wife and two children. It isn't peculiar to teaching alone. The family learns to meet its difficulties, and the children have the advantage of educational facilities close at hand.

A president of a college has opportunities of viewing the forest as well as the trees. As he becomes acquainted with the college staff, he can classify the teachers as excellent, good, fair, and mediocre. Here again, the classification seems to be parallel with the business and professional fields. If he is a man of sympathy and understanding, a president can see the differences in men and women, can come to appreciate the obstacles they face, and can measure the problems that confront many of them. If he is a wise man, he does all he can to make the way easier for them.

It is not to be gainsaid that the work of a teacher is easy, but it is rewarding to those who have purpose, industry, good minds, and a love for young people. If the president looks at the staff of the college over which he presides as employees, as hired hands instead of colleagues co-operating in a great cause, the men and women of the faculty are likely to be unhappy; but a situation of that kind does not exist in the majority of colleges and needs not be counted as an occupational hazard. Good relations are always desirable, and the whole trend in college administration is in that direction. Certainly the professor has a freedom to work and help in the formation of policies to a greater degree than in any other calling where large numbers are employed.

When the advantages of teaching as a calling are summed up and set against the disadvantages, they are, in my opinion, on the plus side. In brief, the teacher has a fairly secure tenure at moderate pay. He is not subject to layoffs and stoppages, and in most cases receives a modest pension after retirement. More important, he has interesting work as a teacher and student. Almost at hand there are laboratory facilities and libraries open to him whenever he wishes to use them. His leisure time is greater than in other callings; recreation and travel, if he has the money, can be indulged in without interference. In the community he has a social position, and many opportunities come to him to lead in local organizations. On the campus he finds congenial, intelligent men and women who add to his happiness as a social being. There is also the possibility of achieving high standing in his field; even fame may come to him as a consequence of his scholarship. Such things offer the opportunity for a successful and pleasant life.

If this be so, then the duty of presidents, deans and professors is plain before them, to encourage able students of good personality to enter the teaching profession. There is great need for them in the faculty of every college. The argument that such students should follow the teacher's calling is fully justified.

M.

Education is a matter of affection and concern for people. This places upon all those engaged in education the obligation to advance its cause. We talk about democracy, but it is necessary to practice it in classroom, on campus, and in all matters dealt with by faculty, students, and friends of the institution. Such is the challenge — a great one, a difficult one! Good sense and an understanding leadership can bring about notable results.

6.

The Status of Students and Their Relation to the College

One of the first things in which I became interested after retiring from the presidency was the background and character of our student body. What were the occupations of the fathers? How well educated were these parents? What grades had the students made in high school and how successful were they in college? As I pursued this study, other facts emerged.

Occupations of the Fathers of Students

Identical studies were made of all students entering in the fall of 1937, 1941, and 1942, a total of 5,610. The percentage from each group varied for the three years by less than 2 per cent except in the case of clerical workers, where it varied 3.5 per cent in one year. The average for the three years is shown in the table on the next page.

Roughly speaking, one-fourth of our students came from families of professional men; and three-fourths from nonprofessional men.

180   The Status of Students

A detailed study of the occupations of the fathers of the 1,870 students entering in the fall of 1937 is given in the Appendix.

Iowa State College is a technological institution. The agriculture and veterinary medicine courses enroll more than one-fourth of the students and rarely admit students not reared on farms. Engineering courses enroll about one-half of the men, and home

EMPLOYMENT OF FATHERS OF STUDENTS ENTERING IN FALL, 1937

Professional Employment	Percentage	Nonprofessional Employment	Percentage
Teachers	3.76	Farmers	32.21
Other professions	6.32	Small businesses	17.25
Engineers and scientists	4.74	Skilled and semi-skilled workers	14.25
Executives in large businesses	8.76	Salesmen	7.13
	23.58	Clerical workers	4.44
		Unskilled workers	1.11
			76.39

economics about nine-tenths of the women. Ten to fifteen per cent of students are enrolled in the Division of Science. This is not a typical institution, but the composition of the student body is probably similar to that of most public Midwestern institutions.

While the children of professional men on the average make better grades than the children of nonprofessional men, the number of the latter is three times that of the former. As a result of this large predominance of numbers, the majority of our best students come from the families of nonprofessional men.

Education of Fathers and Mothers

A study was made of the educational status of the parents of students entering directly from high school, in the fall of 1942. The data available covered the education of 1,642 fathers and 1,646 mothers as reported by the students on their matriculation cards. While this information was not given in a few cases, the reports seemed to be definite and fairly accurate.

THE EDUCATION OF FATHERS AND MOTHERS OF STUDENTS ENTERING DIRECTLY FROM HIGH SCHOOL, IN FALL, 1942

	Fathers	Mothers
	Percentage	*Percentage*
4th grade or less	0.730	0.426
5th, 6th or 7th grade completed	2.740	1.154
8th grade completed	19.350	15.600
Total 8th grade or less	22.820	17.180
Some high school	13.94	12.45
High school graduates	20.95	28.30
Total high school graduates or some high school	34.89	40.75
1 to 3 years college	17.03	26.93
College graduates	15.90	14.60
Ph.D. or 1 or more years graduate work	9.31	0.79
Total degrees or some college	42.24	42.32

Approximately 20 per cent of the parents have not gone beyond the 8th grade,
38 per cent were high school graduates or had completed 1 to 3 years of high school,
42 per cent completed from 1 to 8 or 9 years college.

One Reason for the Increase in College Enrollment

The American people desire an education for their children as good or better than their own. As the educational level of our people rises, college enrollment increases.

The table on page 182 shows, first, that the education of the people of Iowa has advanced; second, that the large majority of our students, 75 to 80 per cent, come from parents who are high school graduates or who have attended college. As the proportion of our population who are college graduates, who have attended college, or who have graduated from high school increases, college enrollment will increase.

High School Grades and Success in College

In any institution where all high school graduates are accepted regardless of grades, many enter who have but slight chance of graduation. Also, here as in all colleges, many well prepared students fail to succeed because they do not work.

Education Completed by Iowans, 1925 and 1940.

	Education of Population 25 Years or Older in 1925	Population in 1925 in Each Degree of Education	Education of Population 25 Years or Older in 1940	Population in 1940 in Each Degree of Education	Students Entering I.S.C. 1942 From Each Group	Entering I.S.C. per 10,000 of Population From Each Group
	Number	Percentage	Number	Percentage	Number	Number
4 years or more college........	33,855	2.54	61,024	4.15	469	77.0
1–3 years college.........	84,087	6.47	101,440	6.90	385	38.0
High school graduate.......	122,087	9.37	257,551	17.50	400	15.5
1–3 years high school.....	135,000	10.40	221,061	15.05	162	7.3
1–8 grades........	898,000	69.00	801,887	54.50	189	2.4
Unaccounted for..	30,000	2.30	28,000	1.90	....	....
Totals......	1,303,029	....	1,470,963	....	....	....

It is certainly striking that 469 students came to Iowa State College from 61,024 men and women who were college graduates, while only 189 came from 801,887 of our population who had not gone beyond the eighth grade. The number of college graduates in the country is growing rapidly. This development alone will stimulate college enrollment in America.

In the following table the number of students is given who, in the fall of 1935, entered from each decile of their high school class, the number of each group who were graduated, and the percentage. (The first decile includes the *lowest* 10 per cent.)

Decile of High School Class	Number Admitted	Number Graduated	Percentage Graduated
1 (lowest)	95	6	6.3
2	93	8	8.6
3	114	21	18.4
4	141	39	27.6
5	190	63	33.1
6	139	58	41.6
7	68	30	44.2
8	281	143	50.8
9	320	179	56.0
10	243	169	69.0

Of those from the lower deciles who graduated, many spent more than four years in residence. Of those in the higher deciles, a considerable number who were not graduated did not fail but transferred to other institutions, largely to secure courses not offered at Iowa State College.

It is evident that any student graduating from high school in the lowest one-third of his class has little chance of graduating from college. Many of those graduating in the lower half of the class would have made a creditable record in a junior college offering terminal vocational courses.

H.

Progress of Students

To say that 40 per cent of the students who enter college are graduated by no means tells the whole story. It was worth while to follow the 1,740 students who entered Iowa State College in the fall of 1935, until they left college. The following table gives the results of the study.

The Status of Students

PROGRESS IN COLLEGE

Of 1,740 students entering Iowa State College, September, 1935, 750 were graduated with averages as follows:

75 averaged 3.120 to 3.875		75 averaged 2.310 to 2.425
75 " 2.860 to 3.118		75 " 2.200 to 2.310
75 " 2.675 to 2.860		75 " 2.108 to 2.200
75 " 2.525 to 2.674		75 " 2.040 to 2.107
75 " 2.425 to 2.525		75 " 1.650 to 2.040

(For the past 5 or 10 years no one has been graduated with an average below 2.000.)

Of the 1,740 students, 990 failed to graduate, as follows:

	Withdrew	High School Record Unpromising	College Averages and School Aptitudes Indicate Probably Able To Graduate	College Grades Above 2.00
1st quarter	191	161	19	11
2nd quarter	113	75	17	21
3rd quarter	223	108	45	70
During 1st year	527	344	81	102
1st quarter	95	46	14	35
2nd quarter	55	30	11	14
3rd quarter	105	41	23	41
During 2nd year	255	117	48	90
1st quarter	76	32	15	29
2nd quarter	49	21	10	18
3rd quarter	49	13	14	22
During 3rd year	174	66	39	69
1st quarter	2	2		
2nd quarter	5	2		3
3rd quarter	15	10	3	2
During 4th year	22	14	3	5
1st quarter	7	5	2	
2nd quarter	2	2		
3rd quarter	3	3		
During 5th year	12	10	2	
TOTALS	990	551	173	266

Progress of Students 185

Of the 225 students graduating from college with averages below 2.20, 111 had been regarded as quite promising on the basis of high school grades; 71 had had fair high school records; 43 had made poor records.

Thus if the 594 least promising (551 + 43) had been excluded, we would have denied admission to 43 who did graduate and to 551 who dropped out.

Of these 594, or 34 per cent, who were certainly poorly prepared for a four year course, many could have made creditable records in a junior college offering terminal vocational courses. The first two years of work in a technological institution are very largely made up of basic courses preliminary to professional work; courses in mathematics, chemistry, physics, zoology, and botany are difficult for, and of slight use to, the students who drop out. A junior college course could be more useful.

The free public junior college offering suitable terminal vocational courses will some day fill a needed place in our educational system.

It seems possible that a more effective counselling system might have saved for graduation at least part of the 173 apparently capable students who failed to make a 2.00 average.

About 15 per cent, or 266, of those who entered withdrew of their own accord with averages above 2.00. Many transferred to other institutions. Many of the latter entered Iowa State College with that in view; as for example, students completing three years and transferring to law and medical schools.

Some interesting conclusions resulted from my extended study of the records of many classes.

The scholastic aptitude test, on the whole, checked rather closely with the high school average as a guide to the student's college record. But neither predicted closely what the individual student would do since so much depends upon application.

One surprising conclusion was that the average of the first quarter's work indicated in a very large majority of cases the academic level the student would maintain throughout college. The idea that the first quarter's grades will be low, due to change of environment, change of study habits and new teachers, and that grades will rise as time passes is wrong. With some exceptions, the first term's average is a good indication of what the average for the four years will be.

H.

Failure of Able Students

Whatever can be said about our accepted tests for high scholastic ability, it is hard to see how anyone can make a really high rating who is lacking in such ability. In the fall of 1947, I decided to interview those entering students who ranked among the highest 10 per cent in scholastic aptitude, and to challenge them to do their best. I called to my office the 240 students ranking in the highest 10 per cent, from 91 to 100 (based on the 1945 edition of the American Council on Education Psychological Examination, by Thurstone and Thurstone). Most of them came in singly, the rest in small groups. After a few minutes' conversation, I told each student three things:

1. He ranked among the highest 10 per cent of the 2,400 who had entered in September. He had inherited from his parents excellent brains.

2. If he would work hard in college he would make high grades and rank near the top of his class.

3. If he would work hard at his profession after graduation, he would rank high in it and earn a generous income. Those at the top in all occupations at fifty years of age were able men and women who had worked hard. No considerable success could come in competition with such men without hard work.

Certainly all of these young people had the ability to make a *B* average. However, at the end of the first quarter, only 101, or 42 per cent, averaged *B*, or 3.0 or better; 103, or 43 per cent, averaged between *C* and *B*; while 36, or 15 per cent, averaged below *C*.

At the close of the second quarter, 17 students who ranked *B* or better the first quarter fell below *B*, while 11 students who were below *B* the first quarter rose above *B*. Slightly less than 40 per cent made a *B* average the second quarter.

While only 101 of the 240 ablest 10 per cent averaged *B* the first quarter, 94 of the remaining 2,160 in the entering group, ranking lower in ability, also made a *B* average.

It is a great reflection on the college that only 40 per cent of the most brilliant young people who entered did superior work in college. I was not able to follow this through. It seems probable that if these students had been in close contact with able instructors in fields in which they were interested, they would have done better; however, their ambition, determination to work and love of learning are pretty well set at seventeen or eighteen years of age. These qualities, rather than brilliance of mind, determine their accomplishment, both in college and in after life.

H.

Upper Class Students Who Make Low Grades

This really is a registrar's job, but almost no registrars have interested themselves in it. A large number of students often survive the freshman year by only a narrow margin and come back as second year students with a grade average below 2.0. Although their average is near 2.0, unless they are carefully watched they may survive two or three years without reaching a general average of 2.0. The only way they can raise their average to 2.0 is to make sufficient *B* or *A* grades, or to repeat courses in which they have made *D* grades, and raise them to *C* or better. Such students are reluctant to repeat courses and are usually unable to make *A* or *B* grades.

When sufficiently rigid probationary rules are enacted and enforced, of course these students raise their grades or are dropped. However, a survey and report on all students above their first year who have an average below 2.0 will usually be enlightening.

This again raises the question of the status of a registrar. If he makes such a report on his own initiative and presents it to the president or deans and nothing is done about it, he will not get up another such report. Often the president is not interested or does not have the time to pursue these matters. If there are several colleges, it is quite certain that the several deans will not act alike on such a report. The registrar himself should have the authority to enforce action, or he should work with some over-all officer who has. There is certainly no advantage to anyone in retaining a student three or four years who never raises his average to 2.0 and who never attains graduation. I am sorry to say that I found such cases during my own administration both at Miami and Iowa State College. Recently at Iowa State the rules relative to students on probation have been so strengthened that I believe such cases are now impossible. However, students who either cannot or will not raise their grades definitely above 2.0 are difficult to handle and need to be persistently watched.

H.

What Proportion of Students Work up to Their Ability?

While of coure all students cannot make high grades, we can expect each student to make grades according to his ability. The question is to gauge his ability and to know what grade is reasonable to expect.

The proportion of students in a college, or in a fraternity, who are working up to their ability is our best criterion for judging the quality of the teaching in a college, or the standards of scholarship in a fraternity.

Each entering student presents two measures of his ability:

(1) His high school average, and (2) his scholastic aptitude rating. I have made several charts for all students entering Iowa State College in September, 1948, and September, 1949, covering the work of several terms. In these charts high school averages are tabulated horizontally in five groups, from 3.50–4.00 at the left to below 2.00 at the right. Scholastic aptitude is tabulated

vertically in ten groups from 90 to 100 at the top to 1 to 9 at the bottom. In each of the 50 squares is given:

>the total number in the group
>the number making 2.00 or better and their average
>the number making a high grade
>the number making a grade below 2.00
>the number who have withdrawn

It would seem reasonable to expect any student who really works, and who is suited to the work he is engaged in doing, to make an average approximately equal to the average of the students falling in his bracket in high school average and scholastic aptitude, who are above 2.00.

For example, a student with a high school average of 3.50 to 4.00 and scholastic aptitude of 80 to 89 should make about 2.89. A student with high school average of 2.00 to 2.49 and a scholastic aptitude of 40 to 49 should make about 2.27. (See chart in Appendix.)

At Iowa State College where practically all applicants for admission who have graduated from any four year Iowa high school are accepted, the numbers who fail to make 2.00 and the numbers who drop out include about 60 per cent of all who enter. In other words, the college graduates about 40 per cent of those admitted.

On comparing the averages made by those who are above 2.00 of different classes following in each group, they are found to be quite closely alike. Thus it seems that these averages probably are a function of the high school average and of the scholastic aptitude. If so, any college might find the table given in the Appendix useful for comparison.

Any institution using Hollerith Machines for tabulating grades can, with some labor, prepare similar tables of their own.

These tables seem to afford a useful basis for comparing the scholarship of one fraternity with another, or of any one group with any analogous group. Of course only about 20 per cent of all entering students can measure up to or above the average rating of their group where only 40 per cent are graduated.

I believe these charts can be used by any college with large advantage in promoting good scholarship.

If two or more colleges determined the proportion of their students working up to or above their expected average, the one making highest would certainly be doing the best teaching.

Fraternities

Men's and women's fraternities loom large on the campuses of our land. The simple and democratic type of organization which prevailed in the last century has been superseded by grand organizations with considerable staffs to supervise and direct the individual chapters. The memberships in these chapters, scattered over the country, now run from forty to as many as two hundred persons. With the growth of chapters and increased membership, the housing problem has arisen on every campus. "Fraternity row" is a feature of many college towns; and with the high cost of housing, the college is brought in to help finance and control building. Through the help of the college, better terms can be secured from banks and contracting concerns.

When this is accomplished, the chapter agrees to pay, through a long-time lease, enough to meet interest and amortization charges; failure to pay or to continue the chapter results in loss to the fraternity. In fact, the college comes to look upon the arrangement for housing chapters as a dormitory question. The financing, building and planning are no longer controlled by the chapter, but pass into the hands of the institution. There is much to be said for the college method of constructing fraternity houses, but it does reduce initiative and responsibility on the part of the fraternity. So it is true that today chapters are being regimented by their own organizations and by the colleges where they are located. As a matter of fact, the members of fraternities are tenants on a long lease basis in houses which may become obsolete before the long amortization process is completed.

The election of a Negro boy to the membership of Amherst's Phi Psi chapter raised a tempest in the tub where the fraternity's soiled linen was washed, in the seclusion of the fraternal cellar. The story was about a year old when Mr. A. S. Romer presented the case in the June, 1949, *Atlantic Magazine*. Mr. Romer was the president of the chapter house co-operative and thus was brought into the trouble area. The account is clearly stated and covers questions likely to be raised more and more often as time goes on. Mr. Romer's article then comes to be something of an historical document to be read carefully by persons interested in the welfare of college fraternities. The focal point in this case is the composition of the national board and the attitude it took on the admission of Tom Gibbs to the Amherst chapter.

To those concerned with the subject, it is a sad fact that the management of national fraternities has passed into the hands of professional officers and the joiner type of alumni, excluding the undergraduate from the management of the fraterity grand chapter. It is true that the undergraduate local chapters send a delegate or two to the national conventions, which meet in some big resort hotel. The business is under close supervision, but the undergraduates are granted an occasional peep into what goes on. It is a far cry from the earlier days of the national fraternity to the present expensive organization with its several paid officers housed in some big city. Today these officers have paid secretaries, field agents and editors to be compensated by the fees charged against each initiate and chapter. These fees, including local charges, amount to $75 to $150 for each new member. In addition, there are house dues and living expenses to be taken care of. So residence in a fraternity house is nearly as costly as that of a city club.

The dean of men at the University of Kentucky was vigorously declared a dictator by the editor of the college paper for interfering in a fraternity matter. The case was one of discipline. The editor declared that students should be treated as adults and allowed to solve their own problems. This is good sense as far as it goes, but it rests upon the proposition that students will take the responsibility and do something when matters go wrong. In this case, the editor felt that the Inter-Fraternity Council should be entrusted with the problem. In institutions where there are more than half a dozen chapters, such a council is certain to exist; but it is my observation that the activities are limited to making rules for rushing and plans for holding the annual dinner, where good fellowship is emphasized. The fact is that the council is composed of representatives of competing chapters who shy away from any controversy that is likely to raise dissension.

In all of this confusion of fraternity comradeship, college rules, student morale, and leadership, there is a challenge. A union of minds, student and faculty, is a real need always; but underneath the problem there should be a foundation of genuine student responsibility that does not rest upon conferences between groups. The fraternity chapter should understand the purpose of a college so that publicity about fraternity doings and the competition between them would be subordinated to educational objectives.

How can higher morale and better student understanding of the college purpose be gained and, once gained, be maintained through the years? The answer involves much preaching of a high order, contacts with parents, conferences with alumni, and close association with student groups. This means hard work on the part of president, deans, and leading members of the faculty, and an understanding of the importance of bringing the fraternities and the college into an attitude of mutual confidence.

M.

Fraternities

When I left Miami, my relations with the fraternities was bad. They acknowledged that the university, as the mother of fraternities, stood for scholarship. Yet the fraternities ranked low in scholarship. So far as I could learn, they cared nothing about their scholarship standing so long as it was high enough to permit their members to remain in college. They recognized only secondary loyalty to the college; their first allegiance was to their fraternity.

When I came to Iowa State College where thirty fraternities flourished, I knew I must do something to establish a sound working relationship between myself and the chapters. In thinking this over, I decided that my aim and that of the fraternity members were the same. I wanted their houses to be well regarded in the community and therefore to be free from all improper conduct. So did they. This was my basic platform.

I invited the presidents of the thirty fraternities to be my guests at dinner once each quarter. We had a good dinner together, and afterward I spoke to them for fifteen to twenty minutes, discussing everything I had on my mind regarding the fraternities and fraternity and college relations. I then asked for questions or suggestions for the betterment of the fraternity system. All questions were answered and suggestions were discussed. We usually adjourned at eight o'clock, after a two hour session. I personally paid for the dinner and felt it was well worth the price. Three or four staff members were asked to attend, and they contributed to the discussions. Practically all of the students whom I invited came. These meetings put a stop to rumors of antagonism between the administration and the fraternities. We came to trust each other. My relations with the fraternities were good.

Two definite advances were made through these meetings: (1) The Inter-Fraternity Council was made up of members elected by each fraternity. It really had no authority. We argued that this body should have authority and should have certain responsibilities. It was finally changed so that the presidents of the chapters became the members of the Inter-Fraternity Council. (2) A rule was unanimously adopted, at my suggestion, by which any fraternity member was to be warned if his average for a quarter fell below 2.0, the requirement for graduation. If his average was not above 2.0 the following quarter, he was required to move out of the fraternity house. As a result of this rule, it was necessary to remove only four or five men a quarter from the thirty houses. Unfortunately, the rule was dropped of necessity in the hard times of 1932 and not reinstated.

It is always offensive to an administrative officer for fraternities claiming great social prestige to be deficient in scholarship. This rule immediately corrected that condition.

As discussed in the Appendix, it is possible to prepare a table based on the data provided by an entering class which will show what college average each student can reasonably be expected to make if his high school average and scholastic aptitude are known. If the fraternities were encouraged to see that every member made a reasonable average, it would put a specific goal before each man, which with proper faculty encouragement would result in a considerable advance in scholarship over a period of years. There would be a great advantage in working with comparatively small groups and having student co-operation in realizing this objective.

I do not regard as sound, movements to remove fraternities from any campus where they are entrenched. The fraternities make a real contribution to the lives of their members. In my opinion, we should, so far as possible, build up a somewhat similar life in college dormitories, embodying the most valuable features of the fraternities, and so make membership in them less of a class line than it now is. We should make dormitory life so attractive that many men will prefer it to life in a fraternity house. I believe this can be done and without very large cost.

H.

Organization of Non-Fraternity Men and Women

It is most desirable to have the non-fraternity men and women so organized that it will be possible for them to enjoy social affairs and athletic competition under their own power. The type of organization developed at Iowa State College came from Purdue University.

A New York alumnus wrote me a severe letter about our very poor showing in football and advised us to find out how Purdue had developed her strong teams. Our director of athletics was sent to Purdue; upon his return, he reported that the only new thing to be found there was that non-fraternity men were organized in wards, on a geographical basis, for athletic competition.

At that time our social director was Mrs. Iza Merchant, a very clever person, popular with the students. On talking over the ward system with her, she suggested that this form of organization could be very useful for social purposes. Mrs. Merchant and the intramural director, Professor Harry J. Schmidt, studying the rooming situation, worked out a division of the town into twelve or fifteen areas, each including about sixty men. Each area or ward, was designated by a Greek letter, e.g., "Alpha Ward."

This type of organization proved to be popular and is still working after eighteen years. There are now thirteen wards in the residence area, exclusive of men living in dormitories and fraternities, each having at least 100 men residing within its boundaries. All men are invited to join, and a large percentage do so. The business of each ward group is handled in meetings conducted by elected officers, a faculty man serving as adviser only. In semi-monthly meetings, a complete program of social affairs and athletic contests is arranged. All social activities, including dances, parties and picnics are under the social director. Athletic events, including touch football, basketball, softball, tennis and horseshoes are under the intramural director.

The meetings and athletic events are open to all. Admission to the social events is by a ward ticket costing one dollar for the entire year. This fee, which is the only assessment made, is used to defray necessary expenses.

The organization affords many of the advantages offered by the fraternities at a slight cost. Many ward leaders develop great expertness in securing co-operation and group solidarity. We regard this system as an important part of our student organization. The 2,233 men and women in our domitories are organized into twenty-eight houses, each with a set of officers. The officers of each house organize the social and athletic life of the members and so contribute much to their college life.

H.

Auditing Student Activity Accounts

In 1912 the accounts of the college paper, the *Miami Student,* were in terrible shape, and the matter was brought to my attention. I asked the business manager, Wallace P. Roudebush, to look into the matter. He reported that no proper accounts had been kept, checks had not been cashed and that it was impossible to balance the books. Mr. Roudebush and I decided that all student activity accounts must be audited monthly. We concluded that most of the managers of student enterprises were wholly ignorant of business methods. We decided that a competent and sympathetic auditor could educate managers of student activities in business methods, as well as keep the records straight.

Mr. Roudebush set up a form of report suitable for all activities and had a quantity printed. He selected a graduate who was agreeable and competent, and we required all student managers to report to her monthly. We also required all managers to deposit receipts with the college treasurer, who deposited them in a common student activity account in the bank.

This idea was so well accepted by the students and proved so satisfactory that we determined to bring the fraternity and sorority managers under the same system. We found that again and again an incompetent fraternity business manager would neglect his collections and run the chapter heavily and needlessly in debt. His successor would be greatly discouraged by the condition things were in, and it often took the fraternity several years to wipe out the deficit.

While some fraternities resented our new ruling, it was put into full operation. At once current deficits ceased, and soon all shortages were wiped out. The result was greatly to the advantage of the fraternities. A small percentage of the gross receipts of each organization was charged, and this covered the expense of auditing.

Upon going to Iowa State College in 1927, I found that not all student activities were under audit. Soon we had all general student activities audited. Some fraternities accepted the audit; others did not. It remained optional with them. I am of the opinion that Miami was the first institution to require the monthly audit of student activities. Today, it is a common practice. This audit has eliminated graft of every kind from student organizations.

For the year ending June 3, 1948, at Iowa State, 251 student organizations took in $468,793.03 and spent $449,772.66. Their total accumulated balances were $122,135.89. These 251 organizations reported above were exclusive of intercollegiate athletics, fraternities and sororities.

H.

YMCA and YWCA

The Christian associations, generally speaking, do not occupy as strong a position in our colleges and universities now as they did twenty-five or fifty years ago. This is probably due to an increase in the number of student activities, the dominance of science and a decline in religion. I dislike to admit the latter; but a recent reading of Dr. Bernard J. Bell's book *Crisis in Education* forces me to make the statement. By the way, it will pay any college president to read that book.

Because religion is not as significant in the lives of many students as formerly, a strong maintenance of the Christian associations fully repays the cost in time and money; that is, if able and suitable secretaries are employed. I have had the good fortune to work with unusually fine secretaries, for both the men and women, who have done valuable work among a large number of the students.

Today, the churches are far more active in student work than formerly. At Iowa State, ten churches have well organized student projects with excellent work centers and capable people in charge. Five other churches have less formally organized work for students. Many students are interested in these church centers. I believe these church student centers have been in no small degree inspired by the work of the Christian associations.

Dr. Bell's severe indictment of the universities for their indifference to religion and religious and philosophical instruction has justification, but I believe he is too severe. For one thing, it is extremely difficult to find an able and inspiring professor of philosophy. I contend that a good teacher is himself an interesting person and can interest his students in his subject. It appears to me that philosophy today is following Greek and Latin into the realm of discarded subjects because of a lack of competent, enthusiastic teachers with fine personalities. Latin was extremely difficult for me, but I had the good fortune to study for two years under a great Latin teacher, Professor W. A. Merill, later of the University of Indiana and the University of California. He interested me greatly in Cicero and Horace and their writings. I worked hard and gained as much from his courses as from any other in my experience.

It is certainly true that a young man leaving college without the love of God and the strength coming from that source can never serve mankind as well or as ably as he could otherwise. The young man depending on himself and his own abilities will almost certainly be selfish and self-seeking. To graduate men without doing everything possible to bring them near to God is heedlessly throwing away at least a quarter of the potential power of our graduates. The YMCA and the YWCA cannot handle this problem alone, but they are of great help. Their services are worth much more than they cost.

H.

The Ship Is Greater Than the Crew

In one of his stories, Kipling has made the apt remark, "The Ship is greater than the Crew." While this statement referred to the business of navigating a great vessel, it may be applied to some of the problems that arise in college life.

Much emphasis has been placed upon freedom of expression through speech, the written word, and printed material, for students as well as for faculty members. But all things are relative; discretion and good sense must be exercised in using such a valuable and highly prized right as the freedom of speech. Most faculty members know this, but it is by no means understood by students who manage, edit and write for the college newspapers, and periodicals. They resent any restriction being placed upon their publications, not realizing what harm can be done by a chance remark or a paragraph heavily laden with cynicism. We have here a difficult and serious problem.

Every college president has been faced with such a situation many times during his administrative service. The defense is that the offending statement did not express the opinion of the college authorities or the judgment of the president and his associates. Nonetheless, the public fails to make the distinction, and there follows criticism and even condemnation of the college as a bad influence upon youth. Even so, restriction of publication and censorship of articles or news are resented by the students. Freedom of the press carries with it responsibility; the failure to recognize that fundamental principle causes many anxious hours for college officers.

The notion that an individual may say what he pleases prevails in many circles; but when certain ideas, comments, and statements are put into print, they have a wide circulation that goes beyond the individual and concerns an institution and its welfare. Hence the value of Kipling's Scotch engineer's remark, "The Ship is greater than the Crew."

These words contain a wisdom which students should understand and heed. Something can be done to secure such an objective through conference with student editors and managers. In these meetings, frankness and an honest discussion of the problem must be the determined procedure, with the idea that censorship and restriction are not the best methods to be followed. The young people must be made to realize that the reputation of the college is in the hands of the student editors and writers who use the college publications as a means of expressing themselves.

The opposite method of dealing with the problem is to give full swing to all and sundry who have anything to do with the college publications, letting the chips fall where they may. Sooner or later, however, an incident will arise that will be serious enough to require administrative inquiry, and the whole matter must be faced again. Hence, the importance of bearing down hard on the maxim, "The Ship is greater than the Crew."

M.

Student Publications and Faculty Control

The student publications at Iowa State College include a daily, an annual, and about a dozen other publications. Each of these can give valuable training to students, but they can also give administrative officers, especially the president, a lot of trouble. It has always been distasteful to me to censor any publication. I would not do it myself, and I could not ask anyone else to do what I would not do. However, each year I called in the chairman of our student publication committee and told him that I was holding him responsible for the election of able, sensible and dependable men and women as editors. This was done; and while, of course, much was printed that I thought foolish, nothing really embarrassing to the college appeared in our student publications.

I said that these publications were to a large extent similar to house publications of business concerns; therefore, they should be loyal to the college. I also pointed out that in addition to our students there were other readers all over the country. Hence any article should be understandable beyond the campus. A conscientious student editor with common sense will not allow objectionable material to appear in a college publication. A college or university in the United States should be a democratic institution; censorship is not compatible with democracy.

At Miami, a professor of English was always made chairman of the committee on student publications. At Iowa State College, the head of the Department of Technical Journalism was appointed chairman. We were extremely fortunate at both institutions in having unusually fine men in these posts, men of sound ideals who got along admirably with students.

I believe the selection of the editors of student publications is a matter of great importance; the faculty person in charge should be certain that reliable students hold such offices.

At Iowa State College this was accomplished by a careful discussion of all candidates for the editorship by those most interested in the publication. Another method that might be used would be to submit the list of candidates for editor for approval of the chairman of the student publication committee; he would be given the authority to strike the name of any irresponsible student from the list. Certainly, the administration is entitled to positive assurance that the editors of student publications are trustworthy men and women with a high sense of responsibility.

H.

Transfer Students

At Miami we had for a time considerable trouble with college tramps—that is, students who enjoyed college life but had no desire to work. They would enter a college somewhere and remain as long as they could. When refused readmission there, they would transfer to another institution. Some such came to Miami University.

I learned that Ohio State University refused to accept a transfer student who had not made an average of C at the college from which he was transferring. The adoption of this regulation by Miami relieved us of nearly all undesirable transfers.

At Iowa State College, nonresident transfer students with less than a C average are excluded. Residents of Iowa are accepted regardless of grades, but extremely few who enter with less than a C average make good. However, we received many of our very best students by transfer. This should be expected since many students having completed one or two years elsewhere would come to Iowa State for agriculture, engineering, home economics, science, or veterinary medicine. Usually they had special interests in those fields which brought them to Iowa State. Transfer students are, on the whole, desirable. After some experience at one college, they have selected another institution as better adapted to their needs. A large majority do excellent work.

H.

Securing Positions for Graduates

Today, practically every college endeavors to prepare its graduates for some field of work. Most colleges and universities try to find positions for all or part of the graduating class. A certain number will continue to study for the ministry, medicine or law. Others will seek fellowships or assistantships in graduate schools or in a college of business and commerce. For all of these, the prime requisite is a high quality of scholarship; poor students are not desired, nor will they be admitted to such fields.

In engineering, agriculture, home economics, medicine, law, the ministry, business and commerce, music, art, forestry, architecture and other specialties in which a baccalaureate degree is to be earned, the majority of students need help in securing employment. Corporations and other employers need assistance in finding men and women of the type they require. Every college should have an employment or personnel department to act as intermediary for its graduates.

The graduates in some fields are in great demand, while those trained in other departments are often difficult to place. Admission to courses or colleges where placement is difficult should be limited. It is inexcusable for a college to urge a man to take some course of study which after it is completed affords no opening in which he can work.

If a college builds up a reputation for thoroughness and for graduating men capable of doing the work for which they are trained, the employment demand will usually absorb the supply. If graduates in a certain field find it difficult to secure jobs, the standards for admission to those schools should be raised sufficiently to cut enrollment to such numbers as can be placed. On the same basis, medical schools could well afford to admit more students, if necessary, by lowering the standards of admission, in order to answer the insistent call for doctors.

Usually the great pressure of numbers at the opening of the college year makes it difficult to identify those who have no serious objective in going to college and who will end in being unprepared for anything. If the purpose of each entrant were inquired into by a skillful man, or by several if the numbers are great, it might be possible to pass on those with purpose and objective and deflect doubtful ones into a channel where they could be more carefully studied. Much effort would be saved if unmotivated students were given a vocational aptitude test and expert counseling before admittance. Some should not be admitted at all; others would enter with a new sense of responsibility and an idea of the necessity for making good. A careful perusal with the student of his high school record in relation to his college work could be made valuable. A close follow-up of such students after admission would soon separate the ones who could and should continue from those who should be dropped.

At Iowa State College only about 40 per cent of those who enter graduate. But practically all who are graduated obtain employment. Of course, too many unprepared students are admitted under the rules of the state board of education. However, it is far better to graduate only 40 per cent of the students to serve in the field of their preparation than to graduate unqualified students.

H.

Student Activity Tickets

The inclusion in the college fee of the price of a student activity ticket which pays for admission to all games, for the college paper, lectures, musical and other entertainments is certainly an advanced step. Otherwise, many poor students would miss valuable phases of college life. Everyone buys these tickets so the price of each item is low and all inclusive college enterprises are adequately financed.

I can see no serious argument against the inclusion of the student activity ticket in the college fee. I believe it is a definite advance toward a democratic college life.

H.

Scholarships and Grants-in-Aid

Dr. Donald Cowling, president of Carleton College made a valuable distinction between scholarships and grants-in-aid. Scholarships were won by a brilliant scholastic record either in secondary school or in college. Grants-in-aid were sums given to needy students to enable them to stay in college; this aid covered part or all of the tuition charge.

In earlier years, I strongly favored loan funds and regarded scholarships as luxuries. Now, while I think highly of loan funds, I believe scholarships are desirable for recruiting able students. Grants-in-aid make it possible for many poor but worthy students to get an education. These students otherwise could not enter and profit from a college course.

The brilliant record of many Harvard graduates must be due in part to the large number of generous scholarships available. The high record of DePauw graduates is undoubtedly due to a large scholarship endowment. Of late, I have been interested in securing as many, brilliant, hard-working students as possible. Scholarships, I believe, are the greatest inducement that can be offered. One able student is worth at least ten mediocre ones.

No nobler memorial can be established than an endowment of $15,000 or $30,000 for a scholarship of respectively $500 and $1,000, to be won through high achievement. I am inclined to believe that better results could be secured if competition were limited to students meeting a high scholastic aptitude test. Thus hard working students of mediocre native ability would be ruled out. Such scholarships should bring to a college high grade students.

H.

Student Loan Funds

I first encountered loan funds through my predecessor at Miami, Dr. Guy Potter Benton. During his term of office Miami had no such funds, and Dr. Benton loaned his own money to needy students and endorsed their notes at the bank. He sustained no losses.

Since I could not loan out my own money, I began in a small way to endorse students' notes at the bank. I also proceeded to raise some loan funds. My first success in securing gifts, in 1912, came in the form of $5,000 from Mr. J. R. Patterson, an alumnus and trustee of generous disposition. This sum was deposited with the irreducible debt of Ohio, at 6 per cent, and the interest only was to be used. The "Patterson Loan" has aided many students. The principal is intact and the accumulated interest now amounts to $11,000. This, of course, draws interest; deducting all losses, the original $5,000 with all interest now amounts to more than $16,000.

We also called on the alumni for small annual contributions which yielded less than $5,000 the first year, but now totals more than $17,000 per annum. At first most of this fund was used for loans. Gradually from this source and through special gifts, adequate loan funds have been built up.

At first I handled all the loans. Unfortunately some bad ones were made and I was consoled only when I learned that over a million dollars loaned to students by a national church organization had been lost. Our rules for loans were made more stringent, and the losses decreased.

At Iowa State College, in 1927, I found a considerable loan fund had been raised and administered by Maria Roberts, dean of the junior college. This money was being very carefully handled with practically no losses. No student was loaned more than $200 a year. No one below the Junior class was eligible for a loan and only juniors and seniors with an average above 2.1. Furthermore, all students borrowing money were required to insure their lives and to deposit the policy as security. At present, lower classmen whose averages are above B may borrow where the need is great. In recent years, Mrs. Margaret Lange handled the loan funds. She made as good a record as Dean Roberts in collections—there were practically no losses.

Some years ago, Mrs. Lange proposed a revolving fund using college money for making loans for less than three months. Students earning their way or students lacking funds at the opening of the term were allowed to borrow from this fund a sufficient amount to pay their fees, provided Mrs. Lange was satisfied they would be able to repay the loan before the end of the quarter. The fund loans from $15,000 to $20,000 a quarter and makes possible the payment to the college treasurer of all fees at the beginning of each term. All student shortages are carried as loans on notes held by the loan fund. Practically all notes accepted by this fund are paid in full with interest during the quarter in which they are made. The smallest interest charged is fifty cents.

Miss Roberts gave students who had repaid their loan in full a certificate which stated that their honesty was established by the way they had handled their debt. These certificates were highly prized. The loans made by Dean Roberts and Mrs. Lange were much more personal than a loan made by the treasurer or by a bank. In every case, the student's grades were examined and considered. His financial resources were inquired into. The possibility of the student's earning part of his expenses was discussed. Each student knew he had been thoroughly investigated, that the loan was found to be necessary and that he had been judged trustworthy. Taking out a loan at the college was an education in business integrity.

Certainly no capable, earnest student should drop out of college for lack of money. There are many jobs about an institution which afford a student the opportunity to earn. Any student can work ten hours a week without detriment to his studies. Some have been known to labor forty hours a week and carry a full academic load successfully. Generally, with as much as twenty hours of labor the class schedule should not exceed twelve hours. However, with some aid from home, a summer vacation job, work during the college year and a loan, any really competent student can get through college.

An adequate college loan fund seems to me to be absolutely necessary. Its administration should invariably be strict.

H.

Student Loan Funds and Scholarships

There is a tendency for students to strive for scholarships rather than borrow. The explanation is simple. A scholarship is an outright gift, while a loan leaves the student at graduation with a debt hanging over him that will take several years to repay. Small loans on short time are made, but general loan funds for the purpose of helping students through college are no longer an important service.

What is to be done with the accumulated loan funds, which amount to a considerable sum? One method is to reduce them to one-third of the capital sums and invest the rest in new scholarships, payable quarterly. The competition for scholarships has grown in the number of applicants and in the quality of those who seek the appointments. This is all to the good, but where is this demand for help to end? One reason for the increase is to be found in the boosting of tuition fees and the cost of living for college students. As a matter of fact, tuition has gone so high as to create a definite obstacle in education. Few families can pay $1,500 to $1,800 for tuition, board and room, through a college year; in addition, what a student can earn at a job during off-hours makes but a small dent in the cost of his education.

The state legislatures are being asked to set up scholarships to help students through college. Congress has before it bills for the same purpose. Private institutions may be permitted to accept students on the principle that the student should be allowed to select his own college. These proposals are the result of the great movement toward free education. They are, in fact, additions to the various social service provisions in the law. But these proposals involve new procedures and techniques in the selection of winners in the competition. How to keep the business of selection from political interference is a problem. The machinery for screening the applicants is complicated and difficult to administer; in addition, the American system of higher education has not yet become stabilized and clearly defined.

Instead of students crowding into the four year colleges, many would be better fitted for valuable work if trained in junior college vocational schools. The universities would then become real professional and graduate institutions. The four year colleges could do what they were expected to do, leaving vocational education to the special schools. When this country reaches such a stage of educational development, the demand for college scholarships may be materially reduced, since many students could then live at home and attend a local institution.

A young man who is something of an athlete can secure a scholarship capable of meeting all his expenses but, in accepting this, he jeopardizes his college work and finds himself at the end of four years looking toward a coaching career or following his game as a professional player. The outcome is by no means satisfactory to the student, nor does it help him obtain a real education.

There are also scholarships offered by industrial concerns in chemistry, physics, geology, commerce and engineering. Most of these are available to sophomores or to upper classmen only, leaving the freshman to get on as best he may.

Many questions are involved in what appears at first a simple matter. To accumulate loan funds is not too difficult; to administer them well requires both judgment and tact. The scholarship problem is not only difficult for the college, but is further complicated by our educational system, i.e., the great number of applicants and the lack of funds to meet their demands. It is wise for the administrator to keep his eye on what is happening in this field.

M.

How a Student Can Get off Probation

In most colleges students with grades below a certain point are placed on probation. At Iowa State College an average of C is required for graduation; when any student falls below C he is put on probation. How may such a student raise his grade average sufficiently to get off probation?

In only two ways: First, by making A and B grades. Second, by repeating enough courses in which he had made $D, E,$ or $F,$ to raise his grade to C or better.

Generally, a student who drops below a C average is not capable of making A or B grades. The second alternative is usually his only hope.

Since it is much easier to get off probation while the student lacks only a few grade points of a C average than it is when he has accumulated many, it is very important that each student be given wise advice as soon as he goes on probation. Far too often this is not the case, and the student is left to struggle as best he can. At least half of the time he does not make it.

As stated, most students placed on probation are those whose level of scholarship is below C. They are not usually capable of making better than C. By all means such students should be compelled to repeat enough D, E, and F work to raise their average to C at once. They are almost always reluctant to do this, but the logic of their situation certainly points to such a course of action.

Students on probation who have made creditable high school grades and whose scholastic aptitude tests are reasonably good should be able to make A or B grades in some courses. If the gravity of the situation is made clear to them, and if a careful survey is shown them of the grades they can make the next term in each subject, it might be wise to have them proceed with all second term courses or to repeat only one course.

All probation students are poor risks. They should certainly be encouraged by proper methods to rise above probation promptly. If this is not possible, they should be dropped, both for their own good and for the good of the college.

There are several reasons why students fail to do creditable work:

1. Lack of ability. This is shown by a combination of low high school grades and low rating on scholastic aptitude.
2. Lack of industry. This may be due to indolence or to too much time given to athletics, student activities, or social life.
3. Lack of interest. Every student going on probation should be required to take a vocational interest test to determine, if possible, whether he is taking the right course of study.

Very few students of moderate ability who honestly put in forty-five hours a week in classroom, laboratory, and study fail to make a C average.

H.

The Status of Students

Intramural Athletics

In 1910-11, I had a sabbatical leave. From September to December, I visited colleges and universities in the East, and then spent six weeks in England and Scotland.

Syracuse University had an enrollment of 5,000 students then. There I viewed the first stadium I had ever seen. This immense structure enclosed a beautiful grass playfield. No one was allowed there except for intercollegiate football. On inquiry, I learned that this was the only playfield at Syracuse at that time. I was greatly impressed by the respect shown football.

Later on, at Oxford and Cambridge, I found forty colleges, each with a sizable playfield, each with teams in every sport. While being shown about one day I was surprised to find two college teams playing football in a field without a single spectator and with the gate locked. What a contrast to Syracuse!

When I returned to Miami, one of my first ideas was to organize intramural sports. We had a director of athletics then who entered into the plan enthusiastically. Shortly thereafter, we had tennis and basketball, each organized in a series of leagues, one with first class, one with second class and one with third class players, all below varsity level, and all having great fun.

Ever since then, Miami has maintained a strong intramural organization of sports; it has done much toward developing the manhood on the campus.

Years later, when our medical director, Dr. Wade Macmillan, retired from his executive work, he organized a gymnasium class of students who were definitely below par physically and barred from regular athletics. Although over seventy at that time, he personally led this class awhile. Then, having one or another of the better students take his place, he would walk about giving individual help. He produced some amazing results. Underweight boys gained decidedly; all improved in muscular development, showing decisively what a wise director can do for undeveloped and defective students.

H.

Intercollegiate Athletics

I regard intercollegiate athletics as detrimental to the intellectual accomplishment of American colleges and universities. A schedule of eight or nine football games, four or five usually out of town, each taking the team away for two or three days, hours of strenuous practice and night classes, result in making creditable scholarship impossible for almost all of the forty or more players on the squad. Basketball, with the excessive number of games, the high excitement and the great evening audiences of students, while not affecting so many players as football, ranks next in unfavorable results on scholarship.

As gate receipts mount, the increased pressure to win and attract large crowds tends to make college football and basketball professional in spirit, if not in practice. The problem becomes steadily more difficult to solve and more necessary of solution.

Where the president has the courage and the support of his trustees, action similar to that of the University of Chicago is possible; there the university plays with teams in its own class in football. I never had the courage to insist on such a course. No one enjoys being defeated. You want to win half the time if possible; and in that effort, usually one or another safeguard against professionalism or semiprofessionalism is pushed aside.

A football game in the fall of the year is a beautiful and impressive spectacle. If it could be retained at a lower tempo, it would be all to the good. I believe a great step in advance was made when the game was put into the hands of thoroughly competent and courageous officials. Another great advancement was accomplished in the introduction of the student activity ticket as a part of the college fee, admitting every student to all the games. Aside from these two improvements, the conduct of intercollegiate athletics has steadily deteriorated over the past fifty years. One of the evidences of this is the fact that some institutions are now paying their football coach more than their president, thus placing a higher value on his services to the institution.

At Iowa State College, in 1927, I was delighted to find intramural athletics well organized under Professor T. N. Metcalf, then head of physical education. This policy has been well maintained since. From four to six in the afternoon, it is a common sight to observe our athletic fields filled with men, and many games in full swing.

I am disturbed by the great disparity today at Miami and Iowa State College, as well as nearly everywhere else, in the money spent on the major intercollegiate teams compared to that used for intramural sports. Of course, the answer is that most of the money comes from intercollegiate football, so that team must be the best possible to attract the large crowds. However, this does not justify neglect to operate at the highest level intramural athletics and corrective gymnasium work, with an ample number of leaders and adequate equipment. Active sports afford a training in courage, sportsmanship and courtesy invaluable to every man.

I might add that ambitious participation in intramural sports tends strongly to reduce the temptation to dissipation. A good workout also helps to eliminate rough-housing and devilment about a campus. All in all, intramural athletics should be given high ranking in every college and university.

H.

Student Health Service

A student health service is important for two good reasons: While the students are in college we are responsible for their health, and we certainly should recognize and discharge this obligation. A sick student in a dormitory or rooming house is usually neglected and is always a nuisance and may even be a source of contagion. Also, a well run college hospital is generally the first introduction for most students to modern medical practice and care; it can lead them to develop proper ideals and health standards.

A modest hospital service can be set up in a small college at little expense. In Miami, around 1913, we opened two or three rooms as a hospital on the second floor of a girls' dormitory. We employed a good full-time nurse and paid a local doctor $300 to come on call. These simple services were surprisingly useful.

A few years later, we employed a full-time doctor at a regular salary, an excellent man who was attentive to business and interested in the work. Later we built a small hospital of twenty beds, adding a charge of five dollars a semester to the student's bill for hospital and medical care. Each student was given a thorough physical examination upon admission. Where a doubtful condition was found, a further examination was given later, with repeated examinations when indicated. The fee entitled the student to four days of hospital care and further days at a low cost.

At Iowa State College, I found a sixty-bed hospital fully equipped with four doctors and a staff of nurses and technicians including X-ray, pharmacist, and a dental hygienist. Here, again, a fee of ten dollars a year with some additional hospital charges met all expenses. At the larger institution, with considerable technological work going on, there were more serious accidents; hospital and medical care were invaluable.

While the idea may not be acceptable to the doctors, I am confident that there should be on the medical staff an osteopathic physician to deal with muscular and bone conditions resulting from athletics among 5,000 men and 2,000 women, and a chiropodist to examine and treat defective feet.

None of our physicians attempted surgery. When surgery was indicated, a thoroughly competent surgeon was called in, or the student was sent to a hospital where he might have the best surgical attention.

H.

Board and Rooms for Students

In recent years, a great advance has been made in the matter of providing board and room on the campus for college and university students. The financing of the dormitories and boarding halls and the sound management of both are matters of serious concern.

Different policies can be pursued and defended in charging for board and rooms. Many institutions definitely plan to make a profit on both items, and in some cases it is a considerable one. Other institutions feel that while they certainly must pay all the expense of operation, at best only a small profit should result. In either case it is essential to know the costs. My experience has been with publicly supported institutions, where the cost must be kept as low as possible.

Student Boarding

Students can be boarded more cheaply where they are served a fixed meal, the cost of which is kept within a certain figure. This plan has a large social advantage as the students enter the dining hall at a definite time and are served simultaneously. Usually they have assigned seats at lunch and dinner, while breakfast is less formal. As those at one table come to know each other well, the social life during mealtime can be quite worth while. Seating arrangements may be changed from time to time advantageously. At Swarthmore, in 1910, I was interested to see three men and three women at each table, where the seating was changed every six weeks.

When meals are served cafeteria style, they invariably cost more, but many idiosyncrasies of individual taste in food are better met in that way.

A policy in regard to cost which I believe to be sound is to aim at a net profit of not less than 5 per cent and not more than 10. No boarding department can be run with no profit and no loss for long, and a small profit must be made as a safety margin. To operate this way, it is essential to know the exact costs.

One of the proper costs is a rental for space used by the boarding department for dining room, kitchen, storage and office. If a separate building houses the boarding department and nothing else, 10 per cent of the cost of the building seems reasonable. If, as is more usual, the boarding department occupies space in one or more dormitories the formula is:

$$\frac{\text{Square feet occupied by boarding department}}{\text{Total square feet of floor space in building}} \times \text{cost of building}$$
$$= \text{cost of space used by boarding department.}$$

Ten per cent of this cost is a reasonable charge.

The cost of heat is best taken as a fractional part of the cost of heating the building, based on the proportion of square feet of floor occupied. As both electricity for power and water used is considerable, they may be metered separately, or they may be taken as a proportion of whole cost for dormitory, as in the case of heat.

The cost of board will then be as follows:

Rental of space used in building	_____
Heat, light, power and water	_____
Management and supervision	_____
Replacement of equipment, 15 per cent of total cost	_____
Supplies	_____
Food, net cost delivered to kitchen	_____
Service, labor	_____
Freight and express	_____
Telephones	_____
Total Cost	_____

$$\frac{\text{Total actual cost} + 5 \text{ per cent}}{\text{Total number of paid boarders}} = \text{charge per boarder}$$

Since the charge for board must be fixed at the beginning of a period, this should be figured on a recent past experience, and the price charged should be altered if necessary for the next term, as governed by the experience for the current period.

The only way the food cost can be closely controlled is to compute the cost day by day and to see that it is kept within the allotted figure per paid boarder.

So far as my experience goes, boys eat more than girls, making a differential of fifty cents or one dollar weekly, in favor of girls, reasonable.

Dormitories

In Iowa and in many other states, state institutions of higher learning are authorized to borrow against anticipated net dormitory receipts for the erection of dormitories.

How much indebtedness an institution may incur on this principle is a matter of policy which the trustees should fix. As a rough basis for determining a safe standard for fixing maximum indebtedness, ten times the average net income from board and rooms for the past five years is suggested. Inasmuch as dormitory occupancy varies more or less with the national prosperity, it is unwise to involve an institution in too much debt. Especially is this true in view of the fact that ultimately all dormitories needed will be erected. There is no sound reason for pushing the erection of dormitories too fast.

Where the law permits and the banks are agreeable, it is much more convenient to borrow on notes from banks. The loans can be paid at varying rates as circumstances dictate and the interest will shift with that prevailing on such loans. The Iowa State Board of Education has followed this plan. In some states bonds are issued and sold; this involves more expense. The interest is fixed throughout the period and often above the rate the banks will charge; the bonds must be taken up each year in fixed amount, no more, no less.

The rate at which the rooms should be rented may be figured in different ways. A fair basis, if it is desired to rent the rooms at as low a rate as possible, would be to charge for the use of the room 3 or 4 per cent of the total cost of all dormitories erected, divided by their normal capacity. This amount should represent the net charge. If we add to the net charge the total actual cost of operation and maintenance per student, we get total rent per student for nine months.

The total cost of operation would include:

Management and supervision _____
Labor: janitors, maids, etc. _____
Repairs and painting (1 to 2 per cent of total cost) _____
Replacement and repairs of equipment _____
Heat, light and water _____
Other supplies _____
Telephones _____
Freight, express and drayage _____
Miscellaneous _____
    Total cost of operation _____

$$\frac{\text{Total cost of operation}}{\text{Normal occupancy}} = \text{cost per student for operation}$$

During 1949–50, it appeared impossible to keep the cost at Iowa State College much below $120 per occupant for nine months. For 1944–45 and 1945–46, the cost was slightly more than half as much. This cost of operation is largely controlled by three items: (1) Management and supervision, (2) labor — janitors and maids, (3) heat, light and water, all of which may vary widely.

One factor relates to maid service: Will the rooms be cared for by maids — beds made and rooms cleaned — or will this be done by the students occupying the rooms? At Miami University and Iowa State College, the rooms are cared for by the occupants. The bathrooms and corridors are cared for by maids or janitors. Full maid service would probably add $25 to $50 per occupant. On the other hand, more supervision than is usually given is needed, if the students are held to a proper care of rooms. A competent man or woman inspecting each room daily would not make a great difference in expense. Such supervision would probably cost $3 to $5 a year per student, but would yield large results.

On the above estimate room rent must vary, based on the average cost of dormitories per student, the rate of interest charged on the investment, the service rendered in labor or supervision. On an average cost of $1,500 per student and 3 per cent interest, $45 would be collected as interest on the investment. At a minimum upkeep figure of $60, the rent would be $105 for nine months. On a cost of $2,000 and 4 per cent interest, $80 would be collected as interest. With full maid service to care for rooms, operation would cost between $85 and $110, making total rent $165 to $190 per year of nine months. At Iowa State College, in 1951–52, a charge of $150 was the lowest we could afford, with two students in each room.

The average cost of dormitories depends not only on style and accommodations, but upon when the buildings were erected. Iowa State College has ten dormitories for men and women, which accommodate 1,920 students. These were built between 1914 and 1942, at a total figure of $2,094,500, or at an average cost of $1,100 per student. By comparison, a dormitory building, erected in 1950 cost $3,400 per student, and housed 268 men.

A useful room size is 18 by 10½ feet with the room running 18 feet from the hall to the outside wall. This includes two closets three feet wide on either side of the door and allows ample room for two students to study at the opposite sides of a comfortable table. Two single beds are easily accommodated.

Comfortable dormitories adequately supervised can contribute much to the value of college life. Usually the provision of heat, light and toilet facilities is superior to that in rented rooms in town. If the organization and supervision is adequate and well managed, the association of students in the dormitories and dining halls can be most helpful, especially to the students who come from homes where the amenities of life have been given little attention and the cultivation of good manners has been neglected.

During the years following World War II, the pressure of providing for the veterans led to great overcrowding in dormitories. Certainly in normal times not more than two students should occupy one room.

There is no question but that fraternity houses contribute greatly to the happiness of college life and to the culture of the men living in them. It is reasonable to expect dormitories to contribute nearly as much.

H.

Our Leaders

Probably between 50,000 and 100,000 men and women in the United States control our future, determine our economic condition, our level of living, our destiny!

Of these, the majority are between fifty to sixty-five years of age and probably their average span of vital influence is fifteen years or less. At that rate, the group would change personnel at from 3,350 to 6,700 a year. Perhaps 5,000 would drop out, and 5,000 younger men and women would fill their places as leaders of the nation. Today, substantially all of these younger leaders are college graduates. We can assume that our colleges and universities confer about 200,000 first degrees a year. If so, 5,000 degrees are conferred upon students who will become national leaders of prime importance, an average of one in every forty who graduate.

As we get into the second half of the century, about 2,950,000 children are entering school at five to seven years of age. About 1,200,000, or slightly more than half who entered, are graduated from high school. There were graduated from college or university four year courses 271,000 in 1947–48.

	Number		Eventual Leaders
Enter school	2,950,000	5,000	1 in 590
Graduate from high school	1,200,000	5,000	1 in 240
Enter college	620,000	5,000	1 in 124
Graduate from college	270,000	5,000	1 in 54

Considering that the great majority of high schools have a relatively small enrollment, less than 240, it is evident that the high schools cannot go far in the selection of prospective leaders. Even in the freshman year in college, one leader in 120 is hard to find. However, before the student reaches graduation, it should be possible by assessing scholarship, personality, character, industry and ambition, to approach an estimate.

A college graduating 50 students might have 1 potential outstanding leader.
”   ”   ”   100   ”   ”   ” 1 to 2 ”   ”   leaders.
”   ”   ”   250   ”   ”   ” 3 to 5 ”   ”   ”
”   ”   ”   500   ”   ”   ” 10 to 12 ”   ”   ”
”   ”   ” 1,000   ”   ”   ” 15 to 20 ”   ”   ”
”   ”   ” 1,500   ”   ”   ” 20 to 28 ”   ”   ”
”   ”   ” 2,000   ”   ”   ” 35 to 40 ”   ”   ”

While colleges cannot prophesy the graduate who will rise to national distinction, they could select a group three to five times as large as the number of their potential leaders and be quite sure it included 90 per cent of such leaders.

The question is — are we doing all we can for these men and women who will later control the destiny of our country? Somewhere between the time they enter college and their graduation day, we should be able to include them in a somewhat larger group which we regard as comprising our most promising students. Some could certainly be recognized while only freshmen. These promising students should receive everything the college or university can give.

In other words, if we would carefully sift out the 5 per cent of best all-round students in a class, beginning with entering freshmen, who had shown real superiority in grades, personality, character, leadership, industry, ambition, or other important qualities, we would find, in the end, about twice as many as we had hoped would achieve distinction. If this most promising 5 per cent were given every useful personal attention we could give them, with skillful teachers in every subject, they would go farther and ultimately serve more generously and more usefully than otherwise.

I would not suggest that we do less for any student than we are now doing, but that the men and women among whom we expect to find the leaders of America should have all that we can give them. That is, they should be in sections under our ablest and most inspiring teachers; they should have our best counselors; they should be followed carefully, and the professor of their major subject should be put in touch with them as soon as they are identified.

It is my experience that persons who are specially gifted are rarely aware of their special gifts. They usually think of themselves as just good, average, or a little above average. Special abilities must be nourished and encouraged. In former years, necessity and poverty stimulated most of the men who became strong leaders and drove them in their youth to make their best endeavor. Today, there is little real poverty and far less necessity. Gifted youngsters must be kept on the track by enthusiasm and encouragement and by opening up the future which may lie before them. Many will not respond to these approaches. Many will be lost to mediocrity through lack of effort. Strong men and women are needed today as never before! Our colleges and universities are responsible for them during the four years. Are we doing our full duty by them?

H.

The president cannot ignore the alumni. In them lies much of the strength of the institution. What they mean to their alma mater depends on what their alma mater is to them, and how she deals with them after they leave the college. The president must use every resource available to unite the college with its alumni in a wholesome manner.

7.

The President and the Alumni

The Alumni

The alumni make up the most important element of the public with which the president is concerned. The students of course are important, but as they are an integral part of the college itself, they should not be included in a consideration of the general public. The alumni are the major product of the college over the years of its previous history. They are largely what the college has made them. If they are cold or lukewarm in their interest, any marked advancement for the college will be impossible.

While the alumni are the most important part of the public with which a college president is concerned, he is very often shy of them because he knows so few, and embarrassed by their criticisms, as for instance on football policy. In many cases the relations of the president with the alumni are poor, but they need not be.

One fact the president should not overlook is that there are always a considerable number of professors and deans on the campus who have a wide acquaintance among the alumni and who give to visiting alumni a good deal of time. The president would do well to identify these faculty members, to rely on their support and make due allowance for the time they spend with alumni. There are always many persons on the staff who are glad to share this burden with the president, and if their assistance is recognized, they will serve in this way more happily.

H.

The Individual Alumnus

"I don't know what to do about the alumni." I have heard that remark many times from the lips of a puzzled president. As a matter of fact, a university president does not know very much about the alumni. He may have a large acquaintance among the graduates of his college or university; but when the numbers run into the tens of thousands, there is a limit to his memory or even to his opportunity. The registrar knows a good many; some of the professors have a considerable following among them, and the secretary of the alumni association develops rather close contacts with groups in the cities. Yet the larger body of alumni carry on with little thought of their alma mater, unless it be in the field of athletics, where they grow enthusiastic according to the success or failure of the teams representing their college or university.

In the heyday of the *Review of Reviews,* the editors were fond of the composite photograph. This kind of picture was made by exposing the negative to a succession of persons. In that way, the editors thought that they might obtain a type characteristic of a certain group. If that were done with the alumni, the average alumnus would turn out to be thirty-five years of age, married, with two children, and living in a mortgaged house. He drives a car of medium price about two or three years behind the current models. His efforts are directed to getting on; his living costs drag him down, and he is a victim now and then of anxiety. Above this average alumnus are men and women who have attained considerable distinction or wealth, but they are not numerous. With such variation in alumni make-up, it is not remarkable that the problem of the alumni in relation to their alma mater is something of an enigma. How can it be solved?

M.

Working Relationship

For several reasons college presidents and even more often university presidents fail to develop close relations with the alumni. For one thing, there are so many of them! Fifty years ago that was not true. Only an exceptional person today can claim a wide acquaintance among twenty to fifty or one hundred thousand alumni scattered over the country.

For the president who has been selected from the college staff, the problem is simpler. A certain number of alumni have worked under him as students and have known him in a less formal relationship. But perhaps two-thirds of those who are appointed to the presidency from outside the institution find the mass of strange alumni a challenge which they are never quite able to meet.

As I had attended Miami University as a student and had served as a professor and dean for twelve years prior to my appointment as president, I was well acquainted with the Miami alumni and counted many of them my close friends. At Iowa State College, however, when I came in 1927, there were 9,000 alumni; when I retired in 1936, there were 14,000; practically all were strangers to me. Fifteen years later, there were more than 40,000.

A further barrier is due to the fact that most letters from alumni are critical rather than commendatory, especially those concerning athletics. As most correspondence with alumni consists in defending the college, the idea tends to develop that they are an unfriendly group.

In numerous institutions, especially those with a large alumni, there is a definite policy on the part of the latter to keep their organization independent of the president's office. This may be due to the feeling that if the occasion arises, the organization should be free to criticise the policy of the president. From whatever cause it springs, such a policy will form a barrier between the president and the alumni.

While in many cases it is not easy for the president to draw close to the alumni, there are a number of policies he can promote which are well worth while in themselves and which will tend to bring about a better relationship between him and the alumni of the institution which he serves.

H.

Established Aids in Alumni Work

There are a number of sources of help now available to presidents and to alumni secretaries with which they should be familiar.

The National Alumni Council holds district and national meetings in which all alumni matters are discussed. It offers advisory facilities and can be addressed through the current president of the council. It is at present looking forward to establishing national headquarters with a permanent secretary. A representative of the college alumni work should attend the national and district meetings of the council.

Three publications of the alumni council contain much valuable information and should be in the alumni office: *Manual of Alumni Work, Alumni Fund Survey,* and *Primer of Alumni Work.*

H.

The Alumni Secretary

This officer began his career in a voluntary, unpaid capacity. As the size of the problems became apparent to the alumni association, the secretary reached the status of a part-time employee. The association discovered the importance of registration of alumni, and of a publication, and so the office increased in importance. These duties and others foreshadowed the full-time secretary, and the association was called upon to provide the funds to meet a considerable budget.

If the alumni cannot raise all the funds required, the college is called upon to meet the deficit. At this point the whole organization may break down. The responsibility is then upon the president and the board of trustees. As a matter of policy, the alumni association should be financed by the alumni without contributions from the college. But a compromise on this point usually brings partial support from the institution's budget at the expense of some other important function of the college, such as an increase in salaries. The president is thus presented with a dilemma which he untangles in most cases by partially granting the request. From past experience, I would say it is better either to do nothing or to support the alumni organization adequately.

M.

The Alumni Secretary

While all these activities for and with the alumni are desirable and important, they are beyond the ability of the president to carry on, due largely to lack of time. Usually an alumni secretary is appointed to head the work, without assistants in a small college, but with a considerable staff in a large institution. If such a secretary has not been selected, the president should co-operate with the alumni and secure the appointment of a suitable man.

What sort of man should be selected as alumni secretary? He should certainly be a graduate of the college he is to serve, preferably one who has a wide acquaintance among the alumni. His loyalty to the college should be beyond question. He should be able to do teamwork amicably and without friction. If he is also an effective public speaker, an outstanding editor, or an able public relations man, it is all to the good. The alumni secretary must understand the college and its aims and must constantly endeavor to aid the alumni to evaluate their college, its program and policies. He must do all he can to build up satisfactory working relationships between alumni officers and leaders and the college administration and the staff. He must work closely with the president.

The alumni secretary holds an important position in the

administration. He heads the thousands of alumni whom he represents on the campus. He also represents the administration and the college to the alumni through the alumni journal and by correspondence. Where the alumni association is an integral part of the college and working closely with the administration, the alumni secretary's work is clear, if arduous. Where the alumni association is separately organized and maintains its independence of the administration, the position of the alumni secretary is often a very difficult one. If the alumni are seriously critical of the college administration, their secretary is torn between representing the critical alumni and defending the president.

The alumni are a powerful and influential body. They have a clear right to make their opinions known. The college is dear to them and they certainly should be well informed of its operation, its weakness, and its strength. The wise president will use every opportunity to inform himself as to alumni opinion and to make clear to the alumni, especially the executive committee of their association, all his plans and hopes for the welfare of the college. With the cordial support of the alumni, the president's position will be greatly strengthened. This support is worth working for.

As the alumni secretary is the representative on the campus of all alumni activities and interests as relate to the college, he has a heavy mail. He is the chief avenue of information through which the alumni apply for help of all kinds. Faculties change rapidly, and an alumnus desiring information or aid turns instinctively to the alumni secretary, who knows the institution and is on the ground. Answering alumni letters alone is an important job.

It must be this secretary's enthusiasm and drive that will keep the alumni clubs going, that will maintain alumni contributions and that will uphold all the many activities of alumni important to the welfare of the college.

The alumni office should be in a convenient central location and should maintain a friendly informal atmosphere.

H.

Elements of an Effective Alumni Program

One of the chief responsibilities of the alumni secretary is to maintain complete files of alumni addresses and biographical notes on each alumnus' activities. The former are usually kept in card files and the latter, in vertical folders. For each alumnus who passes his 70th birthday, a brief but comprehensive biography should be prepared and printed in permanent form every five years. When this is done his material in the files may be destroyed.

The encouragement of class activities is important, including class meetings and luncheons during reunions at the college and the election of class secretaries.

The organization and encouragement of alumni clubs in all logical cities is an important part of the alumni secretary's work.

The alumni secretary aims to act as an intermediary between individual alumni and the college. He strives to answer letters of inquiry from the alumni fully and carefully. Through the alumni journal he endeavors to keep the alumni up-to-date on all current matters of interest at the college.

The alumni secretary himself or a member of the alumni office staff heads the work of soliciting gifts from alumni.

At commencement and homecoming, the alumni secretary is the key man who sees that all the plans of various classes work out. He and his assistants are at the service of all alumni groups. H.

The Alumni Association

Too often the alumni association is a deserted child left on the college doorstep by those who were willing to bring it into the world, but not to support it. It would be worth while to look at the history of alumni associations in order to find out what they are now doing and what has been their record of accomplishment. It is too long a story to go into here, but the topic would be worth the time of some wide-awake candidate seeking a degree in the educational field.

I am of the opinion that many college presidents have been greatly disappointed in the failure of alumni associations to be helpful. The exceptions to this are more often present in the privately endowed institution than in the publicly supported college and university. The reasons for this may be found in the older traditions of some institutions, in the affection that the alumni have for the colleges in which their parents were students, and in the further fact that the students pay for a larger part of the cost of education. At any rate, the alumni of many institutions have but a lukewarm attachment to their alma mater and afford it inadequate support.

To keep an alumni organization going, a college usually is compelled to put money into it. This money is used to pay a part of the secretary's salary and to meet the cost of printing a periodical. The funds raised by the association, after much prodding, supplement the appropriation given by the institution toward the support of the alumni association. Thus the alumni, so far as their organization goes, cannot sponsor criticism of the college without endangering the financial support they receive from that college.

Most college presidents would welcome a free association of alumni that could act on its own initiative and weigh the advances and shortcomings of their alma mater independently. Very little of this type of comment is to be found in the alumni press; and in consequence, higher education lacks the benefit that might come from free alumni associations. Presidents observe little interest displayed by the alumni in the educational program but find a great drawing power in college and university athletics. The latter is something that can be seen, talked about in street and club, and that stirs the patriotic spirit of the alumnus, if and when his college is the winner.

The main obstacle in the way of a larger interest in the purpose of the college is lack of knowledge of what is going on. At banquets and dinners the president may have a place on the evening program, yet hesitates to enter upon any extended discussion of college problems. An active, independent alumni association with a live, sympathetic secretary could bring the educational procedures to the attention of the alumni and arouse an interest that would produce constructive criticism. At present, in most institutions, there is no constructive criticism that finds its way to the president. Sometimes the critics go underground and little by little undermine the college administration. This is, of course, unfortunate and may bring about disastrous results.

There is then need for free, open talk, argument, and consideration of educational problems on the part of the alumni. An association raising its own funds and publishing a periodical without expense to the college would prove a valuable agency which undoubtedly would contribute greatly to the advancement of education.

M.

The Alumni Association

The president should certainly stand cordially behind the association and give it all the help and encouragement possible.

All the officers should be elected by the association without guidance or hindrance. All officers and members of the executive committee should be elected for definite terms with limits on re-election. It is highly desirable that these several alumni responsibilities be passed around among the most interested members.

There should be small dues required of members of the association and all of them should receive the alumni journal.

The officers should have definite responsibilities of which they are aware, and they should be encouraged to discharge them efficiently.

H.

Alumni Clubs

Considerable numbers of alumni are employed and live in the large centers of population. Can these be gathered into a group that would maintain a local club? The number of alumni may vary from twenty-five to several hundred persons, enough anyway to justify a meeting with the secretary of the association.

A dinner is planned and a program for the coming meeting is provided. If possible, the president of the college comes to the dinner. He visits with the alumni, greets them at a reception, and finds the committee has allowed him twenty minutes to talk about education after the dinner. The rest of the time is spent in singing and listening to recollections of college days. The emphasis is upon fellowship and the progress of alma mater's athletic teams. Can this type of program hold the group together until the next annual meeting? The answer is that it may do so, depending largely upon the enthusiasm of a few alumni. In the long run, the local club will flicker and die out, after which another effort is necessary to rekindle the fires. Such procedures are wearing and expensive and not particularly effective.

Probably a certain amount of good will that may prove valuable is developed at the meetings, but a real understanding of the college purpose, its problems, difficulties, and future is not in evidence. The secretary of the association should be in accord with the president of the university concerning the purpose of alumni gatherings and thus use them to inform the alumni what the problems are and how they can be of help. The first and important thing to be done is to build in the minds of the alumni a background of understanding of the viewpoint in higher education, followed by a thorough presentation of the part their alma mater plays in the educational process.

M.

Alumni Clubs

Inasmuch as the composition of alumni clubs varies greatly with their location, each club should have full freedom to determine its own activities and programs. New York will differ from Cincinnati; both of these will differ greatly from a town of 10,000 drawing many members from the surrounding country and villages. Each club in order to succeed must adapt its activities to suit its own needs.

Probably a social program is essential to the success of most clubs.

One thing should be guarded against: Often clubs build up a program for a meeting that is too full. If a representative of the college accepts an invitation, he should have a reasonable time to speak and should not be made to feel that his address is a waste of time and that everyone would rather dance.

H.

Alumni Reunions

The Dix plan for reunions provides for consecutive meetings of classes every five years. A definite time is set and plans are made to bring class members together. The purpose is to maintain interest and to continue the friendships of college days. This may be all to the good, but the testimony of many alumni is that the meetings are rather perfunctory and hardly worth the travel and expense involved. Each class has its own program consisting of a luncheon, a meeting and a general alumni dinner. Little is heard about the college and what it is doing. The older alumni find themselves strangers upon a campus larger and more impressive than in their day. To them the reunion is disappointing and without much profit.

Here again is a wasted opportunity because the time and the event of reunion is not planned as a college function, but for an alumni gathering instituted by the secretary of the association. In some places the alumni have a part in the conduct of the college through a board of visitors which actually confers with college authorities and helps to plan for and even to criticize their alma mater. Through this method the alumni enjoy real cooperation with the college administration and feel that they have a part in the direction of their college. In most instances, alumni are just company for a day—a pleasant relationship, but hardly a helpful one.

M.

Alumni Reunions

Any occasion which brings back to the college numbers of alumni provides an opportunity to acquaint them with some phase of the college life and work. These opportunities should be taken advantage of.

Anything that will tend to renew an interest in and affection for the college is valuable. Each institution and staff member concerned with the alumni, must work out his own plan for the accomplishment of this objective under the guidance of the president or of the alumni secretary. Alumni come back but seldom. If something can be offered which will renew their interest of student days, it will be remembered longer than the pageant of a football game.

H.

Alumni Publications

A careful study of alumni publications would be helpful to all who carry the burden of compiling, organizing, printing and distributing them. These printed periodicals vary from four to eight folded sheets to pamphlets and full-dress magazines. The contents are on the whole rather dry reading, but they do serve as bulletins in which events taking place on the college campus are brought to the attention of the reader. All of them contain items of deaths, marriages, births of children and new jobs or appointments. A good deal of space is devoted to athletics and kindred activities and very little to educational matters.

Most of these publications show evidences of hurried compilation and lack of careful planning. This can be accounted for by the varied and detailed duties of the alumni secretary who is editor, messenger, typist, treasurer, bookkeeper, reporter, and traveler. He emits a sigh of relief when his efforts are put into type form and come off the press ready for distribution.

M.

Alumni Publications

For many years I have read alumni publications, chiefly those from the five institutions with which I have had personal relations. They vary greatly and all, I believe, give news items of alumni by classes and certainly contain much of interest to their subscribers.

The divergence lies almost wholly in the remainder of the magazine. Some contain considerable heavy reading, highly technical articles, and material of slight interest to the general reader. On the other hand, some are far too heavily loaded with athletic information of slight interest to most older alumni.

Of course an alumni magazine must serve people from twenty to eighty years of age; the bulk lies between thirty and sixty. It seems to me that these people are particularly interested in articles with cuts of the most distinguished alumni in different fields and with accounts of recent accomplishments of alumni. They are also concerned with new developments in policy, in buildings and improvements, in items about entering freshmen and the honors won by graduates. Many are also interested in accomplishments and honors won by their old professors.

Some alumni magazines are full of good material. There is enough available on any campus to make such a magazine acceptable to the alumni if handled with skill.

H.

The Alumni Register

This is the key to all alumni work and so is of vital importance. To be of any real use it must be kept up to date. When once brought up to date, it is probable that one capable person could maintain correct records of 25,000 alumni.

If the alumni association does not have sufficient funds to finance this work properly, the president should certainly see that supplementary funds are available and that such records are properly maintained.

H.

The Class Secretary

This officer can be and often is a useful part of an alumni organization. When each class receives its diplomas and the members are guests of the institution at an alumni dinner, the spirit of alma mater runs high, and those who are present at the fraternal gathering feel that they must have a class secretary to keep the records and to send information from time to time to the new alumni. Like most efforts of this kind, the early enthusiasm of the new group slows down after a little while, and the poor secretary finds it more and more difficult to keep up the records. In a large institution with several colleges, a secretary should be elected from the graduates in each college.

M.

Class Contributions

With growing expenses and declining returns on endowments, colleges are turning to the alumni to help make up deficits. The Yale University alumni for many years have contributed large sums annually to meet the deficit occasioned by expenditures over ordinary income. In other institutions a similar plan has been used to raise funds. Experience shows that it takes a long time to build up a substantial list of regular subscribers, but it is well worth the effort. The results are to be found not only in the money contributed, but in an increased interest in the welfare of the college.

On the whole the women's colleges are more successful in organizing alumnae effort than the coeducational and vocational institutions. It would be worth while to study carefully what they have done and how they have succeeded in interesting their graduates.

M.

Class Contributions

In some institutions each class, upon the occasion of the fiftieth anniversary, makes a generous contribution to its alma mater. These contributions sometimes amount to $100,000 or more; but, of course, such gifts can come only from large classes which include a number of wealthy members.

The majority of alumni make but small contributions yearly, yet in the aggregate these total a considerable sum. Since the bulk of the money is usually unassigned, it is available for the purposes which the alumni secretary and the president regard as most important. I have found this fund of real value even when small.

H.

Alumni Can Provide a Living Endowment

The alumni can and shoud prove a great financial aid to their alma mater whether privately or publicly supported. They can be organized as a living endowment. At Oberlin College when an alumnus joins the "Living Endowment Union" he agrees to pay five per cent interest on $____ each year. In a private institution, it is not uncommon to secure annual gifts from fifty per cent or more of the alumni. In a public institution twenty-five per cent is considered good. The annual gifts will average at least five to ten dollars, and in many cases more than that.

Such aid is important enough to justify an organization under a competent manager. The training received from a college has been a large factor in the earning power of most alumni. In practically no case did the tuition paid cover the expense of the training secured. In a very real sense each graduate can be charged with owing his alma mater a considerable sum. For a four year course this might easily amount to from $500 as a minimum to nearly $5,000. Of course, the college expects its graduates to repay this debt many times in services to the people of their respective communities. In most cases the debt is so paid. Where it is possible, cash in whole or in part payment is most acceptable. I am simply urging the point that an alumnus owes his college a substantial sum, not to be begged, but collected. A very important part of the work of the alumni office is the organization which appeals to the alumni for funds and presses these claims.

In 1947, some 384,000 alumni gave $9,628,000 to some 150 institutions in small annual gifts.

H.

Alumni Are a Source of Large Gifts

While a wide annual collection of small gifts should be sought, both for the needs of the college and to gain a place on the alumni benevolent list, larger gifts and bequests can also be secured. A careful record of wealthy alumni should be maintained, and so far as possible they should be kept advised of the work, needs and prospects of their alma mater. The university president should consider obtaining large gifts as one of his important responsibilities.

H.

Financial Campaigns

Financial campaigns are carried on in various ways as circumstances may justify: by the alumni secretary himself, by an assistant working under the secretary's direction, by the alumni president or by an assistant working under his direction.

Aside from these annual drives for current support of special or general causes, a constant quest is maintained for large gifts to be used toward endowment, buildings or other purposes. The number of large gifts and bequests to colleges and universities is astonishing. If the president is not familiar with the methods of raising funds, he would do well to consult one of the recognized fund-raising organizations which work with colleges. The names of fund-raising agencies can be found in the *Alumni Fund Survey*.

H.

Placement of Graduates

At Iowa State College, a technological institution, I took the stand that the college should do everything in its power to see that each graduate be placed in a position for which he is trained.

If he cannot be so placed, either the training is ineffective or we are graduating more students than the field of occupation can absorb.

A proper organization of this placement work is important. It will of necessity differ from one institution to another, but certain basic needs should be met. Any organization seeking a graduate should have its letters of inquiry reach a man at the head of the placement work who knows the current seniors and who can answer inquiries intelligently. When the representatives of an employing company calls at the campus, this personnel officer should be able to bring to his office all students who are desired for conference and also all professors whose opinions will be helpful, rather than that the prospective employer should wander over the campus in a vain effort to contact these persons.

Iowa State College employs full-time personnel officers for engineering and home economics. In agriculture, science, and in the placement of graduates in teaching positions, several part-time persons are so employed. Seniors in the engineering, agriculture, and science colleges are assisted in the preparation of a printed "Personnel Sheet" * on which appears a reproduction of a photograph of the student and a fairly complete biographical sketch. This latter includes an outline of the person's professional preparation and some account of his participation in student and social activities of high school and college. These "Personnel Sheets" are widely used by the personnel offices. The student pays the cost of printing 100 sheets and it is well worth it.

Individual alumni and alumni clubs could give valuable help to placement officers both in securing initial jobs for graduates and in suggestions for promotions to those already employed.

H.

Recent Graduates as Critics of Teaching

The recent alumni really know the college. If a systematic inquiry were made within one or two years of graduation of all

---
* See Appendix, page 320.

graduates, or of 300 selected members of the last two classes, valuable and dependable information might be obtained as to who are the able teachers and who are the unsatisfactory ones. Important data could be secured on what is being well done, and what poorly done in the general operation of the institution. Of course, if such an inquiry were to be made, it should continue throughout a number of years in order to produce the best results. I regard such an inquiry as a worth-while project.

H.

An Alumni Advisory Council

Alumni advisory councils should be appointed from among the men who have been out of college twenty or thirty years and whose advice could be depended upon in matters affecting the college. If the institution includes several colleges, a council should be appointed for each college by the president, after he confers with the deans. Each council should meet with the dean and professors once a year. One member should be replaced each year. These councils, properly conducted, would give the alumni some confidence that their college is progressive educationally and in contact with world affairs. The alumni would undoubtedly feel honored to serve on such a council. In some institutions each department has an alumni advisory council.

H.

Alumni Can Send Able Students

In many cases committees of the local alumni organizations have the authority to assign scholarships to brilliant local students. Such help goes far toward encouraging fine, able young people to attend college. When the average quality of most student bodies is considered, this assistance can be important. The alumni can check on applicants for admission, and scholarships awarded for high merit can do much toward raising the quality of the students who are admitted.

H.

Alumni Can Aid With the Legislature

In state institutions one or two members in each county can inform state senators and representatives of the needs of their institution and can answer questions relative to the institution. These selected alumni should meet at the college early in the fall preceding the opening of the legislature and inform themselves regarding impending legislation. This same alumni group should keep their fellow alumni in their counties advised about the college and its financial needs. Such committees should be selected jointly by the president of the college and the president of the alumni association.

H.

Alumni May Nominate Trustees

In private institutions it is a general practice to have all or part of the trustees selected from the alumni. In public institutions the trustees are elected, or more generally, appointed by the governor. Often the governor appoints members in order to pay political debts. Some such appointments have proved to be excellent, while others have not. Many of these political appointments are made because the governor does not realize the great importance of such a post.

The president does not feel free to nominate trustees. Since, usually, some trustees whose terms expire are eligible for reappointment, the trustees themselves do not feel free to recommend for or against the reappointment, or to nominate others for the vacancy.

Here the alumni, through their executive committee or through a special committee, are in a strong position to exercise their power for the good of the institution. They can appropriately make nominations to the governor and point out the suitability of their nominees for the post. While the governor might not always make appointments from among those so nominated, certainly the alumni's interest would tend to keep his appointments on a higher level.

The appointment of trustees of our state institutions of higher education is among the most important made in a state.

H.

Alumni of Especial Importance

There are two groups of alumni in whom a college is always interested: those who are holding important positions and who are, or are becoming, men and women of large service and distinction in the nation, and those who are active in the alumni organization and on whom its secretary can count for help in all alumni matters. Both groups are of interest to the alumni secretary, and he can usually make up a list of each group, basing the list on the men and women in each active alumni area. I believe it will be found that both groups will include not more than 3 to 5 per cent of living alumni. It will usually be found that about 80 per cent of college graduates rise quickly to positions of influence and responsibility in their respective communities. While only a few reach wide prominence, every college can well be proud of the services its alumni are rendering in every type of leadership.

The alumni are proud of the graduates of their college who are attaining distinction, and stories of their success with photographs are among the most interesting material in any alumni magazine.

Aside from the help the college can give them, the alumni can in turn render valuable service to the college when called upon.

H.

Distinguished Alumni

Every college and university is proud of distinguished alumni. As I have contemplated this matter from time to time, I have had difficulty in deciding just whom to include in that classification. Recently, I set up a tentative scale of seven degrees of distinction:

(1) Of national distinction.

(2) Of regional distinction or of distinction in one of the 5 cities of more than 1,000,000.

(3) Of state-wide distinction or of distinction in one of the 11 cities of 500,000 to 1,000,000.

(4) Of distinction in one of 78 cities of from 100,000 to 500,000.

(5) Of distinction in one of 880 cities of 25,000 to 100,000.

(6) Of county-wide distinction or of distinction in one of 1,630 cities of 5,000 to 25,000.

(7) Of distinction in one of 14,700 towns of under 5,000.

Of course, in each of our larger cities there would be many people of lower rank in distinction as well as those of city-wide distinction.

With this tentative scale a careful effort was made to rank two groups of graduates who have completed or largely completed their life work and whose biographies were available. These were the graduates of Miami University, 1826 to 1873, 1,045 in number; and graduates of Iowa State College, 1872 to 1889, 1,033 in number. The results of these two studies follow:

DISTRIBUTION OF ALUMNI IN SEVEN DEGREES OF DISTINCTION

MIAMI UNIVERSITY 1826–1873: 1,045 Graduates

Degree	1st	2nd	3rd	4th	5th	6th	7th	Without Distinction	
Graduates	5	13	16	59	142	254	437	118	
Percentage	0.5	1.2	1.6	5.6	13.5	24.5	41.8	11.3	100.0

IOWA STATE COLLEGE 1872–1889: 1,033 Graduates

Degree	1st	2nd	3rd	4th	5th	6th	7th	Without Distinction	
Graduates	3	6	29	49	130	221	337	258	
Percentage	0.3	0.6	2.8	4.7	12.6	21.4	32.6	25.0	100.0

While perhaps less than 2 per cent rose sufficiently high in distinction to be widely recognized and only somewhat less than 3 per cent won state-wide distinction, it is a matter of great pride that from 70 to 85 per cent of all graduates could be classified as distinguished in that they gave useful leadership in their own communities, a leadership in business, law, medicine, or the ministry, which was greatly needed.

If this classification could be further refined and adopted by all alumni secretaries and used, it would be of help in estimating the relative distinction of our American college graduates.

H.

Publication of an Alumni "Who's Who"

Today the University of California has more than 100,000 alumni, and fifty other institutions now have more than 20,000. It is quite impossible for many institutions to publish a complete alumni catalog. However, it would be entirely possible for any institution to publish every five years a brief biographical sketch of each of the 2 to 5 per cent of its most distinguished alumni. This should be a joint enterprise of the college and the alumni office.

A start on such a list could be made by collecting the biographies of alumni in *Who's Who in America, Who's Who in Business and Commerce, Who's Who in Education* and *American Men of Science*. Some of these might not warrant inclusion. If the names thus selected were submitted to committees of the various alumni centers, other names could be added. Such a publication carefully edited every five years would be useful to any institution in many ways, and would be a fitting recognition of its distinguished graduates.

H.

An administrator must recognize the importance of maintaining able men and women on the college staff. This consideration should have priority over all others. In every selection, emphasis should be placed not only upon scholarship and teaching ability, but upon character, personality, health, family life, and affiliations.

8.
The Importance of Teaching

Teaching Is a Faculty Matter

The teaching is done by the faculty. Standards of scholarship are fixed by the faculty, and the degrees are voted upon by the faculty. The president has little to do with actual teaching. It is not his job. However, he can do much to maintain and sometimes raise standards and improve the quality of teaching. With the support of the trustees and through the budget, he can also expand or limit the scope of the teaching offered. His greatest influence is wielded through the type of men he recommends to the trustees for appointment to the staff. Here he can emphasize character, research ability, teaching aptitude, personality, or whatever quality he regards as essential to the welfare of the students and the institution. He can do much to maintain the morale of the teaching faculty by the way he supports freedom of speech, tenure, faculty participation in management, the library, and all things highly valued by the faculty. Through his emphasis on its importance over the years, he can materially improve the teaching. The faculty will respond to standards and ideals which are steadily upheld by a president.

There is an old saying, "The stream never rises higher than

its source." This is certainly true of an educational institution. Such institutions have great inertia; with changes in administrative leadership the response is slow, both up and down. But the proverb holds. No college or department rises above the standards set by the president, by the deans, and by the heads of departments.

Character, scholarship, personal relations, culture, ideals, and home relations are affected by the attitude of those in authority. The president influences by his personal ideals everything in the institution and, among others, the teaching. This source of influence should be kept noble, meaning upright, unselfish, considerate, and discerning.

H.

Teaching Is a Faculty Matter

In the preceding comment on "Teaching Is a Faculty Matter," my colleague makes the declaration, "The president has little to do with teaching; it is not his job." The fact is that the president is much concerned with teaching, and he should be, for the leadership rests upon his shoulders whether he likes it or not. Certainly in the college of a thousand students or less the president is the director of all plans and purposes of education. When their president is without a clear philosophy of education, large institutions are likely to wobble in their course.

My colleague calls attention to the control of education by the faculty. His statement is true, but the faculty consists of men and women of special interests, organized in departments, divisions, and schools or colleges. Constant conflicts arise about courses, requirements, registration of students in classes, and other matters. Who is to direct the ship on its course? The answer is, the president.

It is stated that this officer is overwhelmed with budgets, building matters, public relations, money raising, and other affairs of importance. Unfortunately, that is the fact, but it indicates that the emphasis is on the wrong point. The whole tendency in modern life is to become entangled in the secondary, the maze of day-to-day events, and with gadgets, both material and visionary. It is no wonder that the president is overwhelmed with the business of keeping the place going, and in consequence cannot give what he would to education. Nevertheless, I still would say that the president's job is education. The man who fills the place should have a philosophy of education and understand what education means in our modern social order.

A case in point is that of the college of arts and sciences as it stands today. Little by little, the general purpose of the college is being depleted by the introduction of vocational training, as witnessed by the pre-medical and pre-nursing courses, and those offered to medical technicians. After a period of years the instructors in these groups want larger recognition and so fight for the organization of a school or college in which to carry on a larger and more specialized course of instruction. This sort of whittling down is going on everywhere, resulting in reducing and hampering the college of arts and sciences, supposedly the very center of the higher education program.

If the purpose of the institution is to vocationalize the education it offers, then the college of arts and sciences becomes a service college where instruction is limited to training in language, science, and mathematics covering a period of about two years. To this sort of instruction, a variety of vocational courses are tied, their teachers hoping someday to have a college or school of their own in the institution. Who is going to direct, modify, or stop this destructive drift? Will it be the faculty or the deans? Not likely. The problem will rest right on the shoulders of the president. Education is his job.

M.

The Articulation of Students

The pace of the first year in college is faster than that of the last year in high school. Competition is stiffer, as the proportion of able students among college freshmen is higher than in a senior high school class. Students who sailed smoothly through high school are often stranded in college before they are aware of it.

The slight effort put forth in their high school days does not furnish enough momentum to carry them in college.

On the other hand, some high schools afford excellent training; their graduates on entering college often are obliged to repeat courses which they have already mastered. These students are among the ablest entrants, and such an introduction to college may have a most discouraging effect.

Stated another way, each entering student is an individual problem. His high school preparation should be carefully considered, with his assistance, and his college work should be carefully arranged in the light of what he has done and how he has done it. Repetition should be avoided, and the total load should be arranged somewhere between twelve or fourteen hours and eighteen or twenty hours, according to the individual's ability.

Far too often, especially in our larger institutions, student registration is a wholesale job with too little attention given to individual differences. Each applicant is fitted to an average schedule which may be right for 60 per cent, but is too light for 10 per cent and too heavy for 30 per cent of those entering.

No matter what policy of admission and registration is pursued, it remains a fact that some freshmen are extremely able, some, average, and some, poor. More effort should be made than is generally the case to differentiate between the students in these several classes. The best students should be enrolled in a superior group and excused from the more elementary subjects in which they already excel. By some method we should avoid boring these students with the repetition of work which allows them to make high grades without serious study. I am satisfied that nothing is more detrimental and discouraging to a brilliant mind than to be held back in a class of poor students moving at a slow pace.

If a student is to be properly registered, it is essential to consider what his occupation is to be, or at least in what broad field his chief interest lies. Yet students with brilliant minds, of which there are a considerable number, often find it difficult to limit themselves to any one occupation, as they are curious about, and interested in, many. However, they will usually know whether their chief interest lies in the humanities, in science and engineering, in art, or in some branch of agriculture. Even with this vague objective, it becomes clear that certain subjects should be taken in the freshman year.

Until a freshman states his field of interest, broadly or specifically, no one can counsel him wisely as to what courses he should take. We must add purpose to interest if we are to secure the best work from an individual.

In case a student remains uncertain in which field his occupational interest lies, he should be required to take a vocational aptitude test. This will afford considerable guidance to the professor in charge of his registration.

If adequate consideration is to be given to each individual freshman, certainly several thousand cannot be registered in one or two days. Freshman registration must be spread out over a longer period than is now customary. When we consider that the financial cost will be from $800 to $1,800 for the student himself, and $300 to $1,000 or more per year for the institution, and also that the care in registration may make or ruin the student's chances of success in college, a few days more of time seems of small consequence. Unfortunately, colleges, like people, have a strong inclination to do things the easiest way.

For many youths the *free* local junior college, similar to those in California, is the desirable institution of higher learning. Only those who averaged B in high school are well prepared to enter college; between 10 and 15 per cent of these fail. For those who average below B, the free local junior college is the ideal link between the high school and the college or university. The junior college allows the student to try out college at no higher expense than that of high school. It offers substantially the first two years of college and various terminal vocational courses. C average at the junior college level should admit a student to the university or to any four year college. If he is in earnest, the experience saves him money and in no way impedes his progress in college. If he does not succeed, he can transfer to a vocational course or drop out. We need the free junior college, and it will inevitably come into general use.

The articulation between the sophomore and junior years

also deserves careful consideration. In the main, the first two years in college are a preparation for the last two. Is the student fiinishing the first two years prepared to enter the junior year of the course he has elected? Do his college average and his grades in fundamental subjects indicate he is qualified? He certainly should not be promoted or allowed to enter the junior year unless his college average in his first two years is fully up to the average required for graduation. If the requirement for graduation is an average of 2.0, the student should be fully up to this average before admission to the junior year. The end of the sophomore year is the time to drop a student who won't work or who lacks sufficient ability. He may be halted until he repeats enough work to raise his average to the college requirement, if this seems advisable. Why encourage incapable or uninterested students to go further? It would seem, also, that for such students further inquiry should be made as to the wisdom of their selection of an occupation.

When we come into the senior college, the inefficient have been eliminated; the ablest stand out, and their objective in life is clearly defined, or certainly more clearly defined than was the case two years earlier. It is at this time that a large development in the student's intellectual life is to be expected. All students who are competent to enter upon graduate work or schools in the professional fields, such as medicine, law or theology, should be taking the required or desirable pre-training. Students in the senior college have by this time a pretty clear idea how to study; and while able teaching counts tremendously, it is not so essential with upper classmen as with freshmen and sophomores.

H.

Teaching

Of our 1,850 colleges and universities, 138 conferred the doctor of philosophy degree and 438 the master's degree in 1948–49. About 1,400 institutions confined their teaching to undergraduates as an essential objective. In the eight universities conferring from 118 to 496 doctorates and from 940 to 4,793 master's degrees, research and graduate teaching are major occupations. In about 100 more institutions, research and graduate work require from one-tenth to one-third of the time of the staff, largely dividing the attention of many faculty members between teaching undergraduates and postgraduates.

While many believe that supervising graduate and research work improves the quality of undergraduate instruction, I hold the opposite view. I believe the division of interest tends to lead the teacher to neglect one or the other, usually the undergraduate group. Even in a great university where graduate work and research are matters of prime consideration, teaching still remains the leading purpose and problem of the institution. Even here it should be held of more importance than research.

Let us first admit, as we must, that in more than 1,300 colleges in which there is no formal recognition of research as an institutional objective, much of the teaching is far from inspiring. My estimate would be that from 5 to 10 per cent is unpardonably poor, and at least 15 to 20 per cent more is far less effective than it should be. This is due primarily to two things, the scarcity of good teachers and the fact that many students in our American colleges have no serious interest in scholarship. This lack of interest on the part of the student body discourages good teaching.

In our great universities and to a decreasing extent down through the leading 300 which serve graduate students, another factor enters. On the whole these institutions have ample funds to offer attractive salaries to the best teachers, but they generally require the doctor's degree and research ability as a requisite for employment. A really large proportion are employed on the basis of their publications and the excellence of their research accomplishments, with very slight consideration given to their effectiveness as teachers. This latter statement would by no means apply equally to all departments in any single institution. I am not alone in the belief that there is more or less poor and unskilled teaching in every college and university, and that the teaching in our great universities, especially in the freshman and sophomore years, is inferior on the whole to the teaching in our best colleges. A definite campaign should be maintained in every institution for improvement of teaching. Here and there in certain departments such a policy is energetically pursued, though rarely.

It is my opinion that a qualified person working out of the president's office should have as his chief duty the maintenance of teaching standards. Such a person, if fully supported by the president and if courageous, persistent, tactful, and persuasive, could make tremendous improvements in the teaching carried on in an institution over a period of years.

In most colleges there is a natural turnover in the staff of about 20 per cent each year; the percentage is less in small colleges and more in large universities where many assistants and graduate instructors are employed. The first effort of such an officer as has been described should be to check on the teaching ability, experience, and success of every person considered for appointment, and to veto those of whom he cannot approve. This pressure should be heavier on freshmen and sophomore teachers than on those whose teaching would be confined to advanced classes.

This officer's second objective should be to establish, in each department, in-service training of inexperienced teachers. Much could be done by assigning a young instructor to a staff member with a definite reputation as a good teacher, with the understanding that each would visit the other's classes and discuss teaching freely from time to time. Classes or seminars on teaching could well be conducted in large departments.*

His third effort might be bent toward identifying the least inspiring, least capable and least acceptable teachers and, so far as possible, removing them from the staff, or at least from teaching. Employment could generally be obtained for these individuals outside the teaching profession. As soon as every department realized that the president was backing this movement for good teaching, there would be a response.

A sound salary policy to go with such a plan would be to pay the same salary to a first-class teacher who did no research as to a first-class research man who did no teaching or whose teaching

---

* See interesting article by W. W. Charters, *School and Society*, Vol. 13, pp. 494–97.

was poor. The man who combined able teaching and brilliant research should receive higher pay.

During my service at Iowa State College I did all I could to promote good teaching, and some progress was made. Were I to start again where I started then, I would go much farther along that line. I regret keenly that enthusiasm and inspiration are far too often lacking in college teaching. Many deans and department heads fail to appreciate any effort made by a teacher to express enthusiasm or to inspire students. They support a policy of "take it or leave it." They favor teaching formally and giving the class the essential facts. Of course, many earnest, hard-working students do respond to average teaching, but they would certainly be more responsive and so would many other members of the class, if they felt the professor was enthusiastically interested in his subject.

The presence of numbers of indifferent, cynical and critical students in a class can kill interest. True learning can be acquired only by sitting at the feet of a master. Where a teacher is conscious of a critical audience, he becomes cautious, restrained, and guarded; enthusiasm is impossible. The best remedy I know for such a situation lies in a division of the class according to ability and interest. In each section the teacher's purpose will be clearer, and better teaching will be done. I feel that in every freshman class, at least, the most promising students should be taught separately and by the most capable teachers. Among these select students are those who will later be our ablest leaders; certainly they should have the very best instruction that can be provided. This policy is followed unswervingly on the athletic field; it is a sound policy in the educational area. I do not mean that other students should be neglected, but that the most promising should have the special attention of excellent teachers.

H.

How the Work of a College May Be Judged

Those in authority in nearly every college or university wonder from time to time just how well their teaching faculty is doing its job; but strangely enough, they are never able to find out. It is a rare administrator indeed who possesses anything like accurate knowledge either as to the teaching ability of the members of his staff or the quality of teaching done by his faculty as a whole. He may possess abundant information of other kinds concerning the men and women whom he has employed for this purpose, but his files will reveal nothing as to the actual efficiency of their work.

In part, the explanation lies in the fact that college faculty members as a group do not like to be supervised or, for that matter, observed by their superiors in the performance of their classroom work. It is not easy to justify such an attitude. A direct consequence is that many students in nearly every institution suffer constantly at the hands of poor teachers without that condition ever becoming known to the administrative officials. Obviously, some objective measure of the quality of teaching done by our higher institutions of learning is urgently needed.

A suggestion that seems worth considering in this connection is that the quality of teaching of any given institution, taken as a whole, may be judged by the proportion of its students who are found to be working at or above their indicated ability levels. It is not difficult to determine this with considerable accuracy.

It is quite generally agreed among investigators that two of the best indices of the ability of any given entering student are (1) his score on some standardized aptitude or mental test and (2) his average grade in high school. In some institutions, these two scores are combined, with one or both weighted; and the composite score so obtained is regarded as a fairly satisfactory index of the student's ability to do college work. It is true, of course, that there are many students whose subsequent work does not measure up to these early predictions.

It is likewise certain that many work below their true ability levels while in college, and this fact may account for the differences between their predicted and actual performance. It follows that the predictive scores may actually be more nearly accurate than is commonly thought to be the case.

At any rate, it is feasible to divide each entering class of students by means of these predictive scores into five groups, *A, B, C, D,* and *E,* placing in each group the same proportion of the class as normally receive the corresponding average grade in their subsequent college work. If this should be done, it would become an easy matter to check each student's average grade at the end of each semester or quarter against his predicted average, and in this manner to determine how many have fallen below their indicated ability level.

The percentage of students making grades up to or above their predicted level would be a fair measure of the quality of the teaching of the faculty, taken as a whole. The justification for this is that really good teaching keeps a student working at or near the highest level of which he is capable. It is not unreasonable to say that the greater the proportion of the student body of any given institution to be found working below its ability, the poorer the quality of the teaching in that institution. Indeed, this assumption seems warranted even after full allowance is made for the fact that the predictive scores are themselves not entirely accurate.

In precisely the same manner and by the same figures, the efficiency of the respective major departments may be compared. That is, it would be easily possible to determine for each major department the percentage of its students who are working up to or above their indicated ability. There is reason to believe that some startling differences would be revealed among the major departments of nearly any institution in this respect, just as there would be among the institutions themselves, taken as a whole, if they should be compared in such a manner.

H.

Lecturing

It has always seemed to me that the lecture method is greatly overrated. Especially in the elementary work generally offered in the first two years of college. There is little justification for lecture courses. Modern textbooks cover all subjects taught in elementary courses adequately, and class discussions with explanations at difficult points would serve more effectively.

Years ago, the head of the Economics Department at the University of Chicago, in discussing the value of the lecture system, said that when a new instructor was brought into his department he was always asked if he had any lectures suitable for use there. Usually the man had. If so, he was told to have them mimeographed and given to his class as a basis for quiz and class discussion. After having been used in this way, corrected and brought up to date, the material was printed in book form by the department. This plan usually did away with lecture courses.

On any campus there are few superior lecturers. The efforts of many are dull and uninteresting, in short not as effective as quiz and discussion with a good textbook. Most of us acquire information more readily through the eye than through the ear. So long as the lecturer talks, all the class can do is take notes which are rarely as clear as a text. If at the end of each class period the professor would sketch briefly the material in the next assignment giving some explanatory help on the more difficult points and arousing interest in the matter to be covered, the results would be much more successful than those obtained from the average lecture.

I am familiar with the stand taken that classes may be so large they can be handled only through the lecture method. This attitude is unworthy of a college professor. The large class should be broken down into sections small enough for class discussions. Even if the discussions were led by the ablest students in the class, more thinking would be done and more advancement would be made than in lecturing a mass group whose interest would be difficult to hold.

I am convinced that more thinking will result, a better mastery of the subject will be gained, and more interest will be inspired by a combination of quiz, discussion, and problem-working than by lectures. Probably one basis for judging the effectiveness of the work of a college or university would be to rate it inversely on the proportion of lectures given. There is no question but that it takes less effort on the part of an instructor to read a lecture, once written, to a class than to organize and direct discussion, quiz, and problem-working. If the ease of the professor is of chief concern, the lecture system should be strongly maintained.

H.

Lecturing

On a sunny morning in May when the windows of the academic buildings are opened to the gentle breeze, a visitor to a campus may not hear "the voice of the turtle in the land," but he will hear the voice of lecturers on every side. Now and then a few words come through to his ears, but they mean little. The visitor is concerned with the amount of talk that he hears as he walks slowly along the paths that cross the campus. The talkers are lecturing; they are talking for fifty minutes.

The lecture system has its merits, but as a method of instruction, it has been greatly abused, especially in undergraduate courses. Such subjects as languages, mathematics, and to a lesser degree the sciences do not use the lecture method of instruction, but the social sciences and literatures are steeped in it. When a professor is dealing with material that is scattered and not well systematized he has to rely on the lecture as a means of conducting his courses.

In subjects where there are good textbooks, the lecture is wholly supplementary; then instruction is best advanced by questions and discussions aided by assigned reading. In the graduate courses, the lecture is the thread, the connection holding data and conclusions together. After all, the center of the course is the student. He should be brought into the instruction process and given an opportunity to have a part in the development of the course he is taking. By such a method the teacher soon discovers how well his teaching is reaching the minds of the students in the classroom. Such teaching is a give-and-take method for both teacher and student.

M.

Visiting College Classes

In spite of the great prejudice against visiting college classes for purposes of judging the quality of the teaching, it still remains true that in no other way can it be determined.

As suggested elsewhere, this could probably be most agreeably done by assigning an inexperienced teacher to an able teacher and arranging to have them intervisit and discuss their teaching problems. The experienced teacher could learn the type of work the young teacher was doing and could report his findings intelligently to the department head or the dean.

At Miami University I arranged to devote the necessary time to some class visitation. I decided on visiting the classes in the social sciences; and at a meeting of the staffs in these subjects I explained my purpose and promised two things: First, if I visited one section of a man's classes, I would also visit the other classes he taught. So I would in every case spend three to five hours in each teacher's classroom. Thus no teacher would be judged by one class only. Second, I would enter with the students, sit in the back of the room, and remain until the end of the hour, leaving with the class. I believed these two conditions of visiting to be essential. No one took offense from these visits, and there were always enough complimentary things to be said that the edge was taken off such adverse criticism as was offered.

Today, with literally thousands of inexperienced teachers entering upon their work annually, there is no way to help them or to guard students from the effects of poor teaching without class visiting. And yet it is exceptional to find systematic visiting of classes in our colleges.

H.

Fellowships for Promising Young Teachers

As we need from 6,000 to 10,000 teachers each year to fill the ranks of those who retire or die, every effort should be made to attract toward a teaching career all college graduates who have shown real aptitude and interest in the profession.

Many undergraduates are used as part-time instructors, and some show an exceptional aptitude for teaching. If fellowships for able teachers were offered in each department of the universities, those who accepted them would probably enter definitely into the teaching profession. Their research should be divided between the field of knowledge in which they are specializing and the department of education.

Most of our college teachers have gone through the graduate school with little or no emphasis having been made upon teaching. Usually their research is in their special field, whether it be of science or the humanities. Thus they enter their teaching experience after a period of absorption in the highly scientific objective of their thesis with no thought of the problems of teaching and with little enthusiasm.

If those definitely expecting to teach could prepare their thesis on some problem involved with teaching their chosen subject, if they could teach some classes in the subject, under supervision, they would be more interested in their profession. Fellowships in universities open to students who show definite promise of becoming able teachers would contribute greatly to the advancement of good undergraduate teaching.

H.

The Doctorate as a Requirement for a Professorship

The bachelor's degree presumably indicates that the man or woman who holds it has attended college somewhere for four years. In the same manner the doctorate indicates that the holder of that degree has studied in an institution of higher learning for at least three years beyond his baccalaureate and has some understanding of the techniques of research. Presumably, he has a deep and wide knowledge in his particular field; and presumably, he can carry on independent research. However, neither of these presumptions is true in all cases. Many holders of the doctorate never attempt research after their theses are accepted.

This fact leads one to believe that the degree should discriminate in some way between the able research man and the man of creditable scholarship. It has been suggested that the degree be conferred "with highest honors" on the man truly able and eager to carry on independent research; "with honors" on the man of fair research ability; and the degree without embellishment on the man showing little promise of success in independent research.

There is also a wide difference of opinion as to what constitutes a satisfactory thesis study, with chemistry and physics at one extreme and sociology and education at the other. This difference is accentuated by the fact that a great majority of all entering for the doctorate in education are experienced teachers, advanced a number of years from their baccalaureate degrees. Practically all candidates in physics and chemistry enter directly from their baccalaureate degree. A large percentage of these plan to go into research later. On the other hand, nearly all candidates in education expect to continue teaching or to enter upon executive work in education; thus their interest in research is secondary. While there is a strong feeling in scholastic circles that the one degree, that of Doctor of Philosophy, should be the sole award for three or four years of advanced study, this conviction forces the degree to cover widely different types of scholarly endeavor, different in content and different in regard to research. There is much to be said for awarding two types of degrees.

The present attitude that no young person is fitted to become a college professor until he has won his doctorate is unfortunate. In some fields, such as those of chemistry or physics, this stand can be strongly defended. In English, literature, music, art, speech, elementary foreign language, architecture, landscape architecture, and other fields where native artistic endowment or literary appreciation are called for, the requirement seems rather farfetched. It raises the question whether the quest for the doctorate may not destroy or seriously impair the high qualities which fit the individual to lead and inspire. Teaching skill should be esteemed above degrees.

The engineering schools are now facing the problem of what weight to attach to the doctorate as a requisite for their professors. There are certainly some positions which require research technique and advanced learning in mathematics and physics and which should exact the doctor of philosophy degree. However, there are many others where the years required for the doctorate could be better spent in active engineering work, if the success of the students is to be the main concern.

All this, and the theme might be further elaborated, adds up to the fact that demand for the doctorate as a prerequisite for a full or associate professorship in every field is unwise.

At the same time, it appears that the requirements for the doctorate might well be raised. It is customary to admit as candidates only baccalaureate graduates who rank in the upper one-half or one-fourth of their class. However, too many students showing little ability in research are allowed to persist through four or five years when they are awarded the degree. Surely only men of outstanding ability and intelligence should be so honored. Men of less capacity would be sufficiently recognized by a master's degree. It is not easy to draw the line. Students admitted to fellowships who work faithfully for their major professors place the latter under personal obligations which the professors too often repay by recommending such students for advanced degrees.

Possibly the post-doctoral course as now offered at the Institute for Advanced Research and soon to be offered in other research centers will select very able men and produce great research workers.

Certainly the future of America, and indeed of the world, depends on the great creative thinkers who are developed. Of the 3,500 to 5,000 receiving the doctorate each year, perhaps 10 per cent, or 350 to 500, scattered over some sixty fields of knowledge, stand out as brilliant creative thinkers. We should certainly strive to graduate more of them. A study of the lives of the greatest American leaders today might point out some weaknesses in our college and university courses and degrees.

H.

What Does It Cost To Graduate a Student?

During a recent visit my brother brought up the question, what does it cost to graduate a student? To get his attitude, I may say that he is a successful lawyer, on the practical side. The question is one that comes up now and again, and will be raised more and more often in the future. Businessmen are inclined to challenge higher education by asking that question. Certainly more criticism is now directed toward education than at any time in my recollection. Real estate interests speak loudly about the cost of schools and demand reduction of taxes. In state and national budgets education faces a sharp competition for a share in the tax dollar. And privately endowed colleges compete with insistent requests for a share in the funds given by individuals to special causes. Consequently, when the question is asked, "Is it worth that much?" there should be an answer.

In reply, I requested further clearance of the subject from my brother, which elicited the statement that the amount must be around $15,000. This sum is arrived at by interest and deterioration on capital invested in the college plant plus operation costs, the sum of which is then divided by the number of students graduated. We took a hypothetical case where the investment in plant and equipment amounted to $5,000,000. The interest, deterioration, and repairs, if based at 8 per cent of cost, which is low, would be $400,000. To this was added, say, $600,000 more for salaries, supplies, and other expenses, all of which aggregate to the amount of $1,000,000. A graduating class of two hundred would, with this kind of reasoning, bring the cost of the product (graduates) to $5,000 for the last year. Counting a four years' college course, the total would reach $20,000. To this must be added the student's living expenses. Thus the price of educating and graduating one student is $25,000. My lawyer brother raised the question, "Is it worth that much?"

The large sum of $25,000 cannot be charged against the two hundred graduates since there are twelve hundred other students in the hypothetical college receiving instructions at the same time. If the denominator is increased, the annual student cost drops to $718, which is quite reasonable.

But my antagonist, who likes to bait an educator, declared that there are too many people going in for college educations. What are you going to do with them? My answer is that education may have, and often does have, a value in making life more interesting and useful whether one digs in a ditch or sits in the seats of the mighty. This placing of emphasis on vocations has many objections not clearly recognized. Education should not be limited to white collar workers. Yet there is a great pressure on all institutions to provide professional and vocational training. Sometimes this is done without a survey of the field or a careful estimate of the capacity of the occupation to absorb newcomers. The meaning is clear that our educational system is faced with a changing social order.

M.

What Does It Cost To Graduate a Student?

McVey's discussion of the cost of graduating a student appears to me to raise several important questions. It is important to know: How much does it cost? Is it worth the cost?

As close as I can judge, dividing the cost among all students in average attendance during the college year, the total cost to the colleges of the country varies from a minimum of about $400 to a maximum of $1,300. It is probable that the $1,300 includes a considerable expenditure for research. The student fees among these colleges vary from $125 to $800, and the net cost to the colleges varies from $275 to $500 a year.

The minimum for room and board will probably vary from about $450 to $700 for the college year. Books will cost from $35 to $60—perhaps will average about $50. All other minimum expenses, laundry, traveling expense, recreation, and incidentals, range from $175 to $500 or $600. These approximate figures would make the minimum cost to the student, exclusive of clothing:

	Low	High
Tuition	$125	$800
Room & Board	450	700
Books (*average*)	50	50
Incidentals	175	600
	$800	$2,150

A student might attend a state institution for as little as $800 a year and could attend one of our more expensive private universities or technical institutes for as little as $2,000 to $2,200.

If the student has a scholarship or works for wages while attending college, these figures will be reduced.

The cost to the institution, exclusive of the amount of tuition charged, as stated above, will probably vary from $275 to $500 a year. Adding their cost together:

	Low	High
Cost to the institution	$275	$500
Cost to student	800	2,150
	$1,075	$2,650

For the four years this would cost in total from $4,300 to $10,600. These would be minimum figures; perhaps we should say from $4,500 to $11,000.

The college student also loses what he could earn if employed. Taking this at $2,400 a year and deducting room and board at an average of $60 a month or $720 for 12 months; and incidentals at an average of $40 a month or $480 a year, we have a total deduction of $1,200, leaving a net loss of $1,200 a year or $4,800 for four years. We thus arrive at:

Low	High
$4,500	$11,000
4,800	4,800
$9,300	$15,800

In round numbers this amounts to $9,500 to $16,000 as the cost of educating a college graduate.

As the interest at 4 per cent on these sums equals $300 and $640 a year, it is evident that the individual who has received a college education must earn from $380 to $640 more a year than the average high school graduate to warrant the expense financially. It remains possible that, even if he earns no more, the cultural satisfactions and social connections may fully justify the expense. However, we believe that on the average the college graduate will earn more than the interest on the cost of his college education above the average of the high school graduate. We believe it does pay financially on all students who complete their college courses and are graduates.

There is, however, another factor that should be given consideration. A notable fraction of college graduates come to occupy positions of responsibility and leadership where all the training and knowledge acquired in college contributes to their success and value. These positions of vital leadership are essential to our national prosperity. They grow more difficult and burdensome each year, and college and university training for them is generally essential.

There seems to be no way to determine in advance which youths will develop into these vital leaders. The training of those who will give the nation great leadership is essential; so much of the cost of college training may properly be charged to training national leaders.

There is one other viewpoint on this matter of cost. Every parent considering sending a son or daughter to college should certainly consider the youth's high school average and, if available, his scholastic aptitude test grade. If these are unpromising, it is probable he will not complete a college course, and it probably will not pay to send him to college. This matter should be discussed carefully by the parent and child with the high school principal and with the admissions officer of the college. Unless the necessary money is easily available it might be wiser to save it. Today many families are denying themselves seriously to send youths to college who cannot or will not justify the expense.

H.

The president should be fully aware of all graduate and research work carried on by his institution. Both are expensive and neither should be undertaken without carefully counting the cost or without approval by the trustees. A little done with outstanding excellence will mean much to the reputation of the institution. Only outstanding scholars should teach graduate students.

9.

Graduate Work and Research

Research and Its Importance

Scientific research, beginning about seventy-five years ago on an organized basis, has grown to be one of the most important activities in the world. Today all important industries are spending huge sums on research and are relying upon their research staffs to open up new areas of service to the public.

The main training ground for the research worker is the university. About 140 American institutions are offering training for the doctorate in from one to thirty-five fields. Less than fifty of these institutions are training 90 per cent of our research workers.

As time goes on, some additional institutions, from twenty to thirty of them, will probably enter this field; a number of those already engaged will expand their offerings considerably. Before World War II we were giving the doctor of philosophy degree to about 3,500 candidates yearly, but 5,293 in 1948–49. While these men and women have met the requirments of their respective institutions for the degree and have undoubtedly done some research work, a very large proportion have shown no marked ability in this line and will publish little beyond their doctor's theses. How many will qualify as able research workers by the product of their later life, it is impossible to say. I would estimate that not more than 10 or 15 per cent will become distinguished research workers, and not over 15 per cent more will earn their living on the basis of their research output. These figures will vary with the field of study.

The truth is that while the 10 or 15 per cent of the graduate students who have real talent for research should be stimulated to develop this ability to its maximum, those of mediocre research ability should be given adequate training and inspiration to become teachers, with less emphasis placed upon research. Of our 1,850 colleges and universities, probably 1,000 desire that their professors hold the doctor of philosophy degree, but are wholly indifferent to any research they may do. The requirement that staff members obtain the doctorate as a proof of their advanced scholarship is increasing. In the face of this demand, it is undesirable to exclude those from the graduate schools who do not excel in research ability. It appears to me that some clear distinction between the graduates who excel in research ability and those who do not so excel should be made in the degree conferred upon them. My idea would be to graduate the able research man Ph.D. *summa cum laude,* and the scholar simply Ph.D., or give the former the D.Sc. and the latter the Ph.D.

The university, as distinguished from the college, needs not only able research men to direct the research training of candidates for doctor of philosophy, but also men who are skillful teachers, regardless of their research experience. Through a confusion in policy, the universities and some colleges employ men with the doctorate who are second or third rate at research and will accomplish little in that field, and who at the same time are not competent teachers. The university needs both good research men and good teachers. Very few excel in both lines. I have no criticism against employing men with the doctorate as teachers, if they are capable as such. But especially for freshmen and sophomores we need excellent teachers, to whom research should be a secondary matter.

In any case, there is a larger demand for able research men

than the universities can supply. The percentage of men and women graduating with a first degree who have the qualities demanded for research is small. These same persons are offered many inducements by industry, business, the law, medicine, engineering, and other fields. The graduate school can hope to secure only a small proportion of these outstanding graduates. I believe that if the best minds were recognized in the freshman year and challenged with the advantages of a life of research or research and teaching, many would be attracted and could be recruited to the graduate schools. Also, their undergraduate courses might thus be shaped to give them the foundation needed for their proposed graduate work. To expect to recruit many such men for advanced work toward the end of their senior year is futile; it is too late then.

Research, like teaching, is under the direction of the faculty. The president has little to do with it. Even in the preparation of the budget he fixes only the larger appropriations; specific sums for individual research are usually arranged by the deans or department heads.

Professors dislike to be pinned down in research work. They object on the ground that no general statement can be accurate, that each study must be considered on its merits. This is true, but the president in an institution where research is carried on should have some idea of what the professors are talking about. Also, research is a very important matter in our universities; their reputation depends in considerable degree on the research they do and upon its quality. Perhaps half of the entire budget of some institutions is spent on research.

It is important to stress the great differene that exists among various types of research in the time consumed and the cost. A research problem in chemical engineering on the production of a desired product from crude petroleum, involving the development of a method and the construction of a satisfactory pilot plant that will produce the product, will cost a large sum. On the other hand, a research resulting in the production of a few grams of material in the chemical laboratory will be quite inexpensive.

Contrast the difference in time consumed in developing a strain of oats resistant to a rust and producing sufficient seed for distribution to farmers to propagate the strain, with a laboratory study of the physiology of a plant. The former will require far more time than the latter. So research studies differ greatly in time consumed and in money spent.

H.

Cost of Research in Time

The time required by an able scholar to produce a creditable publication differs in the laboratory sciences from the social sciences, and from one subject to another. Estimates made by several leading men reveal that an average of 1,500 hours, varying from 500 to 3,000 hours, are required for the laboratory work on which a scientific paper is based. Not infrequently, after the work has been done it does not justify publication. In addition, probably from 100 to 150 hours are required for library work and writing the report. In research where laboratory work is not involved, much more time for library work and writing is required. Where field work is involved, a great deal of time is consumed beyond campus boundaries.

For the professor who is on the graduate faculty, advanced students are available for most of the detailed laboratory, library and field work. The time consumed by the professor is limited (1) to conferences with the graduate student, from one to four hours a week, for three to five years; (2) to his seminar; (3) to supplementary library work; (4) to writing the paper to be published. While these labors may extend over two, three, or four years, they will probably not occupy more than 200 to 300 hours in total for each research project. The graduate instructor with five to seven students, graduating two men a year with the doctorate, assuming that he signs jointly with the student, should be able to produce two papers a year with not more than 1,000 hours of time consumed. This means half his time.

Of course, as one considers the numbers of a faculty and their output, this estimate, while correct for some, is certainly wrong for many. Departments will vary. Several students may work along similar lines, one helping the other. In another department, each student will be working at a distinctive subject, so different from the others that only the professor can be of much help.

The value of the thesis for the doctor of philosophy degree lies in the student's learning how a master mind works in his field, how it attacks the various problems that arise. The student must come continuously, for a considerable time, into close contact with his chief, who must give him the time needed for detailed discussion. The student also will learn the limitation of knowledge to be found in books. The differences between fields of research and the concern of the professor for his students explain why some men give a student one hour a week; some, two hours or more. Usually, it is the practice of the professor to speak briefly to each graduate student daily. In general, ten graduate students working on research is a reasonable maximum for any professor, although in some cases exceptional men have handled twice this number. Of all the men in an institution directing work for the doctorate, the great majority have from one to five students on research at one time.

While this represents my own opinion after considerable discussion with men whose judgment I respect, there is little agreement among various groups of university research men on the time required for research.

H.

Cost of Research in Money

It is possible to make a crude estimate of the cost of research by dividing the total money spent specifically for research by the number of published papers. This estimate must be inaccurate for two reasons: considerable research results in no papers being published; thus the divisor is too small. On the other hand, considerable research is paid for in the regular educational budget, exclusive of specific research funds, making the numerator too small. These variants tend to balance each other.

At Iowa State College over a period of seventeen years, 1928–29 to 1944–45 inclusive, $9,672,797 was spent specifically for research. During that period, 5,028 papers were published. On this basis, $1,980 was spent, on the average, for each paper. The expenditures for each problem varied greatly. The above expenditures were exclusive of the general administration and operation of the plant. In an organization where all expenses are included, the cost would be from 50 per cent to 100 per cent higher, or $3,000 to $4,000 for each research project. The figures given cover the period as indicated above. This work would cost more now. The National Research Council estimates the average cost of a research project as $5,000.

We might then say that each published research paper represented 1,500 hours in time and $3,500 in money expended. The above figures include no research by the Institute for Atomic Research in which the costs are higher.

H.

Further Observations on Research

Another matter worthy of attention is, What may we expect of a competent research man in production? If he is teaching classes six or eight hours a week, we may regard him as devoting part time to research, let us say 900 to 1,000 hours in the college year. He might reasonably be expected to supervise six to eight research workers and produce, with his students, two papers a year, two students graduating with the doctor of philosophy degree. This is a conservative estimate, and many able men would produce more. The value of a research man who was doing less than half as much should be questioned.

What savings result from using graduate students as instructors? We must assume that nearly all competent graduate students will be subsidized. Using them as half-time instructors certainly saves money. Assume we pay a graduate assistant $1,000 for half-time teaching. If we substitute a full-time, experienced teacher at $3,500 or $4,000 for two graduate assistants, and continue to support the graduate students on fellowships at $1,000 each with no teaching service, our expenses will go up from $2,000 to $5,500 or $6,000. But the quality of the instruction would probably be materially improved.

On the other hand, if only students with a taste for teaching and who are competent to teach are employed, and if they are adequately supervised, they will do good work and will obtain a valuable experience in teaching.

Why is not more research carried on in the usual denominational or independent liberal arts college? In the first place there is too little time. In a college year of nine months, exclusive of Sundays, there are about 235 days. At eight hours a day, a man has 1,890 work hours. After teaching twelve to fifteen hours a week and attending conscientiously to his other college duties, how can a man find the time for 1,500 hours of research? You say that, of course, he cannot do it all in one year. Agreed. But if he produces one paper over a period of three to four years, is that sufficiently inspiring to hold him at work? Of course, he will lack association with interested workers in his special field under those conditions. Usually he would be unable to secure the funds for essential equipment and other expenses. Also, the library of such a college would be inadequate for his needs. We must conclude that research is impossible for 90 per cent of the staff in our average independent college.

As a matter of fact, few men seriously interested in research will teach in an independent college. Usually they will remain in a university where recognition and opportunity for research are present.

If especial skill in the direction of graduate and research work is desired in the president, the dean of the graduate school should be selected for that office. He would be acquainted with all the productive scholars on the staff; he would be favorably known to all of them; he would be honest and dependable. Such a choice for president would usually prove satisfactory.

H.

Allotment of Research Funds

In fairness to those engaged in research, funds must be provided for the work to be done. Sometimes such monetary aid is furnished by industrial concerns that are interested in some specific project; but in most instances, the support for research, especially in the pursuit of individual problems, must be found within the income of the institution. Now and then a legislature will appropriate a fixed sum for research during the biennial period. In that case the college administration must make the decisions and distribute the grants to the departments or individuals who are working on problems.

One method of doing this is to create a committee of eight or nine persons who know something about research. The dean of the graduate school might well be appointed by the president to act as chairman. The committee then sets up general rules of procedure, and after circulating information, invites applications for grants. The applicant states the nature of his project and follows this with a description of the work he wishes to do with a fairly detailed list of the expenditures involved. When the application is received, the committee discusses it; and if in their judgment the project has merit, an inquirer is appointed from the membership of the committee to talk with the applicant. The inquirer can through sympathetic approval secure additional information and a clear concept of the purpose, methods, and possible results of the proposed research. When the committee meets for final action on the request, it will have before it the original papers and the report of the inquirer. Discussion with questions follow, and a decision results that is fair to the research project and acceptable to the guardians of the funds. As the work goes on, the committee should keep in touch with the progress of the research work.

Since I have seen this bit of administration machinery in action, I have confidence in the competence and fairness of such a committee to allocate funds.

M.

When Should an Institution Enter on Graduate Work?

Many of our stronger four year colleges offer graduate work for a limited number of master's degrees. A reasonable estimate of the cost of this work would be to allow one hour per week of a professor's time to each candidate for the degree. If he had only one graduate student, he might squeeze this one in with his regular teaching load; but if there were two or more, his teaching schedule should be cut down at the rate of one hour per graduate student. If his salary were $4,500 and he had three graduate students, on the basis of a fifteen hour load, one-fifth of his salary, or $900, could be charged to the three graduate students.

As soon as an institution moves into work for the doctorate, several other factors enter: (1) At least one professor must be known for creditable research work and the publication of numerous papers. This teacher would quite certainly be receiving $6,000 or more. (2) The library in the field in which the student worked would have to be adequate and this would mean a goodly array of complete files of various journals in that field. (3) There would have to be a fellowship or an instructorship available for each graduate student, as almost every graduate student, especially in science, is supported by some stipend. (4) There would have to be funds available to meet the cost of needed equipment, supplies and special books. I believe that $4,000 to $5,000 should be available annually to meet the expenses, directly and indirectly, of each student admitted to candidacy for the doctor of philosophy degree. A professor with five or six graduate students should not carry more than one-half the regular teaching load, so half of his salary should be charged to graduate work.

Before offering any kind of graduate work for the doctorate, it should be remembered that all departments are ambitious, and the cost of expanding into other departments must be considered. If adequate funds are available, and if the gains are sufficient to warrant the expense, consideration should be given to the fact that more or less emphasis is bound to be shifted from good teaching to research. Is the future growth and support of the institution sufficient to warrant the move?

One other aspect of the matter is important: Our leading universities offer graduate work in from thirty to thirty-five fields. This is a very costly business. The California Institute of Technology and the Massachusetts Institute of Technology offer the doctorate in less than one-third that number of fields, but their type of work affords a natural barrier to expansion. Every institution in the early stages of developing fields for the doctorate should fix limits within which it can work with distinction. Nothing but discredit can result from the degree offered by an inadequately staffed and equipped department. Work could best be supplied in fields where natural advantages are apparent.

I am satisfied that the policy in regard to graduate work is a matter to which trustees should give careful attention. In 1948–49, 138 institutions conferred the doctor of philosophy degree. I question whether three-fourths of these are prepared to offer such advanced work. In the same year, 438 institutions conferred the master's degree, many of which, also, are open to question.

In no institution should graduate degrees be conferred without the approval of the trustees. The trustees should fully recognize the expense of graduate work before permitting it to be established.

H.

Admission to the Graduate School

There are two conflicting factors affecting admission to the graduate school. On the one hand, only the truly able, outstanding students seem capable of doing creditable graduate work; this tends to limit enrollment. On the other hand, all of our graduates are at work in the world; and if some can manage to return to the university for further study, it is a good thing. It seems wrong to shut them out. This tends to lower admission requirements. The situation is further complicated by the fact that many graduates who entered the teaching profession did not make outstanding undergraduate records, and certainly these people need more training.

Conditions of this sort are met by different institutions in various ways. The graduate students of Princeton University were limited before the war to 250 by trustee action. This number was apportioned among the departments as seemed to meet the situation best. No more may be admitted until some graduate student either graduates or withdraws. This keeps the quality of the students very high, and for Princeton it is a sound policy.

Massachusetts Institute of Technology has a similar plan: The number of graduate students is fixed as at Princeton. Neither of these institutions offers graduate work in education, so no problem of training high school teachers is raised. Many graduates do enter college and university teaching, however.

At many institutions students admitted to the graduate school are limited to those who were graduated from college in the upper third or upper half of their class. This eliminates those who were either dull or lazy, yet avoids a rigid limitation on enrollment.

With few exceptions, only the highest 5 or 10 per cent in a class are promising material for graduate work. Of this group, again only 5 or 10 per cent will have real aptitude for original research. However, as large numbers graduating with master's or doctor's degrees do not pursue research after leaving the graduate college, high research ability need not be required of all who are admitted.

Especially in our state universities, the restriction to the upper third or half of the class will exclude some really desirable students. Many from the lower two-thirds who enter the teaching profession prove to be able teachers or administrators, deeply interested in their work. They need graduate instruction both for their own development and for promotion requirements. Records of professional success should be accepted toward admission to the graduate school.

A number of graduate schools specify only a baccalaureate degree for admission. However, this does not mean admission to study for a degree; this privilege is limited by various restrictions.

There is sometimes an embarrassing feature which occurs in dealing with graduate students. A young man of low or mediocre ability will work closely with his major professor, becoming a slave, actually, in the professor's service. The latter greatly appreciates the student's help and continues him for selfish reasons until the professor feels compelled to urge the young man's admission to candidacy for the doctorate, although related departments know he does not qualify. The graduate dean and faculty hesitate to overrule the strong recommendations of the department head.

While the need for men and women with the training required for the master's and doctor's degree is great, American universities have admitted and graduated more such students than has been warranted by the quality of their scholarship.

In 1948–49, 50,827 master's degrees and 5,293 doctor of philosophy degrees were conferred.

H.

Financial Assistance to Graduate Students

A large proportion of all graduate students are on some kind of a subsidy that approximately covers their expenses. I should say that outside the field of education, this is largely true. Students in education, also, are frequently on scholarships or fellowships, but many come to summer school during their vacation or for a year's work when they have saved enough money. They then return to increased salaries as a result of their accomplishment.

The subsidy for graduate work is justified insofar as it helps to prepare teachers more efficiently. Certainly more than half of all candidates for the doctorate degree look forward to teaching as a profession.

In many of our state universities, the fellowships or graduate assistantships awarded graduate students require half-time work in teaching freshmen and sophomore classes. This certainly lowers the quality of the teaching in a large percentage of cases, unless these graduate assistants have been selected carefully for their teaching ability. While some prove to be excellent teachers, many are inexperienced, have little natural teaching skill, and are so absorbed in their own research work or advanced study that they give little attention to their teaching.

If each department using graduate students as instructors would set up an adequate system for training and supervising them, more could be said in favor of the practice. When one talks to the heads of departments, the problem is usually brushed aside with the statement that supervision is being given or that they can't afford it. I was never able to make any appreciable progress along this line. I doubt if any real progress can be made until a college official with sufficient authority supervises the teaching of all graduate student instructors. I am not suggesting that such an official train these men and women himself. He could, however, see that such training was in effective operation in each department, and force the retirement from teaching jobs of all whom he found to be doing poor teaching, thus compelling the departments to take better care of the situation.

Wherever research touches the teaching of freshmen and sophomores it generally reduces the quality of the teaching. In some instances, it is so inferior to good high school teaching that the students are shocked and disgusted.

We must train many more capable men and women of fine character and personality in our graduate schools. In order to secure students of that type, the institutions must offer to meet their financial needs in large part, but not at the expense of proper instruction in the freshmen and sophomore classes.

H.

Authorship in Publishing Results of Doctoral Theses

There is diversity of practice in the matter of publishing theses, partly due to departmental custom and partly to individual policy.

In some cases the paper is published under the name of the major professor with acknowledgment in the paper to the graduate student who has done the work. In some cases it is published jointly under the name of the professor and the graduate student. In other cases it is published under the name of the graduate student alone, with acknowledgment in the paper to the professor directing the work.

To me this variation is undesirable, often misleading, and should be corrected. It seems to me clear that a doctoral thesis should be published under the joint authorship of the directing professor and the graduate student. I hold this view for the following reasons:

1. In most graduate schools, quite a number of the best men are so fully occupied with large numbers of graduate students and their teaching duties that they are unable to carry on independent research. If the graduate student is assigned the sole authorship of the paper, the professor's name never appears. This is ridiculous and unnecessary.
2. If the professor publishes the paper under his own name alone, it is unfair to the student who has spent from one to three years of hard work on the subject. His name certainly should be listed as joint author.
3. **The professor is known in his special field; his name with that of the graduate student would give weight and an appropriate introduction of the new Doctor of Philosophy to the research men in his field. It would give more rather than less significance to the thesis.**
4. A professor occasionally believes that the graduate student has worked so hard and has done so well that he deserves to be given the sole credit of authorship. I would contend that such a man will publish later many more papers under his own name, and that this first paper would receive more attention if published under the joint authorship of professor and student.
5. In the graduating ceremony, frequently the professor under whom the thesis was written presents the man who is candidate to the dean of the graduate school for awarding of his degree. He thus presents his student to the audience. By publishing the thesis under a joint authorship, the professor presents his student to the men in his field of work all over the country.
6. While I have never directed graduate work, I cannot conceive that the part of the major professor in producing the thesis is of minor importance. Even with the ablest graduate students, the influence of the major professor in conference for from one to three years on a piece of research must be profound. The less able student would be only an instrument in the hands of the professor. His subject, his methods of work and all that he did would come directly from that source.

For the above reasons I look forward to a day when all papers resulting from a doctor of philosophy thesis will be published jointly by the professor who directed the work and the student who did the work and received the degree.

H.

Authorship in Publishing Results of Doctoral Theses

My colleague maintains that the name of the professor under whom the dissertation has been written should appear as a joint author on the title page of the thesis. To this position, I take some exception.

The thesis of the graduate student is supposed to be a piece of individual work. It is the business of the professor to discuss with the student the topic and field of the dissertation, and to suggest where material is to be found. The candidate does his search for material, makes his own bibliography, organizes the material, and writes his thesis. The supposition of thesis writing is that the graduate student has reached sufficient maturity to produce a scholarly piece of work. Co-operative authorship with too much guidance stands in the way of independent work by retarding the purpose of a thesis as a doctoral requirement.

I have seen a good deal of abuse arising from joint authorship. A professor has a special piece of work he wants done and uses the graduate student as a helper, and so looks upon him as an assistant, instead of an independent student. In the days when the German university was regarded highly as a source of graduate work, the head of a laboratory required that all theses worked out in his laboratory bear his name as senior author. The procedure is now followed in some of the American universities largely for the purpose of glorifying the head of the department. It can be said that now and then, especially in the field of science, the head has a co-operative piece of work that requires research on several problems. These projects are co-ordinated and constitute a joint piece of research. In such an instance, the names of the workers should appear on the title page.

Nor do I feel with Hughes that more attention would be given to the student's thesis if the name of the professor under whom the student works appeared on the title page. The best aids to the wider circulation of the thesis are the names of the department and the university in which the work has been done. When my colleague writes that he looks to the day when all papers resulting from a doctor of philosophy thesis will be published jointly by the professor directing the work and the student who did the work and receives the degree, I think he overstates his case. What is needed in these days is greater independence and self-reliance on the part of students. This desirable quality, in my opinion, cannot be secured by such supervision as suggested in Hughes' comment.

In addition to the doctor of philosophy degree, the colleges and departments of education in some of the larger institutions have conferred the doctor of education degree without a thesis requirement; but courses have been added which the candidate is required to finish before receiving his degree. The argument for this procedure is that the student learns more by giving his time to his studies. There is something to be said for this requirement for the degree. The candidate hopes to teach or work as an administrative officer and does not expect to do research. Nevertheless, I think the lowering of the requirements for the doctorate in any field is a mistake. A thesis is, after all, a test of a candidate's ability to formulate his conclusions after considerable investigation. The value of such a procedure is very great; in following it, the candidate gains something that no other method affords.

M.

Joint Research—Interdepartmental Committees

As research grows increasingly valuable, it becomes more and more difficult for many desirable projects to be handled by a single man. Important projects tend to fall within two or more usually accepted fields of research.

Corrosion is an example. At the Massachusetts Institute of Technology, research on this subject is under a committee representing chemical engineering, metallurgy, chemistry, physical chemistry, electrochemistry, and marine engineering. Similar committees representing all departments concerned are set up to deal with research on accoustics, air conditioning, heat transfer, housing, and solar energy conversion.

The old research method of one individual's carrying on research alone, in semi-privacy, cannot solve many vitally important problems. Ability to work agreeably with others becomes important. Research used to be a field where extreme introverts were directed. A selfish desire to work alone limits the value of a research man.

H.

Writing Books

Many research men look with more or less scorn on book writing. As a matter of fact, there is scarcely any field where an able man can be more useful.

As the field of knowledge broadens, it becomes more and more difficult to decide what should be included in a textbook. Furthermore, Americans do not excel in writing textbooks that are both clear and interesting. We are prone to use technical language unnecessarily. Englishmen surpass us as intelligible writers on technical subjects. We need more experts in the field of science who can write good textbooks.

Textbooks for pupils in the seventh and eighth grades and high school are of immense importance. These young people must learn the most that they will ever know right there. From four to six years must embrace all they will learn of our total knowledge. What is to be included, what omitted, how much space for each subject, are difficult decisions that ought to be made by the wise and learned. Then to write so that it will intrigue the largest number of students! Many textbooks hold not a shade of fascination for anybody. They are written on the basis of take it or leave it policy. Our future leaders in thinking are there now among the upper grade and high school students, ready to be fascinated and inspired, ready to enter the realms of science or of the humanities for the benefit of the world. Yet there are those who scorn the writing of textbooks.

Outside of textbooks, writers are badly needed—gifted writers who know some field of science. While perhaps a few million men and women more or less understand the advances that are being made in science, there are scores of millions who do not understand any of it. If we had writers who could popularize such advances in books and magazines, they would be of tremendous value in bridging the gap between the pioneers in science and millions of our citizens.

Far too much scientific writing is addressed solely to the learned in a specific field. This is not to say that such articles are not valuable; they are valuable but not enough. One feels that scientists are afraid people outside their field might understand their writings. Hence they use far more technical words than necessary. We need more popular writers who can be understood by the masses and whose writings interest and intrigue them.

An enormous number of college texts lack all elements of fascination and allure. Too often they set the standard for the professor who uses them. They entirely disregard the fact that any man studies eagerly what interests him. No effort is made to charm or excite the student in the great field of knowledge under discussion. One might easily conclude that the writer himself has no genuine interest in his field and writes only under compulsion.

I maintain that any really able writer of books, textbooks for children or college youth, or popular books for the masses, is quite as valuable a staff member as the research man who produces one or two learned papers a year with the help of graduate students, for the benefit of the very few.

H.

University Research Foundations

With the great increase in the volume of research, the problem of patents and the income from patents on the basis of work done on college time and in college laboratories has grown. Perhaps this problem has been especially acute in publicly supported institutions, but the situation is largely the same everywhere.

An increasing number of institutions (52 in 1951) have established research foundations to handle patents based on the discoveries of staff members. The foundations apply for the patents and meet all the costs. The patent rights are assigned to the foundation, which then bears all the expense of defending the patent and assumes all the responsibility for exploiting the production and sale of the patented article. Conditions of operation vary among the several foundations.

Some institutions prefer to ignore the patent problem entirely. They fear the possible commercialism resulting and the deflection of valuable men from research to the pursuit of patents. I doubt if this fear is justified. In the first eleven years after the foundation at Iowa State College was incorporated, 4,070 research publications were issued and 117 patents applied for, only a few of which were of real value. Most research results certainly will not justify financially any attempt to patent them. Patentable research results will always be exceptional.

Of the 117 patents applied for by the Iowa State College Research Foundation in the eleven year period, 10 were rejected, 23 expired, 51 were granted and 23 were pending. The foundation had forty-six active agreements from thirty-nine of which some income accrued.

The average staff member is not a businessman; he has meager knowledge as to the patentability of a process. He hesitates to pay for a patent and has small resources with which to defend a patent in litigation. He has little understanding of the way to handle the business and to exploit the patent. In all these matters a research foundation can be of great aid.

At Iowa State College, the research foundation sets aside a fixed percentage of receipts for administrative expenses and litigation expenses. It thus has available resources for dealing with all expenses regardless of the income from any individual patent. The net resources of the foundation are available only for the promotion of research.

The amount of net income from the patent paid to the staff member who assigns the patent to the foundation varies from 10 to 25 per cent among the majority of foundations.

Patents and income from patents involve difficult questions on any campus where much research is in progress. While certainly a research foundation does not answer all questions or stop all discussion, we feel that it provides the least objectionable way of dealing with patents.

H.

Wider Use of University Foundations

This organization device can be used for other purposes than that of research alone. The placing of research funds in the control of a separately incorporated foundation gives the board operating freedom that it does not have under a college charter. The control of such a foundation by the selection of trustees from the administrative officers, members of the board of trustees and college staff insures that the policies are not antagonistic to those of the college. Public institutions are hampered constantly by state finance officers who demand that all receipts of the state college or university shall be deposited in state accounts and drawn upon only by the approval of the state finance officers. Recently, legislatures have created state building commissions which are given a lump sum to be used by the building commission as its members may determine. Incidentally, the governor of a state where such a commission exists can use the authority placed in the commission to help his political ambitions.

When such developments in state control of an institution's funds are fully established, the freedom of the institution is considerably handicapped; and if the control is pushed to limits, it may result in curtailing the usefulness of the institution. The wider use of a university foundation can be helpful in protecting a public college or university. For instance, scholarship funds established from private gifts can be administered by it. Even gifts for building could be placed with the foundation; and in that way, free the construction from entanglement with contractors and architects who secure jobs as politicians rather than as experts in the building and planning fields.

Some abuses may arise when the trustees conclude that they can go into business and, thus, free from taxation the earnings produced by the operations of the business. This is an evasion of the purposes of the tax exemptions allowed educational institutions. The ethics of public responsibility should eliminate any such methods in conducting an educational institution. There is, however, in the use of a university foundation, a genuine instrument by which an institution can protect private funds against misuse by overambitious state officers.

M.

The religious life of a college is worthy of considerable attention from faculty members and students. In a state educational institution such activity is left to the churches and outside organizations for the most part. There is much to be gained by bringing to the campus outstanding religious leaders who will stimulate and unite the different groups toward a co-operative purpose, that of encouraging the spiritual development of the students.

10.

College Chapel, the Library, and Other Matters

College Chapel

Fifty years ago, daily chapel was held on almost every college and university campus. Usually attendance was required. A hymn was sung, the scripture was read, a prayer was offered, and a second song closed the service. Perhaps some announcements were made. It was a daily, official recognition of an overruling Power with which the institution desired to keep in harmony. Chapel was nonsectarian.

The value of chapel was never debated in the day of the small college; it was accepted without argument. As the institutions grew, students could not be accommodated in the chapel. When fewer clergymen were appointed as college presidents, there was less insistence upon a religious service. When student organizations increased in number and importance, chapel notices became a nuisance. Gradually the service was discontinued.

The writer attended chapel at Oxford, England, before the first World War. All students were required to be present. "Dirty rollers" were students who tumbled out of bed and went to answer chapel roll call in pajamas and overcoat without having performed their ablutions. In the 1920's, I attended an Oxford Chapel again and found practically no one there but the choir and the clergyman. The war was very hard on the college chapel.

And so it was abandoned for the most part. There had been a very real social value in assembling the students and faculty together once a day. How much of a spiritual imprint was made on the average student, it is difficult to say. Certainly, it was appropriate and desirable to have the entire student body bow before God each day and recognize His supreme authority. Few institutions have the facilities and means to continue a dignified, optional chapel service as is still carried on at Harvard University. If required chapel can be resumed; I am for it. An optional chapel requires a paid choir, and certainly the attendance will rarely justify the effort and expense.

H.

College Chapel

In the dictionary, several meanings are given for the word *chapel*; in fact, nine appear in the pages of a recent publication. These definitions begin with the statement that a chapel is a private or subordinate place of prayer or worship. From there the word is extended to mean a room or building for worship in a college or a royal court. In the ninth definition, the word *chapel* is defined as a body of printers belonging to a printing house. Although used in several other relations, in the college world *chapel* is identified with an assembly of students where a varied program is carried on, with scripture reading, a short prayer, sometimes brief remarks, closing with a variety of announcements, changes in schedules, meeting arrangements and pep talks. The chapel services in early days had a purpose now almost wholly lost. As a matter of fact, the daily meeting under the pressure of time schedules has been superseded by weekly or monthly assemblies. Without doubt something of value has disappeared with this change.

In his comment on the value of prayer to a college president my colleague has made a simple but eloquent plea for the spiritual faith of a college president. If prayer can be of great help to him, it would be of equal help to students. A president would do well to meditate upon this problem.

The YMCA, YWCA, and the Gibbon clubs make a contribution to the religious life of a modern college, but the accomplishments of these organizations are limited. In denominational schools, a full-time chaplain can be brought into the staff without difficulty; but in a public institution, this method of dealing with the religious life of the students would meet with criticism from various sectarian groups. It is possible to encourage denominations to erect chapels, dormitories, and even to establish theological schools near the campus of a large university. This has been done in numerous instances, but the value of such efforts rests upon the sympathetic and helpful co-operation of all concerned.

M.

The Library

The importance of a library to a college becomes apparent as one studies the need it fills. Having taught chemistry in a college prior to becoming its president, I took a number of years to realize that the library should be generously supported. It was difficult for me to believe that more money should be spent for the staff than for the books, journals and bindings in a library. It was hard to understand that inevitably a considerable portion of books bought would be used very little, if at all. I did not know that next to the college faculty itself, the library was the most important adjunct of a college.

However, I did finally learn the prime value of a college or university library. In 1932, due to the great depression, our appropriation at Iowa State College was cut 27 per cent; and all faculty salaries were, of necessity, reduced. I explained our financial difficulties to the faculty and asked them if cuts should be made in equipment and supplies or in library support. They were unanimously of the opinion that the library should not be cut; so we carried it on with normal funds, except in salaries. It is certainly a high compliment indeed to say of an institution that its library is adequate in staff, journals and books.

In designing a new library building, convenience in service and use should be the controlling factor, not architectural beauty. A competent architect can meet the utilitarian needs of such a place to the full satisfaction of a good librarian and still produce a beautiful building. Far too often, the architect has been allowed to overrule the librarian and to design a monumental building regardless of its use. Then the librarian is obliged to fit the library into it as best he can. This is a deplorable situation, and more to be regretted with the passing years.

It is now considered sound for a library to provide seating capacity in the reading room for from one-tenth to one-fourth of the student enrollment. This allows for variation in the type of institution and the degree in which it is necessary to use the library for study purposes.

Stacks are rarely large enough to hold all the books. If a separate building fitted with stacks is available as a storage building, one-fourth or more of the collection can be installed there. Many books of value are rarely called for but should be within easy reach when needed.

The problems of a college and a university library differ greatly. In a university where extensive research is carried on, more money might be required to support the library each year. For every field in which an institution does extensive research, a university library should have the leading journals in every language in which they are printed. At present, a few institutions are conferring the doctorate in from thirty to thirty-five fields. Even these great universities are not at the forefront in more than half of their fields; but in their most distinguished areas, and in related subjects, they probably have extensive collections of journals and books. The library budgets of thirteen universities exceed $450,000 a year; of these, eight run from $600,000 to $1,100,000. Annual statistics on library operation and maintenance are available from a number of sources, including *College and Research Libraries, Statistics of Southern College and*

University Libraries, and *Statistics for College and University, Libraries for the Fiscal Year* collected by the Princeton Library.

Quite the most important thing about a library is the librarian. If he is of first class caliber, the money appropriated for the library will be well spent; the service to patrons will be good and every department will have, within the limits of its resources, all the books and journals it needs. Certainly, a salary as large as any dean in the college receives, is due a high-grade librarian.

One serious problem is to secure a librarian who can with equal knowledge and understanding deal with both the humanities and the sciences. Probably in a great university, the head librarian should qualify fully in the more important of the two fields, while an associate librarian should supplement him in the other field.

In my opinion, a university library should not spend money for rare books simply because they are rare. Some scarce and rare books which cannot be borrowed may have to be purchased from time to time for the use of a department. They should not be bought for the gratification of a librarian who fancies such a collection.

The best test of the efficiency of the management of a library is the average length of time that elapses between filing the call slip and receiving the book requested or the information that it is out. This should not consume more than two minutes for any book in current use.

The reference librarians can add enormously to the usefulness of the library. It is astonishing how much information a competent reference librarian can make available quickly.

One fact about a library that greatly astonished me is that it costs at least 4 dollars to put a book on the stack room shelf—that is, to order, receive, catalog and shelve a book. If some person gives the library one hundred books and the library agrees to shelve them, the most will be at least four hundred dollars less the clerical expense of ordering. No gift of books, unless a notable collection, should be accepted where conditions are imposed. Neither should a library accept gifts of books unless they definitely fit into the institutional programs.

When browsing through a library, I have often been disappointed to find many volumes with the leaves uncut and other unmistakable signs that the books have not been used. This will inevitably occur, but probably with not more than 5 per cent of the books in a good library.

In every department, some staff member should be assigned the responsibility of maintaining the books of that department on as high a level as possible. No librarian can keep up with all the books published in every field. However, a competent member of the staff of a department, collaborating with the librarian, can usually handle the selection of books adequately. I have felt that most of the unused books were bought through lack of proper co-operation between the department staff and the librarian.

The subject of the advisability of department libraries always creates argument unless plenty of money is available. There is such an interlocking of departments, every field being forced to rely on work in other related fields, that there must be one library for all. There are exceptions, as in the case of a law library, and possibly in a few other instances. Where funds are available to duplicate all or part of the volumes in the main library, a department library would prove most useful. However, in this instance, it should remain subject to the main library and under the direct control of a librarian on the library staff. Otherwise the department library may quickly degenerate. No department should be permitted to withdraw all books in its field from the main library for permanent deposit elsewhere. Otherwise quite as many people in related fields would be embarrassed for lack of books as were aided by the department library.

Another point relative to handling the library book fund is often in debate. Shall the fund be divided and a certain amount placed at the disposal of each department or shall it be left in a lump sum in the hands of the librarian? Certainly, if the total sum is small, there is something to be said in favor of dividing it and giving each department a few dollars for books. As I see it, wherever the library fund is anywhere nearly adequate, it should be left at the disposal of the librarian. A competent librarian knows pretty well the relative needs of each department, and he can weigh the different requests for books and journals better than anyone else. If a person feels he is being unfairly treated, he can always appeal to the library committee. The earnest desire of the librarian to supply everyone with the books he needs will obligate him to be fair to all.

The library should certainly be close to the president's heart.

H.

The Library

Piles of old magazines, books of ancient origin, and valuable records are to be found in every college library building. Meantime, new purchases, current periodicals and newspapers pour into the acquisitions department. Libraries are understaffed, the piling up of printed material goes on until the pressure for space becomes a matter of major concern, and the functioning of the library as an important factor in the educational plans of an institution is hampered and restricted.

This problem presses for a solution! The obvious answer is simply to increase the size of the building where the books and printed materials belonging to the institution are housed. But to do this is often impossible, because the library building is a unit on many campuses that cannot be increased in size without marring the original building. The question thus presented was regarded as so important that a number of the larger universities not far from Chicago asked one of the foundations to make a survey of the situation and to report a remedy. As a consequence, the surveyors suggested that a large fireproof building be constructed near Chicago where the less used books of those institutions might be stored. A small staff was to be provided to keep the records and a system of exchange so organized that books when needed on any of the member campuses, could be supplied. The plan has great merit.

At the University of Kentucky, a large library building was erected in 1935. The stacks in the building were capable of holding 400,000 volumes. At the end of ten years, the stacks were filled.

It was impossible to add to the building but it was possible to provide storage space in the new maintenance building for 300,000 volumes. When this building is completed, reports and seldom used volumes will be sent there, and the library proper can expand for another ten years without much difficulty.

The answer to the question of space in library stacks for the increasing acquisitions is: First, an adequate library building which will continue to be the center of administration for all the book collections; second, a fireproof storage building located on the edge of the campus; third, provision for a small staff to manage the storage space; fourth, a co-operative exchange system to move the books required in other parts of the campus. The storage building should be planned and built so that it can be added to as the need arises.

There are two questions on which I wish to comment in connection with what has been written. One has to do with the direction and control; the other, with the storage of books as a library problem.

The general proposition is that all books in college departmental and central libraries should be under the direction and control of the university librarian, for in no other way can the book property of the institution be properly guarded, accessed, and placed. Department libraries are notoriously limited in the service they render, especially if there is no one in charge during regular hours. Some member of the department may give part time to the library, and more often a student is employed to be on hand for a limited period. If this library is not closely associated with the central library, a duplication of book purchases follows, and money is not used to the best advantage. If departmental libraries are really needed, and an argument can be made for that point of view, they should be placed under a trained librarian, appointed by the director of libraries.

Book purchases should be made by the director, and all books catalogued in the control office and library so that the seeker after knowledge may learn where the books he desires may be found. Professors have a way of removing books from departmental libraries and placing them on office shelves, a practice that makes accounting of books difficult, if not impossible. All this points to the necessity for definite central control of the book resources of a university.

With the immense influx of publications, the housing and storage of materials will reach a stage necessitating the enlargement of stacks. Many college libraries are filled and all stack space taken. As a result, side rooms and basements are used to house the material. Often the accumulation remains for years without classification and cataloguing. This situation is highly unsatisfactory and a source of embarrassment when a donor wishes to see the books he has given to the library. The directors of libraries are more and more often making a classification of those books that might be used and needed, and those infrequently used. The latter can be placed in storage, thus increasing the efficiency of the central library.

Unadorned buildings, fireproofed and planned for space, can be erected on the outskirts of the campus without marring the building arrangements. In the case of colleges in a congested area, a building can be erected co-operatively which would take care of the storage problem of several institutions. In the course of a decade, the need for more storage space will certainly arise, so the problem must be dealt with on a long range plan. Perhaps the use of microfilms, microcards, and other forms of micro-reproduction will bring relief to storage problems.

M.

The Library Stack Room

I hold some opinions about library buildings which I regard as important, but many librarians may not agree with me. Any college president facing the question of a new library or additions to the library should give consideration to the size of the stack room.

As I see it, a working library should have the smallest possible practical stack room plus a separate and adequate storage stack room elsewhere on the campus. My firm conviction is that promptness in service is a very great advantage to library patrons. If the stacks are not too large, it is possible to hand the patron the desired book within two to three minutes. If the stack room is large relative to the collection, there may be no pressure upon the librarian to arrange the books for prompt service and the time taken in delivery to the patron will be increased from ten to fifteen minutes, as in many of our large libraries.

It is reasonable to consider the problems of library book storage over a period of 1,000 years, as a college or university is one of the most permanent institutions in the world, regardless of what political, economic or social changes may occur. Furthermore, the library is and must continue to be the heart of such an institution.

To be definite, let us consider the libraries of the several leading separate land-grant institutions that limit their work to their major subjects. For any of our ten to fifteen greatest universities, which cover twice as many fields as do the lesser schools, double the book capacity would be required. Using data from the library of a land-grant college as a basis for discussion, we have available the following facts: Library operations were started about 1870 and the library now includes more than 400,000 volumes. About 13,500 volumes a year are added, roughly 7,000 volumes of periodicals and 6,500 books. In future years, it is safe to assume there will be an annual average increase of 15,000 volumes, 8,000 periodicals and 7,000 books. In 1,000 years, that will mean 15,000,000 volumes added to the present 400,000 unless vigorous weeding is done, or micro-reproductions are used at least in part.

During the years of operation some 10,000 catalogued volumes were disposed of. In 1950, this amounted to 1,400 of which most were worn out or obsolete. There is small relief to be expected from the discarding of valueless books unless a more drastic policy is adopted.

The library cited accommodates about 250,000 volumes in the stacks, 10,000 on open shelves in reading rooms and 140,000 housed in a separate book storage building. The library stacks are inadequate, and plans are under way for an addition. Just how much stack room is needed in this library and storage building?

Most periodicals more than twenty-five years old can be

removed to the storage building. When additional stacks in the library are available, files for thirty years could well be retained in the library. Eight thousand volumes of periodicals a year for thirty years would amount to 240,000 volumes of periodicals to be housed in the library stacks.

On the average, books are not useful as long as periodicals, and most books can be moved to the storage building after twenty years. Space in library stack room would be required for 20 x 7,000, or 140,000, volumes. The minimum requirements for the library stack room would then be 380,000, and 500,000 would give a very comfortable permanent storage capacity.

How can we estimate the necessary capacity of a book storage building? I should say it should hold, on the average, (some could be discarded sooner) all periodicals as far back as 100 years. Since files for the last thirty years will be held in the library, those for seventy years must be kept in storage—70 x 8,000, or 560,000, volumes of periodicals must be held in storage.

In a similar estimate, the average book need not be held over seventy-five years. As those twenty years old or less will still be in the library, 55 x 7,000, or 385,000, volumes must be held in storage. This gives a minimum necessary storage capacity of 945,000, or 1,000,000 volumes.

By what process can books be discarded in order to avoid serious mistakes? I suggest that while the storage building need not be built all at one time, sufficient space should be provided to allow a series of stacks to be set aside for discards. Each year the shelves should be gone over and all books apparently of no value and those which have been on hand more than fifty years, or periodicals more than seventy-five years should be removed to the shelves for discarded books. These books could be held for twenty-five years, during which time all volumes among the discards that are called for should be moved back to the regular storage shelves.

When discarded books have been kept for twenty-five years without having been called for, they may be safely sold or given away. This technique of discarding might be modified after some years of experimenting. Perhaps many books could be transferred to discarded book shelves after a shorter period. It seems to me that 1,500,000 would be the maximum number of books for a land-grant college to hold at any time in library and book storage buildings, over the next thousand years.

Three more things should be mentioned: (1) The book storage building while stressing utility should be built to preserve the books. It should be of fireproof construction. It should have the temperature so regulated as to prevent such heat in summer as will tend to destroy the books, or such cold in winter as would make visits to the stack rooms painful. Some means should be provided to regulate moisture and eliminate impurities in the air. Protection must be provided against insects and rodents. (2) It seems practical to store conveniently in stacks three books per cubic foot of space; that is, a space 10 by 10 by 10, or 1,000 cubic feet, of normal stack room space will house 3,000 books. In most institutions a building of such size would not all be needed at one time, and should be designed to be built in sections as needed. (3) The use of microfilms and especially microcards will undoubtedly increase. The microcard carrying forty-eight pages or more on a three by five card has great possibilities. These cards occupy very little space and appear to be much less perishable than microfilms and much more convenient to use. However, so long as a book is available, I believe it is to be preferred to a microcard or film. The wide use of the latter may reduce the amount of storage space needed; it will certainly not increase it.

In spite of the inconvenience, the separate book storage building will contribute more to library efficiency than if it is incorporated in the library building itself. The separate building will necessitate moving books out of the library on their way to oblivion. Books mistakenly transferred can be brought back. The relative uselessness of certain books can be more clearly established in a separate building.

While the above discussion applies directly to institutions offering work for the doctorate and of necessity subscribing to large numbers of periodicals, the same reasoning can be applied to any college library. If only 5,000 volumes are acquired annually, in 1,000 years that will amount to 5,000,000 volumes. Some rational and insistent method of elimination must be followed. I can see no good reason why an undergraduate library should ever contain more than 300,000 or 500,000 volumes. The tendency of the librarian will certainly be to hold on to the books. Some effective plan should be enforced to discard useless books and keep the library down to a size that can be efficiently and economically operated. Our colleges are all young, none more than 200 or 300 years old; and these matters are not yet too pressing, but they must be kept in mind.

H.

A University Press

About forty institutions hold membership in the Association of American University Presses. Perhaps fifteen or twenty additional institutions might well consider establishing a university press.

My experience with a university press has been confined to Iowa State College, from 1927 on. It was established in 1924 to print the student publications of the college. These consisted of the college daily, the annual, and the various other undergraduate publications. In 1924, $10,000 had been accumulated by the several publications, and under the leadership of the head of the journalism department, secondhand equipment was bought and established in a basement room. The Iowa State College Press in 1951 had its own building, had modern and ample equipment, employed about thirty-five full-time and eighty-five part-time workers and has done all this out of earnings without any subsidy. The book department was added in 1934 and in 1951 accounted for 65 per cent of the total volume of business. We feel that the Press is a very important part of the college.

Since every institution has a number of student publications, it would seem rather simple to duplicate this procedure, except that today a sum larger than $10,000 would be required at the start.

The university presses may be classified in two ways: Those which are expected to be self-supporting and those which operate with a substantial subsidy. Again, some operate their own printing plants as at Iowa State College, while others, as at the University of North Carolina, contract their printing. It is convenient to have the printing done on the campus, but financially there is little advantage. Where a subsidy is provided, more books of less general appeal can be published. However, where the press is self-supporting, it still feels a major obligation to produce a number of definitely worth-while books though they may be individually unprofitable. The deficit, if any, is met from earnings on books that have a wide sale.

The Iowa State College Press publishes the *Iowa State Journal of Science,* and the *Farm Policy Forum.* The exchanges received for the former are turned over to the library and are of considerable value. The latter journal has a more general circulation, by subscription.

If a university press is established, it should have the careful attention which Professor Blair Converse of the journalism department gave to the Iowa State College Press at its inception. While this press has received no college subsidy, we have never felt that it was seriously handicapped in accepting manuscripts. It questioned primarily whether or not the material was valuable and well written. Most books that have been published have sold reasonably well. However, it is true that many of these books would never have been published by a commercial publisher. Certainly our press has encouraged the production of scholarly books by the members of the faculty. Three out of four of the authors are from the Iowa State College community.

H.

Art in College Halls

Some twenty-five years ago, Dr. John Rea, professor of English at Miami, asked me for money to put above the blackboard in his classroom a frieze of pictures of interest to students of literature. He said that while a class should never be dull, a series of pictures would give the students additional inspiration. The idea pleased me, and when the pictures were in place, I felt that they lifted both their surroundings and the subjects they interpreted.

Sometime later, I was called to Iowa State College and found enormous areas of bare wall. Following Dr. Rea's idea, I appointed an art committee with a very capable chairman and put $300 in the budget for pictures. I continued this each year as long as I made out the budget. From this small yearly sum, in eight years more than 300 prints of celebrated paintings were purchased, framed and hung on our walls. Later, many more were added. Thousands of boys and girls from humble homes have looked upon these masterpieces in halls and classrooms, and I am sure they have learned as much as a $3,000 professor employed with the same money for one year could have taught them.

H.

Art on the Campus

There is a place on a campus for art. A college should emphasize the use and the spirit of beauty. Such art is not limited to collections of paintings and sculpture, but embraces landscaping, architecture, music, and drama. Art collections, landscapes, and architecture are available to all who come on the campus; thus the visitor in search of spiritual as well as material beauty is favorably impressed.

Most art collections owned by colleges are confined to portraits of eminent members and distinguished alumni. These are interesting enough, but something more is needed if true culture is to be afforded the students and visitors to a college. Large collections are expensive, and to be at their best must be kept clean and exhibited in well-lighted galleries. But the college can own a few fine paintings and place them in strategic positions in halls and reception rooms. As a department of art is developed, the care of pictures can be turned over to its head. For students to enjoy and appreciate the graphic arts, it is desirable to have well chosen reproductions of good pictures available to them. This can be done by creating a lending plan by which the student may have a good picture in his room for a month or a semester at a nominal fee. Fraternities and sororities have been known to turn gladly to such a plan and to use it in giving distinction to their houses. When this is done, the students become interested; thus there is talk and resultant understanding and appreciation of good pictures and art.

Modern art and contemporary art are one and the same thing. All art at one time was modern, but this fact is not taken too seriously by those who have a preconceived idea of what art is. To be good a picture must be within their range of what art should be. So in a scientific day the artist tries to attune his thinking to the new turn in what is proving a disturbing period. To do this he turns to abstraction, realism or surrealism as a means of conveying his message; as a result he finds himself under heavy fire from those who have their own ideas of art. This situation can be a source of grave criticism when an art department sponsors a modern art exhibit. If it is an exhibit of modern art, the visitors do not understand it; thus a barrage of criticism falls on the college and particularly on the art department. "Is that art? Then none of it for me," is the central theme of the criticism. The college loses prestige in the opinion of most citizens, and the cause of art in that community is stymied for the time being.

A good many questions enter into this situation, such as the freedom of expression for the artist. Looked at from a long range view, one can say that it is far from wise to antagonize the public, but by a careful selection of pictures, modern art may in time be accepted in principle. Some of this art is pretty awful and retards the growth of the art spirit when presented to a public that has not been prepared. Hence the wise department head proceeds slowly, and by degrees builds a public taste that is tolerant to the work of the modern artist and thus is eager to see and accept the best in modern art. Just as the army commander can get his skirmishers too far in advance of the main body of his troops, so an art department can go too far beyond the understanding of the public. It is a wise department of art that understands this. Time is the essence in producing a genuine appreciation of modern art, so that the public can tolerate, accept and enjoy what the artist is trying to say.

M.

A Cultural Course for Students

An account of an interesting plan to utilize the support of both town and university in the maintenance of a great program of music and lectures may be of value and encouragement to college heads who have dreamed of such a co-operative enterprise.

The scene is in Lexington, Kentucky; the participants, the Central Kentucky Community Concert Association, the Lecture Forum and the University of Kentucky. For many years the association's budget was limited, and the membership arbitrarily fixed by the size of the hall available; the forum dragged along with a small attendance and a mediocre list of speakers, while the university maintained a program of speakers and musical concerts, which was not too satisfactory. At this point, the university erected a modern auditorium capable of seating 15,000 people and called the new building the Memorial Coliseum. The popular idea conceived the new building as a gigantic basketball court with a large number of seats for spectators. But the university had more extended plans for the use of this fine building, which ideas in due course of time were presented to the association and the forum. The control of programs was left to the association with the university to be represented on the committee in charge of the program.

The university was to pay toward the support of the program two dollars for each student enrolled. The association and the forum were to measure their membership at a minimum of 3,000 subscribers. In the past, the budgets of these two organizations were in the neighborhood of $9,000. Under the new plan, the total budget was as follows: University of Kentucky supplying 7,000 students or $14,000; the association membership, 3,000 at six dollars each or $18,000, a total of $32,000 or three and one-half times the previous expenditures of the two organizations. The university, in addition to the student fees, would furnish the building, lights, heat and staff without cost to the new program. Thus, by combined and co-operative effort, a great and notable series has been provided for both students and citizens.

Under the separate and former organizations, the concerts were limited to five numbers, while the lecture course conducted by the forum included four addresses. The two admission tickets cost the subscriber nine dollars without tax. The new plan called on the subscriber to pay six dollars without tax for the eleven programs of the year. The change and improvement in the offerings are shown by the artists included in the billing:

James Melton, leading tenor of the Metropolitan Opera; the London Philharmonic-Orchestra, conducted by Sir Thomas Beecham; Don Cossack Chorus; Jascha Heifetz, violinist; Elena Nikolaidi, Greek contralto; Arthur Rubenstein, pianist; Dallas Symphony Orchestra, Walter Hendi conducting with William Kapella as piano soloist; Charles Laughton, actor of radio, screen and stage; and Eleanor Roosevelt, United States delegate to the United Nations.

Those familiar with artists and lecture lists need no argument in favor of the high quality of the entertainment offered under this co-operative plan. Complaints of exclusive membership can no longer be made; there are now seats for all. So, outside of possible differences regarding artists, no obstacles appear to stand in the way of the success of this great cultural program.

M.

A Creative Artist on the Campus

Dr. and Mrs. Edgar Stillman-Kelley were on the faculty of the Western College at Oxford, Ohio, for ten or fifteen years. Dr. Stillman-Kelley was maintained on a fellowship, and Mrs. Stillman-Kelley was a teacher of piano. They were both highly regarded, valuable members of the staff.

In 1919, Dr. and Mrs. Kelley came to me and suggested that Miami University invite Percy Mackeye to come to Miami as a fellow in poetry. They suggested that a modest salary and a house would be attractive to him. I presented the matter to the trustees, who became interested in the idea; and in the fall of 1920, Mr. and Mrs. Mackeye and their daughter came to Oxford and entered upon this arrangement. A simple one-room frame studio in which he planned to work and to meet the students was built among the trees of the lower campus at Mr. Mackeye's suggestion.

One evening a week, Mr. Mackeye invited to this studio the students who were interested in creative writing. From fifteen to thirty came and were highly entertained and stimulated by Mr. Mackeye's reading and discussion of poetry. While in Oxford, Mr. Mackeye also wrote several notable narrative poems. This arrangement with the poet continued for four years. Later on, under President Alfred H. Upham, Ridgely Torrence held a fellowship in poetry for several years at Miami University.

On inquiry I learned that no poet can make a living from his poetry; $1,000 a year in royalties is probably the highest amount earned by our most distinguished poets. The same is true of musicians who write symphonies. It is largely the case with sculptors and painters who have not won wide recognition. The idea occurred to me that from fifty to one hundred American universities and colleges could well afford to maintain a creative artist on a fellowship. While he might not teach formal classes, his contribution to the education of the students as a living poet or artist on the campus and in informal conferences with students would be quite as valuable as that of the average professor.

I discussed the idea with President Marion L. Burton of Michigan and interested him in the project. He brought the poet laureate of England to the Michigan campus for a few months. Later, Robert Frost was fellow in poetry at Michigan for several years under Dr. Burton.

At Iowa State College, the sculptor, Christian Petersen, began some work for the college in 1933 under the Works Progress Administration. Since 1937, under President Charles E. Friley, he has served on a fellowship in sculpture, teaching a class and creating numerous beautiful bas-reliefs and statues for the college. He now holds an associate professorship. He has undoubtedly contributed more than the average professor to the education of our students in this technological institution.

If each of our wealthier colleges would support on a fellowship an able young artist, the value to this country would be enormous. At the same time, thousands of students would leave college with some appreciation of creative art and with a wider cultural background.

H.

Appendix

Appendix

Appendix

Detailed Study of Occupations of Fathers of Members of Class Entering in Fall of 1937

The 1,870 students who entered Iowa State College in the fall of 1937 were separated according to the occupations of their fathers. Each student was requested to enter his father's occupation on his registration card. In this class forty failed to do

PROFESSIONAL—24.4 per cent
THE OCCUPATIONS OF FATHERS WHOSE WORK REQUIRES OR IS ADVANTAGED BY COLLEGE EDUCATION

Executives	121	State Highway Commission	2
Engineers	48	County Agricultural Agents	2
College Professors	37	Governor of Iowa	1
Bankers	33	Judge	1
Veterinarians	30	Advertising	1
Lawyers	27	Research Technician	1
Doctors	25	YMCA Secretary	1
Teachers	25	Employment Secretary	1
Dentists	21	Land Appraiser	1
Accountants	13	State Insurance Agent	1
Clergymen	11	Member Board of Control	1
Pharmacists	8	Optometrist	1
School Superintendents	7	Architect	1
Editors, Publishers	6	Forest Service	1
Reporters	4	Instrument Maker	1
Army and Navy Officers	4	Librarian	1
Chemists	3	Farm Manager	1
U. S. Inspectors	3	Bureau of Internal Revenue	1
		Designer	1

447 or 24.4%

314 Appendix

NONPROFESSIONAL—75.6 per cent
The Occupations of Fathers Whose Work Does Not Require a College Education for Success

Occupation	Count	Occupation	Count
Farmers	621	County Officials	3
Merchants	164	Motion Picture Projectionists	3
Salesmen	108	Welders	3
Railroad Employees	65	Florists	3
Post Office Employees	45	Sheet Metal Workers	2
Insurance Agents	26	Lithographers	2
Mechanics	23	Golf Green Keepers	2
Contractors	22	Plasterers	2
Carpenters	21	Tailors	2
Laborers	18	Boiler Makers	2
Machinists	17	Pattern Makers	2
Foremen	14	Policemen	2
Clerks	12	Chefs	2
Plumbers	11	Government Employees	2
Janitors	11	Bricklayers	2
Undertakers	10	Masons	2
Printers	10	Laundry Managers	1
Telegraph Employees	10	Piano Tuner	1
Painters	10	Well Driller	1
Barbers	8	Leather Worker	1
Stationary Engineers	8	Bookkeeper	1
Lumbermen	8	Expressman	1
Buyers	8	Meat Cutter	1
Superintendent of Works	8	Street Commissioner	1
Jewelers	7	Theater Operators	1
Hotel Operators	6	Window Cleaner	1
Hatchery Men	6	Bus Driver	1
Blacksmiths	6	Livestock Commission	1
Truckers	6	Road Maintenance Worker	1
Coal Miners	6	Credit Adjuster	1
Electricians	5	Mill Work Estimater	1
Photographers	5	Cattle Club Secretary	1
Dry Cleaners	4	Cannery Operator	1
Garage Operators	4	State Oil Inspector	1
Bakers	4	Land Appraiser	1
Shoemakers	4	Shepherd	1
Nursery Men	4		

1,382 or 75.6 %

so. Some occupations are vague and difficult to classify accurately. However, the result gave a fairly sharp differentiation between men engaged in professional work or work definitely advantaged by a college education; and men engaged in work for which a college education is not required although perhaps useful.

This study showed a very wide diversity of occupation and a surprising number of college students whose fathers were in relatively humble positions.

Basis for Determining What Rank in Scholarship Any Given Student Should Attain

Every freshman entering college brings with him two ratings which indicate more or less definitely what quality of college work he should be able to do, if he enters on a curriculum suitable to his ability and if he will apply himself earnestly and capably to study.

These ratings are the average of his high school grades and the result of his scholastic aptitude examinations as given in college.

The following table is compiled from the grades earned by the 1,642 students entering in September, 1949 during the three quarters of their first year, and by the 2,637 students entering in September, 1948, during the three quarters of their second year and the first quarter of their third year—in other words, the grades earned by two classes covering seven quarters in all.

Of course many students, 60 per cent, either failed to make a 2.0 average or better, which is required for graduation, or withdrew. Of those who withdrew, about 10 per cent were making creditable grades at the time and most of them transferred to other colleges.

The failure of those who were below 2.0 in average or who withdrew with poor grades was due chiefly to *lack of hard study* or *poor preparation*. Some were entered in work unsuited to their ability, and some very definitely had no serious interest in college studies.

The figures given are computed from all average grades of 2.00 or better. Seven different quarters were used.

While the averages of students in each group, as determined by high school average and scholastic aptitude, varied in the different quarters studied, the variation was slight. The table is made up of the actual averages of the seven quarters for each group.

It seems reasonable to expect any earnest student, entered in work suitable to his abilities, to make a grade equal to the average of those in the same group as himself as determined by high school average and scholastic aptitude, who made a 2.0 average or better.

It should be noted that Iowa State College accepts all high school graduates from Iowa who apply, and all non-residents of Iowa with an average of 2.0 or better.

H.

The Average a Student Should Maintain as Determined by His High School Average and His Scholastic Aptitude

Scholastic Aptitude	High School Average 3.50–4.00		High School Average 3.00–3.49		High School Average 2.50–2.99		High School Average 2.00–2.49		High School Average Below 2.00	
	Students	Average	Students	Average	Students	Average	Students	Average	Students	Average
90–100	161	3.12	107	2.82	65	2.70	29	2.57	1	2.34
80–89	82	2.90	102	2.71	64	2.57	31	2.57	6	2.37
70–79	84	2.92	93	2.70	80	2.58	39	2.56	9	2.33
60–69	44	2.85	69	2.66	77	2.53	27	2.43	9	2.39
50–59	45	2.79*	63	2.59	73	2.51	52	2.40	9	2.39*
40–49	29	2.73	50	2.60	57	2.50	65	2.39	7	2.39
30–39	22	2.67	31	2.54	44	2.38	20	2.42	8	2.36
20–29	18	2.71	35	2.54	48	2.43	41	2.41	14	2.36
10–19	9	2.69*	22	2.49	24	2.41*	20	2.42	4	2.37
1–9	2	2.68	10	2.49	13	2.38	20	2.32	10	2.29

* These averages were too high in proportion to adjacent figures. These figures have been interpolated instead of actual averages.

Appendix

One of seven charts from which the averages given on page 317 were obtained

CLASS ENTERING IOWA STATE COLLEGE SEPT. 1948. SUMMARY OF MARKS AT THE END OF 6TH QUARTER, JUNE 1950

Scholastic Aptitude	No. Stud.	High School Average 3.50 to 4.00	No. Stud.	High School Average 3.00 to 3.49
90 to 100	109	85 averaged 3.05 (8 above 3.75) 4 below 2.00 20 had withdrawn	100	61 averaged 2.83 (22 made 3.00–4.00) 9 below 2.00 30 had withdrawn
80 to 89	64	46 averaged 2.88 (18 made 3.00–4.00) 3 below 2.00 15 had withdrawn	88	55 averaged 2.79 (18 made 3.00–3.83) 8 below 2.00 25 had withdrawn
70 to 79	66	53 averaged 2.91 (26 made 3.00–3.84) 4 below 2.00 9 had withdrawn	82	44 averaged 2.82 (18 made 3.00–3.82) 11 below 2.00 27 had withdrawn
60 to 69	31	26 averaged 2.77 (10 made 3.00–4.00) 0 below 2.00 5 had withdrawn	66	44 averaged 2.65 (11 made 3.00–3.65) 5 below 2.00 17 had withdrawn
50 to 59	34	24 averaged 2.98 (11 made 3.00–3.94) 3 below 2.00 7 had withdrawn	89	46 averaged 2.62 (9 made 3.00–3.61) 11 below 2.00 32 had withdrawn
40 to 49	27	18 averaged 2.89 (8 made 3.00–4.00) 1 below 2.00 8 had withdrawn	52	32 averaged 2.68 (9 made 3.00–4.00) 7 below 2.00 13 had withdrawn
30 to 39	8	7 averaged 2.75 (2 made 3.13–3.37) 1 below 2.00 none withdrawn	27	9 averaged 2.75 (5 made 2.50–3.25) 4 below 2.00 14 had withdrawn
20 to 29	13	9 averaged 2.56 (1 made 3.50) 0 below 2.00 4 had withdrawn	39	24 averaged 2.65 (13 made 2.50–3.52) 2 below 2.00 13 had withdrawn
10 to 19	6	5 averaged 3.08 (3 made 3.00–4.00) 0 below 2.00 1 had withdrawn	30	15 averaged 2.51 (8 made 2.50–3.00) 3 below 2.00 12 had withdrawn
1 to 9	4	2 averaged 2.96 (2 made 2.59–3.33) 0 below 2.00 2 had withdrawn	27	10 averaged 2.60 (6 made 2.50–3.14) 3 below 2.00 14 had withdrawn

No. Stud.	High School Average 2.50 to 2.99	No. Stud.	High School Average 2.00 to 2.49	No. Stud.	High School Average Below 2.00
79	43 averaged 2.68 (13 made 3.00–3.88) 12 below 2.00 24 had withdrawn	51	32 averaged 2.56 (9 made 2.75–3.41) 5 below 2.00 14 had withdrawn	6	1 made 2.92 0 below 2.00 5 had withdrawn
70	36 averaged 2.59 (4 made 3.00–3.36) 10 below 2.00 24 had withdrawn	46	17 averaged 2.52 (5 made 2.75–3.53) 12 below 2.00 17 had withdrawn	14	5 averaged 2.64 (3 made 2.50–3.00) 2 below 2.00 7 had withdrawn
95	37 averaged 2.69 (7 made 3.00–4.00) 19 below 2.00 39 had withdrawn	67	24 averaged 2.53 (8 made 2.75–3.53) 9 below 2.00 34 had withdrawn	21	10 averaged 2.38 (2 made 2.78–3.40) 1 below 2.00 10 had withdrawn
80	39 averaged 2.64 (11 made 3.00–3.84) 12 below 2.00 29 had withdrawn	55	18 averaged 2.57 (8 made 2.50–3.36) 14 below 2.00 23 had withdrawn	26	9 averaged 2.40 (2 made 2.75–2.80) 2 below 2.00 15 had withdrawn
93	38 averaged 2.63 (9 made 3.00–4.00) 19 below 2.00 36 had withdrawn	92	43 averaged 2.45 (16 made 2.50–3.50) 9 below 2.00 40 had withdrawn	30	8 averaged 2.97 (6 made 2.72–3.80) 7 below 2.00 15 had withdrawn
75	32 averaged 2.50 (3 made 3.00–3.59) 9 below 2.00 34 had withdrawn	71	25 averaged 2.44 (8 made 2.50–3.50) 12 below 2.00 34 had withdrawn	20	3 averaged 3.11 (3 made 2.66–3.34) 3 below 2.00 14 had withdrawn
67	33 averaged 2.50 (7 made 2.75–3.45) 7 below 2.00 27 had withdrawn	60	12 averaged 2.61 (9 made 2.50–3.00) 13 below 2.00 35 had withdrawn	24	5 averaged 2.48 (2 made 2.73–2.75) 4 below 2.00 15 had withdrawn
83	27 averaged 2.62 (9 made 2.75–4.00) 15 below 2.00 41 had withdrawn	97	29 averaged 2.53 (16 made 2.50–3.44) 13 below 2.00 55 had withdrawn	36	9 averaged 2.59 (3 made 2.93–3.64) 6 below 2.00 21 had withdrawn
48	12 averaged 2.66 (3 made 2.75–3.73) 3 below 2.00 33 had withdrawn	78	22 averaged 2.44 (9 made 2.50–3.14) 11 below 2.00 45 had withdrawn	27	4 averaged 2.75 (4 made 2.52–3.00) 4 below 2.00 19 had withdrawn
38	10 averaged 2.50 (3 made 3.00–3.18) 2 below 2.00 26 had withdrawn	84	17 averaged 2.37 (7 made 2.50–3.00) 6 below 2.00 61 had withdrawn	46	8 averaged 2.29 (4 made 2.50–2.59) 2 below 2.00 36 had withdrawn

IOWA STATE COLLEGE
DIVISION OF ENGINEERING
PERSONNEL SERVICE
AMES, IOWA

> Student's photograph here

Degree: Expect to receive the B. S. Degree in Electrical Engineering, June 1951.
College Address: 125 N. Hyland, Ames, Iowa.
Home Address: 1911 Warren, Bellevue, Nebraska.
Personal Data:
  Date of Birth: November 18, 1926. Place of Birth: Bellevue, Nebraska. Height: 6 ft. Weight: 160 lbs. Married. Health: Excellent. Ancestry: Father, American; Mother Swedish. Church Affiliation: Presbyterian.
  Father's Occupation: Carpenter Forman.
  Hobby or Outside Interests: Reading, Stamp Collecting, Hunting, Popular Record Collecting, Bowling, Golfing.
  Special Talent or Accomplishments: Basketball Referee, Typing.
  College Work Enjoyed Most: Electronics. *Second Choice:* Physics.
High School Information: Bellevue (Nebraska) High School.
  Major Activities: Athletics, Junior and Senior Class President, Junior and Senior Class Plays, Staff Member of School Paper and Annual.
College Information:
  IOWA STATE COLLEGE: 9 Quarters.
    Technical Societies: AIEE-IRE, Local (2,3,4), National (4).
    Honor Fraternities: Eta Kappa Nu, Tau Beta Pi, Guard of St. Patrick.
    Social Fraternity: Sigma Chi, President.
    Organizations Outside the College: Boy Scouts of America (Life Scout).
    Activities: Engineer's Carnival (3,4); Interfraternity Council (3,4), Social Chairman (3), President (4); Veishea (3,4); Engineering Division Open House Chairman (3), Open House General Chairman (4).
    Special Recognitions: Activity "I" Award (4).
  OMAHA UNIVERSITY (Omaha, Nebraska): 4 Semesters.
    Activities: Columnist, School Paper (1), Route Chairman; Ma-ie Day Parade (2); Freshman Football, Intramural Athletics (1,2).
  Earned 100% of total college expenses.
Business and Industrial Experience:
  Nebraska Public Power System, Bellevue, Nebraska. 2 months—Junior Engineer.
  Bates and Rogers Construction Corp., Bellevue, Nebraska. 3 months—Cement Finisher's Helper.
  Messner's Motor Service, Bellevue, Nebraska, 3 years (part time)—Station Attendant.
  Omaha World Herald, Bellevue, Nebraska. 3 years—Master Carrier Salesman.
  Electrical Engineering Dept., Iowa State College, Ames, Iowa. Present—Network Analyzer.
Military Service Record:
  U. S. Naval Reserve: September 1, 1944—July 1, 1946. AT 2/C. Attended Aviation Radio Technician School. Instructor Fleet Electronics Training Unit.
References:
  Prof. M. S. Coover, Head, Electrical Engineering Dept., Iowa State College, Ames, Iowa.
  Mr. M. D. Helser, Dean of Junior College and Director of Personnel, Iowa State College, Ames, Iowa.
  Mr. John M. Messner, Owner and Manager, Messner's Motor Service, Bellevue, Nebraska.
  Mr. Howard N. Eriksen, General Manager, Nebraska Public Power System, Columbus, Nebraska.
Available for Employment: June 1951.

  Personality Ratings and Scholastic Records will be furnished upon request by the Engineering Personnel Office of Iowa State College, Ames, Iowa.
  All the above information was supplied by the student; its accuracy has not been checked by the college.

Index

Index

Index

Admissions officer, importance of, 113
Advertising, college and university, 135
Alumni
  advisory council, 240
  aid with legislature, 241
  association, 229–31
  class contributions, 236
  class secretary, 236
  clubs, 231–32
  distinguished, 242
  financial campaigns, 238
  nominate trustees, 241
  placement of graduates, 238
  program, elements of effective, 229
  provide living endowment, 237
  publication of alumni "Who's Who," 244
  publications, 234–35
  recent graduates as critics of teaching, 239
  register, 235
  reunions, 233–34
  secretary, 226–27
  work, established aids in, 226
  working relations with, 225
Alumnus, the individual, 224
Architecture is important, 146
Art in college halls, 304
Art on the campus, 305
Articulation of high school and college, 249
Articulation, sophomore and junior years, 251
Artist, creative, on campus, 308
Assembly, university, 86
Athletics, intercollegiate, 211
Athletics, intramural, 210

Auditing student activity accounts, 196
Authorship in publishing results of doctoral theses, 281–83

Boarding students, 214
Books, writing, 285
Boyd, W. R., influence in Iowa, 51
Budget committee, 171
Budget, 127
Building plans, 145

Catalogs, 134
Chapel, 291–92
Classes, visiting, 260
Campus, planning, 143
Campus sites, 141–42
Clerical services, 125
College
  hospital, 212
  how work may be judged, 255
  press, freedom of, 199–200
  teacher has a good life, 174
Consultants, help from outside, 37
Cost to gruaute a student, 263–65
Cost of a poor appointment, 156
Council, university, 85
Culture course for students, 307

Dean of men, 104
Dean of women, 100–02
Deans
  appointment and contributions, 94
  college, 98
  elimination of, 94
  limited appointment, 96
  selection, 168

324 Index

Deans and Department Heads
  election, 88
  leadership, 36
  reducing salaries on demotion, 37
Democracy in college administration, 167
Department heads, 107
Doctorate as a requirment for professorship, 261
Dormitories, 215

Enrollment, one reason for growth, 181

Faculty
  classifying members, 36
  housing, 148
  recruiting new members, 152
  turnover, 156
Fellowships for promising young teachers, 260
Financial officer, 88, 92
Football coach's salary, 173
Fraternities, 190, 192

Graduate school, admission to, 278
Graduate school dean, 36
Graduate students, financial assistance to, 280
Graduate work, when should an institution enter on, 276
Graduate work and research, 269
Graduates, securing positions for, 201
Grants in aid, 203
Guilds control higher education, 166

Houses, dormitory, organization of, 195

Inaugurals, 4
Intercollegiate athletics, 211
Interviewing prospective staff members, 155
Intramural athletics, 210
Inventory, how to use, 127

Landscape architect should plan campus, 143
Leaders, identifying in college, 218
Lecturing, 259

Legislature
  change in attitude toward education, 57
  its technic in dealing with requests, 60
  padding requests for funds, 61
  presenting needs to, 58
  use of alumni with, 61
Library, 293, 297
Library stack room, 299
Loan funds and scholarships, 204, 206

Nominating committee, 171
Non-fraternity men and women, organization of, 194

Occupations of fathers of students, 311
Ohio State University, professorial appointments, 37

Parliament, college and university, 83, 86
Pensions, 158, 161
Personnel blank used at Iowa State, 320
Plans for buildings, preparation in advance, 145
Plant maintenance, 116
Prayer, great source of strength to president, 21
Presidents
  age of 300 presidents on election, 72
  assistants the board should provide, 65
  emeritus, his attitude, 44
  emeritus, how to utilize, 43
  entertainment problems, 30
  evidence of a good appointment, 75
  exceptional expenses, 32
  and the faculty, 151
  intangibles and imponderables, 19
  how long he should serve, 41-42
  need for a wise counselor, 70-71
  new, advances he may make, 8, 54
  new, questions he should ask, 3
  old, effect on institution, 43
  personal influence, 20
  previous employment on election, 73

Presidents *(continued)*
  puzzling problems, 34
  raising funds, 57
  removing unsatisfactory men, 79
  responsibility for leadership, 40
  selection of, 73
  should know their staff, 151
  speaking engagements, 38–39
  treatment by legislature, 58, 61
  unsatisfactory men, 77
  what is expected of him, 6, 76
President's
  dog, 29
  house, 26–27
  secretary, 18
  time, 11, 15, 17
  wife, 22, 24, 25
Probation, how a student can get off, 208
Professional meetings, attendance of faculty, 137
Professor, removal as unsatisfactory, 34
Provost, 93
Public relations, 138

Recruiting new faculty members, 152
Registrar and his functions, 108
Research
  cost in money, 273
  cost in time, 272
  foundations, 286
  funds, allotment of, 275
  interdepartmental committees, 284
  its importance, 269
  observations on, 274

Sabbatical leave, 161
Scholarship and grants-in aid, 203
Scholarship rank, basis for determining for any student, 313
Senate, university, 85
Ship is greater than the crew, 198
Stenographic bureau, 125
Student
  activity accounts, auditing, 196
  activity tickets, 203
  boarding, 214
  health service, 212
  loan funds, 204
  publications and faculty control, 200
  articulation high school and freshman year, 249
Students
  education of parents, 180
  failure of able students, 186
  high school grades and success in college, 181
  occupations of fathers, 129
  progress in college, 183
  proportion working up to ability, 188
  and their relation to college, 179
  transfer, 201
  upper class, who make low grades, 187
Superintendent of buildings and grounds, 116
Surveys of colleges and universities, 129, 131

Trustees
  appointment of, 48
  appointment to staff, 53
  calibre of appointments, 59
  centralized and individual boards, 48
  committee on efficiency and cooperation, 50
  committee on student affairs, 50
  finance committee, 51
  formulation of policies, 62
  Hughes' experience with, 49
  influence of W. R. Boyd, 51
  judicial and nourishing boards, 50
  and the legislature, 57
  McVey's experience with, 47
  matters of concern to, 53
  president chairman of board, 64
  president should attend all meetings, 49
  Dr. H. S. Pritchard's addresses, 51
  responsibilities, 52
  size of board, 56
Teaching, 252
  a faculty matter, 247–48
  importance of, 247
  and research, 163
  supervision from president's office, 254
Twenty-year plan, 136

326 Index

University foundations, wider use of, 288
University press, 303

Vice-President
  in charge of business, 66
  in charge of faculty and curricula, 68, 93
  in charge of public relations, 69
  duties of 3rd vice-president, 69
  on economy and efficiency, 69
Visiting college classes, 260

Words, organization of, 195

YMCA and YWCA, 197